CORNELL STUDIES IN CLASSICAL PHILOLOGY

EDITED BY

HARRY CAPLAN   JAMES HUTTON

G. M. KIRKWOOD

VOLUME XXXIV

St. Jerome as a Satirist

A STUDY IN CHRISTIAN LATIN THOUGHT AND LETTERS

BY DAVID S. WIESEN

ST. JEROME
AS A SATIRIST

A Study in Christian Latin
Thought and Letters

BY DAVID S. WIESEN

Swarthmore College

CORNELL UNIVERSITY PRESS

ITHACA, NEW YORK

To MY PARENTS

Preface

ST. JEROME'S contemporaries were the first to recognize, usually with extreme displeasure, the satiric features of his writings. An anonymous critic who had felt himself wounded by Jerome's barbs charged him with being a *satiricus scriptor in prosa*. Sulpicius Severus, writing within Jerome's lifetime, speaks of the widespread disapproval aroused by his caustic exposure of the vices of the clergy. At a later period Cassiodorus was struck by the *mordacitas* with which Jerome "broke the necks of the proud" and avenged himself on his personal enemies. In the high Middle Ages, John of Salisbury included St. Jerome, with Horace, Persius, Juvenal, and Seneca, as a satiric censor of men and morals. Indeed, Jerome's excoriation of his age heavily influenced John of Salisbury's own penetrating lampoons of the society of Henry II's court. Jerome's antifeminist satire, in particular his tract *Adversus Iovinianum*, proved to be an inexhaustible gold mine for medieval poets. For example, Chaucer modeled his Wife of Bath in part on St. Jerome's descriptions of shrewish behavior. The scholarly fifth husband of the Wife of Bath would enrage his mate by laughing uproariously as he perused night and day the misogynistic writings of

> a clerk at Rome
> A cardinal, that highte Seint Jerome,
> That made a book agayn Jovinian.

In the Renaissance, Erasmus goes so far as to state that Jerome expresses himself most characteristically and forcefully when he is hurling vitriolic invective at heretics and personal foes.

The mordant element in St. Jerome's writings and the resemblance of this element to the satire of the pagans have not entirely escaped the attention of modern scholars. In his Yale dissertation *Latin Satirical Writing Subsequent to Juvenal* (Lancaster, Pa., 1915), Arthur Weston devoted a brief chapter to St. Jerome. Stanislaus Seliga in an article in *Eos* (XXIV, 1933) discusses "Quibus contumeliis Hieronymus adversarios carpserit." The same author returned again to this subject in an article, "De Hieronymi scriptorum colore satirico," contributed to the *Charisteria Gustavo Przychocki* (Warsaw, 1934). However, Charles Favez has not unjustly characterized the work of Seliga as "un catalogue de *contumeliae.*" M. Favez's own article, "La Satire dans les 'Lettres' de Saint Jérôme" (*Revue des Etudes Latines*, XXIV, 1946), deals with only one portion of Jerome's works and is, as he himself admits, not a thorough treatment of the topic. The article of Miss M. E. Pence, "Satire in St. Jerome," in the *Classical Journal* (XXXVI, 1941) is a very short discussion of some of the better-known passages. Thus, although St. Jerome's satire has prompted abundant comment and curiosity from his own lifetime down to the present day, no full and general study of this subject has hitherto been undertaken. The aim of the present work is to fill this gap by investigating the origin, nature, and purpose of St. Jerome's satire with special regard for its relationship to the classical satire of the pagans.

I have attempted to include in this study the entire corpus of St. Jerome's writings with the exception of such tattered fragments as are gathered by Dom G. Morin in the *Revue Bénédictine* (XX, 1903). In treating the *Letters* I have consulted both the edition of Jérôme Labourt in the Budé series and Isidor Hilberg's text in the Vienna Corpus of Christian Latin authors as well as older editions. Labourt's seventh and penultimate volume appeared too late for consideration here. Unfortunately, a large number of Jerome's writings are available only in Migne's reprint of Vallarsi's edition of 1766–1772. These volumes in the *Patrologia Latina* are disfigured by misprints and other patent errors which I have been obliged arbitrarily to correct in quoting passages. The first printings of the *Patrologia*, completed before 1868, when fire destroyed Migne's workshop and molds, are the freest of error, but these early impressions are now rather difficult to obtain. Of printings subsequent to 1868, the latest are generally the best, since some of the more egregious errors, which had crept into the texts reset after the fire, were removed with each successive impression. Hence I refer to the most recently published volumes whenever these have been available to me. Since the numbering of the columns was changed with each fresh publication, it is important to note exactly to which reprint reference is made:

Migne, *Patrologia Latina*	Reprint of
XXII	1854
XXIII	1883
XXIV	1865
XXV	1884
XXVI	1884
XXVII	1866
XXVIII	1890
XXIX	1865

For Jerome's commentary on Isaiah I have consulted the edition of S. Reiter in the Vienna Corpus and for the commentary on Jonah the text of Dom P. Antin in the *Editions du Cerf*. Dom G. Morin's edition of the homiletic works in *Anecdota Maredsolana*, 1897–1903, has been employed. Some of the exegetical and homiletic works have recently appeared in the seventy-second and seventy-eighth volumes of the *Corpus Christianorum*.

and I have also used these texts. All English translations of passages from St. Jerome are my own.

For the chronology of Jerome's life and works I have usually accepted the findings of Ferdinand Cavallera as authoritative, but in cases of dispute I have also taken into account the opinions of Grützmacher and Pronberger.

I wish to express here my warm gratitude and deep appreciation to Professor Herbert Bloch, of Harvard University, whose great knowledge of the age of St. Jerome and whose gracious interest in this study have been unfailing and indispensable sources of instruction and encouragement. I am also greatly indebted to the kindness of Professors Harry Caplan, James Hutton, Gordon M. Kirkwood, and Friedrich Solmsen, who read parts of this work and offered many learned suggestions of the greatest value.

Thanks are due also to the Clarendon Press, Oxford, for permission to quote from Wendell Clausen's edition of the *Satires* of Juvenal, copyrighted 1959.

D. S. W.

Swarthmore
January 1964

Abbreviations

Anecdot. Mared.	*Anecdota Maredsolana, seu Monumenta Ecclesiasticae Antiquitatis ex Mss. Codicibus nunc primum Edita aut denuo Illustrata.* Maredsous, 1897 and 1903.
Cavallera	Ferdinand Cavallera. *Saint Jérôme, sa Vie et son Oeuvre.* 2 vols. Paris and Louvain, 1922.
CC	*Corpus Christianorum, Series Latina.* Turnhout, 1953 ff.
CSEL	*Corpus scriptorum ecclesiasticorum Latinorum.* Vienna, Leipzig, and Prague, 1866 ff.
Grützmacher	Georg Grützmacher. *Hieronymus: Eine biographische Studie zur alten Kirchengeschichte.* 3 vols. Berlin, 1901, 1906, and 1908.
Luebeck	Aemilius Luebeck. *Hieronymus quos noverit scriptores et ex quibus hauserit.* Leipzig, 1872.
PG	J. P. Migne. *Patrologiae Graecae cursus completus.* 162 vols. Paris, 1857–1866.
PL	J. P. Migne. *Patrologiae Latinae cursus completus.* 221 vols. Paris, 1844–1864.
TAPA	*Transactions of the American Philological Association.* 1869 ff.

Contents

	Preface	vii
	Abbreviations	xi
I	St. Jerome and the Satiric Tradition	1
II	O Tempora! O Mores!	20
	Letters	23
	Historical Works	47
	Polemical Works	51
	Exegetical Works	54
	Conclusion	61
III	The Church and the Clergy	65
	Letters	68
	Polemical Works	90
	Homiletic Works	93
	Exegetical Works	95
	Conclusion	110
IV	Women and Marriage	113
	Letters	119
	Polemical Works	148
	Exegetical Works	160
	Conclusion	164

V Heretics, Jews, and Pagans   166
    Heretics   167
      Letters   173
      Polemical Works   178
      Homilies   179
      Exegetical Works   180
    Jews   188
    Pagans   194
    Conclusion   197

VI Personal Enemies   200
    Anonymous Enemies   200
    Jovinianus   213
    Vigilantius   218
    Rufinus   225
    St. Augustine   235
    St. Ambrose   240
    Conclusion   244

VII Retrospect and Conclusion   247
    St. Jerome's Own View of His Satire   247
    Conclusion   264

    Bibliography   273

    Index   285

ST. JEROME AS A SATIRIST

*A Study in Christian Latin
Thought and Letters*

CHAPTER I

St. Jerome and the Satiric Tradition

SATIRE is defined by the fourth-century grammarian Diomedes as follows: *Satura dicitur carmen nunc quidem maledicum et ad carpenda hominum vitia compositum, quale scripserunt Lucilius et Horatius et Persius.*[1] Diomedes here describes two aspects of satire, its poetic form (*carmen*) and its abusive and scurrilous content, the purpose of which is the castigation of human vice and folly. Satire then, in the strict sense of the term, meant to the Romans a definite form of poetic composition. Considering content alone, modern scholars may classify Julius Caesar's

[1] H. Keil, *Grammatici Latini*, I, 485. That this definition is older than the fourth century can be seen from Suetonius, *De Poetis* 20, in A. Reifferscheid's edition. A. Rostagni's edition (Turin, 1956, 11) contains the following description of Horace, Persius, and Juvenal: *Hi enim universorum delicta corripiunt nec vetabatur eis pessimum quemque describere, nec cuilibet peccata moresque reprehendere.* Since G. L. Hendrickson has shown that Varro's Menippean satires were probably not known formally as *saturae* at the time of their composition but that this was a later designation, they and their literary descendants may be omitted from the discussion of the ancient view of satiric form. See Hendrickson's "Satura—The Genesis of a Literary Form," *Class. Philol.,* VI (1911), 129–143.

Anticatones as satire or include in the same category Seneca's eighty-sixth letter, with its mordant description of Roman bathing habits.[2] From the modern point of view the novel of Apuleius is a highly satiric work.[3] The Romans, however, would not have classified such prose works strictly as satire.[4] Nevertheless, so clearly had verse satire in the hands of Lucilius, Horace, Persius, and Juvenal become a literary means of attacking men and morals that other forms of composition in which cutting invective played a leading role could be considered satire, even though the traditional verse form was not maintained. Thus in later antiquity the word *satiricus* began to be used without regard to form in a sense approximating that of our word "satiric." St. Jerome, although he left to posterity virtually no verse compositions, refers to himself on four occasions as a satirist in the larger sense of a penetrating and vituperative critic of human behavior.[5] Since Jerome himself did not restrict his concept of

[2] Arthur Weston, *Latin Satirical Writing Subsequent to Juvenal* (Lancaster, Pa., 1915), 7 and 9. Hereafter referred to as Weston.

[3] Schwabe in Pauly-Wissowa-Kroll, *Realencyclopaedie*, II, 250; Weston, 14–15.

[4] U. Knoche, *Die Römische Satire* (2d ed.; Göttingen, 1957), 1. He rightly insists on the formal significance of the term *satura*, but he seems to overstate his case in saying that it was impossible for the Romans to understand satire in a wider sense, since he later admits (pp. 45–46): "Und spätesten in den wirren Jahrzehnten die dem Untergang der römischen Republik vorangingen, konnte man auch die Invektive schlechthin als *Satura* bezeichnen, mochte sie nun in Versen oder in prosaischer Form abgefasst sein." J. W. Duff, *Roman Satire* (Berkeley, 1936), 13, also emphasizes the formal nature of the *satura*. Cf. G. L. Hendrickson, "Satura tota nostra est," *Class. Philol.*, XXII (1927), 46–60.

[5] Letters 22. 32 and 50. 5, where Jerome specifically speaks of himself as a successor of Horace and Juvenal, and Letters 40. 2 and 117. 1, where he refers to a charge brought by his enemies that he had been writing satire. The only verse compositions we have from the hand of St. Jerome are the two *epitaphia* of Paula, Letter 108. 33. The use of the word *satura* or *satiricus* in the larger sense of our word satire is rare. In spite of Lewis and Short, Ammianus Marcellinus xvi. 6. 3 does not provide an example of *per saturam* meaning "in a mocking manner." Cf. Sallust *Jugurtha* 19. 5.

the satiric to its narrower and more formal meaning, he provides justification for regarding as satire and studying as a unit those elements in his writings which express caustic, scurrilous, and abusive judgments of society in general or of individual men.

It might at first appear strange to speak of satiric writing in Latin literature as late as the fourth century, for formal satire shared in the general decline of Latin letters which had begun in the second century. We do hear of several obscure satirists contemporary with Juvenal, a Turnus, a Silius, or a Sentius Augurinus, but they are mere names, and the rest is silence.[6] Perhaps of all literary forms satire is least able to be conceived in an atmosphere of intellectual apathy or brought to birth in a society that does not permit the free expression of social criticism.[7] Yet the vigor of the pagan satiric tradition had by no means been completely exhausted. The fourth century after Christ, the period into which St. Jerome's earlier life falls, witnessed the sudden reawakening of interest in the classical writers of satire. Our earliest evidence is provided by the Christian apologist Lactantius, whose works are filled with references to Lucilius, Persius, and Juvenal.[8] Ammianus Marcellinus offers clear evidence of the revival of interest in Juvenal, who, after having been virtually unnoticed for centuries, now becomes one of the most widely read of Latin authors.[9] Describing with bitter disgust the ignorance and luxury of the Roman nobility, Ammianus says: *Quidam detestantes ut venena doctrinas, Iuvenalem et Marium Maximum curatiore studio legunt, nulla volumina*

---

[6] Weston, 11–13. The date of the satire of Sulpicia on Domitian's reign is very much disputed. See Schanz-Hosius II⁴, 560. Cf. F. Munari, *Epigrammata Bobiensia*, II (Rome, 1955), 91–95.

[7] Of course even Horace (*Sat.* ii. 1) and Juvenal (1. 151–171) keenly felt the danger of insulting the powerful.

[8] See below, pp. 16–18.

[9] Friedlaender's edition of Juvenal, *D. Junii Juvenalis saturarum libri V* (Leipzig, 1895), I, 81–85; U. Knoche, *Handschriftliche Grundlagen des Juvenaltextes, Philologus*, Supplementband XXXIII (1940), Heft 1, 34–40.

praeter haec in profundo otio contrectantes, quam ob causam non iudicioli est nostri.[10] Other evidence of Juvenal's popularity confirms Ammianus' testimony. The works of the Gallic poet Ausonius contain many reminiscences of the satirist, as do those of Claudian.[11] Servius quotes Juvenal more than seventy times.[12] A pupil of Servius, perhaps named Nicaeus, wrote notes to accompany his revised text of Juvenal about the end of the fourth century.[13] Another commentary, which is attributed to a pagan scholar sometimes called Probus, was written between 352 and 399.[14] These commentaries, intended to facilitate the reading of Juvenal, are further proof that the satirist aroused keen interest in the fourth century.

Of the other satirists, Lucilius is frequently mentioned by Ausonius and Jerome, as well as by Lactantius.[15] But their knowledge of Lucilius is probably derived either from florilegia or (and this is especially true of Jerome) from references in Cicero and Horace, since it is most unlikely that the text of Lucilius was still extant in the fourth century.[16] Nevertheless, the large num-

----

[10] Amm. Marc. xxviii. 4. 14. Few readers would disagree with the sentiment of E. A. Thompson that Ammianus was himself stimulated by disgust with the Roman nobility "into writing satire which in depth of feeling would bear comparison with Juvenal himself" (*The Historical Work of Ammianus Marcellinus* [Cambridge, 1947], 14).

[11] H. A. Strong, "Ausonius' Debt to Juvenal," *Class. Rev.*, XXV (1911), 15, and G. Highet, *Juvenal the Satirist* (Oxford, 1954), 297–298. Also P. Fargues, *Claudien, Invectives contre Eutrope* (Paris, 1933), 7 and 14.

[12] Highet, *Juvenal*, 186.

[13] Friedlaender's Juvenal, I, 81; Knoche, *Hand. Grund.*, 46–48.

[14] Friedlaender's Juvenal, I, 82; Highet, *Juvenal*, 299.

[15] For Lactantius see below, p. 16. See Auson, *Ep.* XI. 11 and XVI.

[16] F. Marx, *Lucili carmina reliquiae* (Leipzig, 1904), LX. Cf. U. Knoche, *Röm. Sat.*, 25, and C. Kunst, *De S. Hieronymi studiis Ciceronianis (Dissertationes Philologae Vindobonenses,* 1918), 181. Both Marx and Knoche believe in the existence of a moralistic florilegium from which Lactantius derived his knowledge of Lucilius. But an examination of Jerome's references to Lucilius as collected by Luebeck reveals that they were all derived either from Cicero or Horace.

ber of allusions to this satirist in late antiquity suggests that what remained of his writings was still highly regarded.

In contrast to the decline in the reading of Lucilius, the popularity of Horace continued unabated. Indeed, one scholar who has carefully investigated Horace's "Fortleben" finds far more references to him in Christian writers of the fourth century than in those of the preceding century.[17] Horace's fear of becoming a school author was amply fulfilled, and the poet's language and thought were, until the very end of the ancient educational system, imprinted on the minds of all educated Romans.[18] The thorough studies of M. Hertz have revealed that there is scarcely a fourth-century writer who cannot be shown to have been acquainted with Horace's works, the satiric as well as the lyric.[19]

Persius too, in spite of the difficulties his text presented, seems to have found a wide body of readers in the fourth century. Our major *testimonium* comes from St. Jerome himself. Addressing his great enemy Rufinus and defending the method of exegesis which he had used in his commentary on the Epistle to the Ephesians, Jerome says: *Puto quod puer . . . legeris . . . commentarios aliorum in alios, Plautum videlicet, Lucretium, Flaccum, Persium atque Lucanum.*[20] Jerome thus suggests that Persius was one of the major authors read and expounded in the schools. The interest in Persius during St. Jerome's lifetime is further evinced by the revision of the text undertaken by Flavius Julius Tryfonianus Sabinus in the year 402.[21]

---

[17] E. Froebel, *Quid veteres de Horatii poematis iudicaverint* (Jena, 1911), 39.

[18] Horace's fear is expressed in *Sat.* i. 10. 76 and *Epist.* i. 20. 17.

[19] M. Hertz, *Analecta ad carminum Horatianorum historiam* (Breslau, 1876–1882).

[20] *Contra Rufinum, PL* 23, 428C–429A.

[21] The subscription of Tryfonianus is quoted by Conington in his edition of Persius (Oxford, 1893), p. xxxvii. See also W. Clausen's edition of Persius and Juvenal (Oxford, 1959), p. vi.

Another satiric work which appears to have achieved wide currency in St. Jerome's day is the so-called *Will of a Pig* (*Testamentum Grunii Corocottae porcelli*).[22] In the preface to the twelfth book of his commentary on Isaiah, in describing the lack of intellectual vigor characteristic of his age, Jerome adds: *Testamentum autem Grunii Corocottae Porcelli decantant in scholis puerorum agmina cachinnantium.*[23] Again, in his polemical work against Rufinus Jerome says, *Quasi non cirratorum turba Milesiarum in scholis figmenta decantet: et testamentum Suis, Bessorum cachinno membra concutiat, atque inter scurrarum epulas nugae istius modi frequententur.*[24]

It may be said then that in the age of St. Jerome the inherited corpus of satiric writing formed part of the popular reading matter. Jerome's caustic exposure of personal and social failings should be seen as a sign of the renewed vigor of the satiric outlook and of the satiric form of expression. One might well inquire why the satire of Horace, Persius, and Juvenal aroused so great a response in readers of the fourth century. It may reasonably be conjectured that the decadent society of the twilight years of Roman civilization found in the satire of the pagans a reflection of its own moral problems. The similarity between the defects the pagan satirists discovered in their society and those which Jerome perceived in his own age enabled the Christian moralist to adopt the sentiments and sometimes even the diction of the pagans in his censure of the contemporary world.

Among all the writers of his day St. Jerome was uniquely suited by his learning as well as by his temperament to combine the inherited body of pagan satire with a new and vigorous Christian satiric spirit into a literary attack on the vices of society

---

[22] Text in Buecheler's 6th ed. of Petronius (Berlin, 1922), 268–269.
[23] *PL* 23, 425A.
[24] *Contra Ruf.*, *PL* 23, 430C.

and of personal enemies. Through his extensive reading Jerome gained a knowledge of pagan literature perhaps unrivaled in his own day. The enormous erudition of Jerome not only in Christian letters but also in the secular literature of the pagans is demonstrated on every page of his voluminous works, was generally recognized by his contemporaries, both friends and enemies, and has been abundantly and repeatedly demonstrated by the diligence of modern scholarship. "While I was a youth, I was carried away by a wondrous ardor for learning," confesses Jerome.[25] Scholars need only examine St. Jerome's own writings to discover the way in which he acquired his pagan learning, for he himself has left us abundant evidence concerning his secular education.[26] Even as a young man under the tutelage of the famed *grammaticus* Aelius Donatus, whom Jerome often mentions with pride as his teacher, he became so thoroughly absorbed in his rhetorical studies that he would run to the law courts in order to hear in actual use the modes of expression he had learned at school.[27] Many years later, as an old man, he would dream of the rhetorical training of his childhood.[28] Jerome's feeling for literary style was profound. In attacking the theological opinions of Rufinus, Jerome considers his opponent's inelegant language as a serious defect.[29] Extremely careful about his own style, Jerome spent much effort in polishing his diction, even in short letters to friends.[30] Indeed, Jerome's interest in

[25] Letter 84. 2.

[26] The best account of Jerome's education is by Grützmacher, I, 113–136.

[27] *Comm. in Gal.*, PL 26, 365A. On Donatus see Eusebius' *Chronicle*, ed. Fotheringham (London, 1922), 321; *Contra Ruf.*, PL 23, 429A; *Comm. in Eccles.*, PL 23, 1071A, and CC 72, 257.

[28] *Contra Ruf.*, PL 23, 441B.

[29] *Ibid.*, 429B-C.

[30] Jerome's frequent apologies for the hasty language of his letters imply that he considered their style of importance: Letters 75. 1; 118. 12; 129. 8.

secular literature was the cause of great grief to him in the course of his life.[31] His famous account of a dream in which, having been accused in heaven of being a *Ciceronianus* rather than a *Christianus*, he swore before the tribunal of God never more to read *saeculares codices* reveals the depth of Jerome's fear that it was wrong for a Christian to derive enjoyment from pagan letters.[32] A. S. Pease has shown that the frequency of citations from classical literature diminishes strikingly immediately after this vision.[33] Nonetheless, in his seventieth letter, to Magnus, and in his polemic against Rufinus, Jerome was compelled to defend his reading of pagan literature against the charge that such reading was unchristian.[34]

Of all aspects of St. Jerome's writings none has aroused more interest than his use of pagan authors. Since Emil Luebeck laid the foundation for this investigation in his dissertation of 1872, a host of scholars have carefully combed Jerome's works in order to discover exactly which pagan authors he had read and what his attitude toward them was.[35] Thanks to the efforts of Hilberg, Pease, Courcelle, Ellspermann, Eiswirth, and Hagendahl, we now have a clear picture of St. Jerome's learning[36] and can see on the one hand that, as far as Greek literature is con-

---

[31] Nonetheless his learning was a marvel to contemporaries. The admiring testimony of his own and later ages is collected in *PL* 22, 214–232.

[32] Letter 22. 30.

[33] A. S. Pease, "Jerome and Pagan Literature," *TAPA*, L (1919), 157.

[34] Note Rufinus' attack on Jerome's reading of the pagans in his *Apology against Jerome*, *PL* 21, 588D.

[35] For Luebeck's work, see list of abbreviations.

[36] I. Hilberg's edition of the Letters, in *CSEL*, LIV–LVI (Vienna, 1918); A. S. Pease, "Jerome and Pagan Literature," *TAPA*, L (1919), 150–167; G. L. Ellspermann, *The Attitude of the Early Christian Writers toward Pagan Literature and Learning* (Washington, 1949), 126–173; P. Courcelle, *Lettres Grecques en Occident* (Paris, 1943), 37–115; H. Hagendahl, *Latin Fathers and the Classics* (Göteborg, 1958), 91–382; R. Eiswirth, *Hieronymus' Stellung zur Literatur und Kunst* (Wiesbaden, 1955). E. Basabe, "San Jeronimo y los Clasicos," *Helmantica*, II (1951), 161–192, adds little new.

cerned, Jerome "fait étalage d'une erudition à bon marché."[37] On the other hand Jerome's acquaintance with Latin literature has proved to have been far greater than originally supposed by Luebeck. Indeed the studies of Hagendahl have revealed Jerome as a skilled mosaic artist who fitted into his writings an enormous number of paraphrases and actual quotations of pagan authors. Among the authors cited by Jerome, the comic and satiric poets figure prominently. Plautus was one of his favorite authors when he lived in the desert.[38] In later years, as Rufinus charges, Jerome could not resist teaching the comic poets to the young boys committed to his care.[39] Even the early investigations of Luebeck discovered twenty-five passages of Terence cited by Jerome, thirty-four from Horace's *Satires* and *Epistles*, and sixteen passages of Persius.[40] This enumeration takes no account of Jerome's repeated references to some of these passages, nor does it include his innumerable paraphrases and borrowings of individual lines which he subtly and skillfully blends into his writings.[41] Jerome's acquaintance with these writers will appear the greater when it is realized that many of these passages are recalled from memory.[42]

The infrequency of direct references to Juvenal in Jerome's writings may seem to indicate a serious gap in his acquaintance with pagan satirists. Yet, although Jerome never mentions Juvenal by name, he refers to him often enough to show that he had read his works. Jerome thrice uses a phrase from Juvenal's first satire, *manum ferulae subducere*, with the meaning, "to

---

[37] Courcelle, *Lettres*, 62.

[38] Letter 22. 30.

[39] Ruf. *Apol.* ii. 8 (PL 21, 592A).

[40] Luebeck, 110–115, 162–167, and 195–198.

[41] The discovery of many of these obscure references to pagan authors is one of the great merits of Hagendahl, *Latin Fathers*.

[42] Jerome himself insists that the references he makes to secular literature are remembered from his childhood reading of these works; *Comm. in Gal.* iii, *praefat.*, PL 26, 427B.

receive a secular education."[43] Other references to Juvenal are more oblique.[44] One of the more surprising reminiscences occurs in Jerome's translation of Ezekiel 3:7, where the phrase *adtrita fronte* may recall Juvenal 13. 242.[45] The close similarity in spirit and content between the first book of Jerome's *Adversus Iovinianum* and Juvenal's sixth satire will be discussed when Jerome's satire on women is handled.[46]

But the satiric and comic poets were not the only pagan writers who were of value in Jerome's training as a satirist. It must be remembered that in his dream Jerome was accused of being a *Ciceronianus*, for, *ubi thesaurus tuus, ibi et cor tuum*.[47] Much of the technique and vocabulary of Jerome's satiric invective has close parallels in the polemic of Cicero's speeches.[48]

[43] *Contra Ruf.* i. 17 (*PL* 23, 430A) and Letters 50. 5 and 57. 12.

[44] The other references are Letter 52. 5 *adtrita frons*—Juv. 13. 242; *Vita Hilarionis* 12 (*PL* 23, 34B), *Nudus latrones non timet*—Juv. 10. 22; Letter 61. 3, *nosse mensuram suam*—Juv. 11. 35; Letter 66. 13 and *Adv. Helvidium* 20 (*PL* 23, 214B), *pavimenta verrunt*—Juv. 14. 60; Letter 27. 3, *bipedes asellos*—Juv. 9. 92. The first of these allusions was pointed out by A. S. Pease, *TAPA*, L (1919), 167, n. 11. The second, fourth, and fifth references are disputed by G. Highet, *Juvenal*, 298, n. 11. The phrase *quae tamen rara avis est* in *Adv. Iovin.* I. 47 (*PL* 23, 290B) must surely be a reference to Juv. 6. 165, for the meaning of the phrase is exactly the same in both passages, namely that good and sweet women are virtually nonexistent. Hagendahl, *Latin Fathers*, 145 and 156, is wrong in referring the phrase to Persius 1. 146 or in explaining it as merely proverbial.

[45] *PL* 29, 999B. If Pease is correct in connecting *adtrita frons* in Letter 52. 5 with Juvenal 13. 242, the same must be true of the passage in the *Vulgate*. The phrase *rubore frontis adtrito* is found in Letter 22. 29.

[46] See below, Chapter IV.

[47] Letter 22. 30. P. de Labriolle, in *Miscellanea Geronimiana* (Rome, 1920), 227–235, and F. Z. Collombet, *Histoire de Saint Jérôme* (Paris, 1844) I, 122–142, have tried to show that the dream was a rhetorical fiction. The dream is defended by Cavallera, II, n. D. Certainly the investigations of Pease (*TAPA* 1919) and of Eiswirth, *Hieronymus' Stellung*, show that the dream represents psychological if not literal truth.

[48] The subject has been studied by W. Süss in *Giessener Beiträge zur Deutschen Philologie*, LX (1938), 217–229.

Cicero's courtroom invective will be treated in the discussion of those passages in which it appears to have influenced St. Jerome.

But perhaps above all external influences, the richest source of Jerome's satire was his own proud and irascible nature. Jerome might almost be called an *anima naturaliter satirica*. Ambitious and vain, he would not suffer lightly any questioning of his intellectual authority.[49] A fanatic partisan of whatever cause he adopted, whether adamantine orthodoxy, severe and enthusiastic asceticism, or the overriding authority of the papacy, Jerome considered all opposition to his cherished principles as a personal insult and replied with violence. His contemporary Palladius, the historian of early monasticism, says that the true value of St. Jerome's writings was concealed by his βασκανία, the equivalent of *invidia*.[50] In the *Dialogus* of Sulpicius Severus, one of the interlocutors, after describing the bitter tongue of Jerome, adds with magnificent understatement: *Unde a quibusdam, quos nominare nolo, dicitur non amari.*[51] Jerome's temperament led him into an endless series of quarrels in which the personal and intellectual elements are inextricably confused.[52] One of Jerome's most important modern biographers describes him as "reizbar," "fanatisch," "unduldsam," "rücksichtslos," "heftig," "eitel," "zänkerisch."[53] He comments that Jerome had a special talent for perceiving the weaknesses of men. Further-

---

[49] Hence the constant and bitter complaints which appear in the prefaces to Jerome's biblical commentaries. Hence also the quarrel with Saint Augustine, which did not become violent only because of Augustine's great restraint. See below, Chapter VI.

[50] "Lausiac History," ed. C. Butler, in *Texts and Studies* (Cambridge, 1904), VI, no. 2, 108, 7. The dislike was mutual. Jerome says, *Palladius, servilis nequitiae . . . Num et illius ingenio nobilitatique invidemus?* This remark seems to be a direct reply to the charge of *invidia*. Cf. Cavallera, I, 196, n. 2.

[51] *Dialogus* i. 9; p. 160 in Halm's edition (*CSEL*, I).

[52] These quarrels are discussed, with undue partiality toward St. Jerome, by J. Brochet, *Saint Jérôme et ses Ennemis* (Paris, 1905).

[53] G. Grützmacher, *Hieronymus*, I, 14, and II, 179.

more, "er hatte geradezu Freude daran, andere zu verletzen."[54] Even the favorably disposed biographer Cavallera admits that "il y avait néanmoins dans son caractère des traits peu sympathique."[55] In his essay *The Personality of St. Jerome,* Cavallera goes so far as to speak of Jerome's ill-humor, irascibility, rancor, violence, and penchant for exaggeration.[56] To these qualities we may add a penetrating sense of the ridiculous or perverse in human behavior. When these traits of character are combined in Jerome with a thorough acquaintance with the comic and satiric poets, who sharpened his ability to describe with caustic power the faults he perceived, the result was forceful and often brilliant satire.

But we must not suppose that St. Jerome was the earliest Christian writer in whose works the satiric element was strong. Rather he was the continuator of a Christian satiric tradition. In the dark years of Latin literature, between the second and fourth centuries, when those who valued their lives and social positions would not speak out against the commonly accepted standards of behavior, the satiric spirit lived and flourished in the works of a class of writers who were steadfastly opposed to the morality and religion of the society in which they lived and who would not have hesitated to risk even their lives in expressing this opposition. In the writings of the Christian apologists satire became a natural mode of stating this wholehearted opposition to the pagan world.

The works of Tertullian abound in satire, as we might expect

[54] *Ibid.*, I, 14 and 156.

[55] Cavallera, I, 195. The different evaluations of Jerome's character and motives in Grützmacher's and Cavallera's biographies are indicative of the distinct Protestant and Catholic traditions in Hieronymian scholarship. As might be expected, Hagendahl prefers the Protestant Grützmacher, Bardy, the reviser of Labriolle, the Catholic Cavallera. See Hagendahl, *Latin Fathers,* 147, n. 2.

[56] He deprecates these qualities as the blemishes of a brilliant and admirable character. See *A Monument to St. Jerome,* ed. F. X. Murphy (New York, 1952), 17 and 19.

from "une âme de colère et de passion."[57] A recent scholar has characterized the tone of Tertullian's writings as *tumens, indignans, comminans, invidiosus.*[58] In *De pallio* the satiric element is so strong that the work has been thought to be based on an earlier satire, perhaps a Menippean satire of Varro.[59] But other works of Tertullian are also rich in satiric passages, a few examples of which may be cited here.[60] Tertullian thus describes the religious festivals of the pagans:

Grande videlicet officium focos et toros in publicum educere, vicatim epulari, civitatem tabernae habitu abolefacere, vino lutum cogere, catervatim cursitare ad iniurias, ad impudentias, ad libidinis illecebras! Sicine exprimitur publicum gaudium per dedecus publicum. Haecine solemnes dies principum decent, quae alios dies non decent. . . . Honesta res est solemnitate publica exigente induere domui tuae habitum alicuius novi lupinaris![61]

The tone of this passage is determined by two characteristic traits of satiric writing, irony and the use of exaggeratedly detailed description in an attempt to ridicule.

Like many satiric writers Tertullian directs some of his sharpest barbs against the behavior of women:

Quid item tanta ordinandi crinis operositas ad salutem subministret? Quid crinibus vestris quiescere non licet, modo substrictis, modo relaxatis, modo suscitatis, modo elisis? Aliae gestiunt in cincinnos coercere, aliae, ut vagae et volucres elabantur, non bona simplicitate.

---

[57] P. de Labriolle, *Histoire de la Littérature Latine Chrétienne* (Paris, 1947), I, 155.

[58] G. Säflund, *De Pallio und die stilistische Entwicklung Tertullians* (Lund, 1955), 59.

[59] J. Geffcken, *Kynika und Verwandtes* (Heidelberg, 1909). Opposed to this view is M. Zappala, "L'inspirazione cristiana del 'De Pallio' di Tertulliano," *Ricerche Religiose*, I (1925), 132–149.

[60] G. Highet, *Juvenal the Satirist* (Oxford, 1954), 183 and 297, discusses the faint traces of Juvenal in Tertullian's works.

[61] Tertullian *Apologeticum* (ed. H. Hoppe, CSEL, LXIX, 1939), 35, 2–4.

Affigitis praeterea nescio quas enormitates sutilium atque textilium capillamentorum, nunc in galeri modum quasi vaginam capitis et operculum verticis, nunc in cervicum retro suggestum. . . . Vos vero adicitis ad pondus, colluras quasdam vel scuti umbilicos cervicibus astruendo.[62]

Then again in *De virginibus velandis:*

Vertunt capillum et acu lasciviore comam sibi inserunt, crinibus a fronte divisis apertam professae mulieritatem; iam et consilium formae a speculo petunt, et faciem morosiorem lavacro macerant, forsitan et aliquo eam medicamine interpolent, pallium extrinsecus iactant, calceum stipant multiformem, plus instrumenti ad balneas deferunt.[63]

Tertullian's writings were much admired by St. Jerome. Jerome remarks in one of his letters, *Quid Tertulliano eruditius, quid acutius?*[64] It has recently been pointed out that he was one of the earliest Catholic writers to show an interest in Tertullian, who had suffered a *damnatio memoriae* because of his defection to the Montanist heresy.[65] This interest is ascribed to "une parenté psychologique entre Tertullien et Jérôme." But the relationship between Tertullian and Jerome was much more than psychological. In Jerome's two major satiric attacks on women and marriage, his twenty-second letter and his polemical work *Adversus Iovinianum*, the writer expressly borrows from Tertullian's antifeminist writings.[66] The relationship between the two writers will be pursued further in the discussion of Jerome's satiric attacks on women.[67]

[62] *De cultu feminarum* (ed. Ae. Kroymann, *CSEL*, LXX, 1942), II. 7. Cf. *De virginibus velandis* XVII. 1 (*CSEL*, LXXVI, 102).

[63] *De virg. vel.* XII. 3 (*CSEL*, LXXVI, 97).

[64] Letter 70. 5. But see *Adv. Helvid.* 17 (*PL* 23, 211B), where Jerome rejects Tertullian as a heretic.

[65] C. Mohrmann, "Saint Jérôme et St. Augustin sur Tertullien," *Vigiliae Christianae*, V (1951), 111.

[66] Letter 22. 22 and *Adversus Iovinianum, PL* 23, 241A.

[67] Below, Chapter IV. For another early Christian satiric attack on the pagan gods, see Minucius Felix, *Octavius* xx–xxviii.

But Tertullian was only one of the Christian writers gifted in satiric expression. His successors in the Christian satiric tradition found a natural object of attack in the pagan gods. The Christian poet Commodianus subjected the pagan deities to penetrating ridicule.[68] In prose, Arnobius' sharp onslaught against pagan religion in the last four books of *Adversus nationes* reveals that apologist as a satirist of acid eloquence. Arnobius' skillful use of irony has been compared to Voltaire's.[69] Although it is hardly possible to illustrate his vitriolic wit by quoting excerpts, a few passages may at least give some idea of his method of attack. In his third book Arnobius describes life among the gods in highly satiric terms:

O pura, o sancta atque ab omni turpitudinis labe disparata atque abiuncta divinitas! havet animus atque ardet, in chalcidicis illis magnis atque in palatiis caeli deos deasque conspicere intectis corporibus atque nudis, ab Iaccho Cererem, Musa ut praedicat Lucretia, mammosam, Hellespontiacum Priapum inter deas virgines atque matres circumferentem res illas proeliorum semper in expeditionem paratas. havet, inquam, videre deas gravidas, deas fetas gliscentibusque per dies alvis alias intestini ponderis morositate cunctari, parturire alias tractu longo et manus obstetricias quaerere, illas telis gravibus et dolorum acuminibus fixas heiulare, tortari et inter haec omnia suppetias Iunonis implorare Lucinae.[70]

---

[68] Text of Commodianus in *CSEL*, XV. His date is much disputed. See P. Courcelle in *Revue des Etudes Latines*, XXIV (1946), 227–246.

[69] Labriolle, *Histoire*, I, 288. There is an error in Labriolle's chapter on Arnobius. On page 277, note 1, he refers to Jerome's Letter 20. 5 as a source for the story that Arnobius wrote *Adversus nationes* to prove his sincerity as a Christian convert. Arnobius is indeed mentioned in the passage cited but only as follows: *Septem libros adversus gentes Arnobius scribit.* The reference should be to Jerome's *Chronicle* under the year 2343.

[70] *Adversus nationes* (ed. A. Reifferscheid, *CSEL*, IV, 1875), iii. 10. See also the elaborate commentary of George McCracken, Arnobius, *The Case against the Pagans*, in *Ancient Christian Writers*, VII and VIII (Westminster, Md., and London, 1949).

In Book IV, mocking the large number of gods included under one name, Arnobius paints a scene such as might occur at a sacrifice to Minerva:

Si, cum divinas apparamus res adgredi atque aris flammantibus sua reddere constituta, Minervae omnes advolent ac de istius nominis possessione certantes poscant sibi singulae apparatum illum sacrorum reddi: quid in medio faciemus? . . . dicet enim forsitan prima illa quam diximus: meum nomen est Minervae, meum numen, quae Apollinem genui, quae Dianam et ex mei uteri fetu caelum numinibus auxi et deorum numerum multiplicavi. immo, inquiet quinta Minerva, tutinis,[71] quae marita et puerpera totiens castitatis purae inminuta es sanctitate. . . . quid dicis, inquiet secunda haec audiens.[72]

The ridiculous argument continues and waxes more violent as the five Minervas stake their claims and trade insults. In another passage of ridicule Arnobius recounts the illicit loves of Jupiter and concludes:

Ut videatur [Juppiter] miserabilis prorsus ullam non esse causam ob aliam natus, nisi ut esset criminum sedes, maledictorum materia, locus quidam expositus, in quem spurcitiae se omnes sentinarum e conluvionibus derivarent.[73]

Arnobius' chief weapon in his attack on pagan religions is a satiric caricature in which every absurd detail of pagan belief is exaggerated to monstrous proportions.[74] In contrast, Lactantius, the pupil of Arnobius, wins a somewhat different place in the history of satire. Although not himself an original satirist, nevertheless in the *Divine Institutions* he makes abundant use of the

---

[71] The text is corrupt here.

[72] *Adv. nat.* iiii. 16. Mockery of the large number of gods is found even in pagan satire. See Juvenal 13. 46–47.

[73] *Adv. nat.* v. 22.

[74] Cf. Weston, 231–236. Weston's few pages do scant justice to the unceasing stream of ridicule to which paganism is subjected in Arnobius' three last books.

classical satirists to support his strictures against pagan religion.[75]
Thus in the first book he suggests that the stories told in all
seriousness about the gods sound more like satiric tales from
the pages of Lucilius or Lucian.[76] The worshipers of vain
images are addressed with a line of Persius.

> O curvae in terris animae et caelestium inanes.[77]

The images themselves are ridiculed with a passage of Horace
which St. Jerome later uses with exactly the same purpose:

> Olim truncus eram ficulnus, inutile lignum
> cum faber incertus scamnum faceretne Priapum,
> maluit esse deum. deus inde ego, furum aviumque
> maxima formido.[78]

Lactantius uses as material in his attack on pagan religion the
remarks of Persius in his second satire against the dedication of
golden vessels to the gods.[79] Subsequently he attacks philosophy,
mocking its comparative newness among men, *quod inridens
Persius*

> postquam, inquit, sapere urbi
> cum pipere et palmis venit,

tamquam sapientia cum saporis mercibus fuerit invecta.[80] Another
attack on pagan superstition is supported by Persius 2. 29:

> qua tu . . . mercede deorum
> emeris auriculas? pulmone et lactibus unctis?[81]

---

[75] Lactantius' use of pagan literature is discussed by Hagendahl, *Latin
Fathers*, 63–88. For Jerome's verdict on him, see Letter 58. 10: *Lactantius
. . . utinam tam nostra adfirmare potuisset quam facile aliena destruxit.*

[76] *Div. inst.* (ed. S. Brandt, *CSEL*, XIX, 1890), i. 9.

[77] *Ibid.*, ii. 2; Persius 2. 61.

[78] *Div. inst.* ii. 4; Horace *Sat.* i. 8. 1 Cf. Jerome's commentary on
Isaiah, *PL* 24, 453D.

[79] *Div. inst.* ii. 4; Persius 2. 68–69.

[80] *Div. inst.* iii. 16. Persius 6. 38–39.

[81] *Div. inst.* vi. 2.

To his attack on the intellectual failings of the pagans Lactantius adds a severe critique of their moral and social vices. To reinforce his description of their dark and vicious life he makes use of seven lines from Lucilius:

> Nunc vero a mani ad noctem, festo atque profesto,
> totus item pariterque die populusque patresque
> iactare indu foro se omnes, decedere nusquam
> uni se atque eidem studio omnes dedere et arti,
> verba dare ut caute possint, pugnare dolose;
> blanditia certare, bonum simulare virum se;
> insidias facere, ut si hostes sint omnibus omnes.[82]

Thus the Christian apologists reveal in their writings not only a rich gift for satiric invention but also the ability to make use of the inherited corpus of satiric material in their attacks on the pagan enemy.

Lactantius carries the tradition of Christian prose satire, which began with Tertullian in the late second century, down to the early fourth, the period of Constantine and the beginning of Christianity's triumph. But in the last bitter battle between Christianity and paganism the expression of the Christian satiric spirit was not confined to prose alone. Two bitter verse compositions testify to the vigor of satiric writing in the age of St. Jerome. The anonymous *Carmen contra paganos* is a fanatic attack on pagan religion and on the prefect Virius Nicomachus Flavianus, the leader of the pagan revival at the end of the fourth century. The somewhat calmer *Carmen ad senatorem*, also anonymous, is a satiric onslaught on an aristocratic renegade from Christianity.[83] Another verse attack on paganism,

---

[82] *Ibid.*, v. 9 (Marx, 1228–1234) Cf. vi. 4, where Lucilius' definition of *virtus* is quoted at length.

[83] O. Bardenhewer, *Geschichte der altkirchlichen Literatur* (Freiburg im Breisgau, 1912), III, 566-569; Weston, 57–63; H. Bloch, "The Last Pagan Revival in the West," *Harvard Theol. Rev.*, XXXVIII (1945), 230–232.

Prudentius' *Contra Symmachum,* also contains powerful satiric elements.[84] In these poems victorious Christianity adopts the bitter tone of satiric invective as a caustic solvent for the lingering traces of paganism.

These poems, which all belong to the end of the fourth century and hence are contemporary with St. Jerome, reveal how natural it was for Christianity to use satire as a weapon in its struggle to mold society according to its new principles. Exactly the same task of edification lay behind much of the satire of St. Jerome, for Jerome's effort to promote a higher standard of Christian behavior is a continuation of the apologists' appeal for a Christian reform of society. As a naturally harsh and caustic personality and as a scholar thoroughly acquainted with the methods of ridicule employed by the pagans, Jerome was extremely fond of using satire to expose and castigate the faults he could perceive in men and morals. The task of the following chapters will be to show this in detail.

[84] Weston, 49–56. One of the lengthiest and most brilliant satiric attacks on the pagan deities is found in the works of Jerome's younger contemporary, St. Augustine, *De civ. Dei* iv. 8–12.

CHAPTER II

O Tempora! O Mores!

IT is a commonplace for satirists to castigate the age in which they live, to compare contemporary society unfavorably with the past, and to declare that the vices which they lampoon are peculiar to their own time. In his first satire Juvenal expatiates on the question, *Et quando uberior vitiorum copia?*[1] The satirist goes as far as to say in his thirteenth satire:

> Nona aetas agitur peioraque saecula ferri
> temporibus, quorum sceleri non invenit ipsa
> nomen et a nullo posuit natura metallo.[2]

Persius expresses his weariness with the empty life of his day in a line which Jerome twice quotes:

> O curas hominum, o quantum est in rebus inane![3]

Seneca contrasts the decadent luxury of his own age with the manly simplicity of Scipio's time. At the beginning of his satiric description of Roman bathing habits he tells us, *Magna*

[1] *Sat.* 1. 87.

[2] *Sat.* 13. 28–30. In line 28 *nona* is Clausen's reading. Others read *nunc* with the P manuscript. For the sentiment, cf. *Sat.* 6. 1–20 and 11. 56–161.

[3] Persius 1. 1. This line probably comes from Lucilius. See Marx, I, 9. For St. Jerome's use of the line, see *Anecdot. Mared.*, III, 2, 130, and III, 3, 83.

ergo me voluptas subiit contemplantem mores Scipionis et nostros.[4] Ammianus Marcellinus too takes the time of Scipio as the high point of human morality as he contrasts the swollen hypocrisy of Roman social life in his own day.[5] Ammianus suggests that the vices of the nobility, which he describes in great detail, are peculiar to his own age.[6] Of course, the contrast between the evils of a modern age and the purity of a time long past was also popular as a *locus communis* in the schools of declamation throughout the imperial period.[7]

The same deprecation of the age in which he lived and the same unfavorable view of its morality in contrast to the past are found in St. Jerome's writings. The attitude of a fourth-century Christian moralist to contemporary society was of necessity somewhat ambiguous. On the one hand there was considerable reason for optimism. The swift progress made by the forces of Christianity in the latter part of the fourth century was unmistakable. Writing about the year 400, St. Jerome declares, probably with some exaggeration, "The gilded Capitoline is filthy, all the temples of Rome are covered with soot and cobwebs . . . and a flood of people runs past the half-ruined shrines to the tombs of the martyrs."[8] About the same time Jerome addressed a letter to two Goths, Sunnia and Fretela, who had asked him for guidance through the textual difficulties of the Psalms. Jerome begins his letter with some highly optimistic remarks on the condition of society:

[4] *Epist.* 86. 4. Cf. *Quaest. nat.* i. xvii. 8 for a similar idealization of Scipio's age.

[5] Amm. Marc. xiv. 6. 11. Note the characteristic *at nunc* with which both Seneca and Ammianus introduce their satiric description of present decadence. Cf. Juvenal 11. 120: *At nunc divitibus cenandi nulla voluptas.* Also Juvenal 14. 189: *Haec illi veteres praecepta minoribus, at nunc. . . .*

[6] Amm. Marc. xxviii. 4. 17.

[7] For the *locus communis de saeculo*, see J. de Decker, *Juvenalis declamans* (Ghent, 1913), 22–38.

[8] Letter 107. 1. For date, Cavallera, II, 47. Cf. Prudentius, *Peristephanon*, II, 509–529.

Dudum callosa tenendo capulo manus, et digiti tractandis sagittis aptiores, ad stilum calamumque mollescunt; et bellicosa pectora vertuntur in mansuetudinem christianam. Nunc et Esaiae vaticinium cernimus opere completum: "Concident gladios suos in aratra, et lanceas suas in falces; et non adsumet gens contra gentem gladium, et non discent ultra pugnare.⁹

In spite of the obvious attempt at flattery, these words do at least show that Jerome's view of society and morals was sometimes favorable and approving. Yet such expressions of optimism are rare. Jerome saw more clearly than most of his contemporaries that he lived in the twilight of Greco-Roman civilization and that night could not be long delayed. In his commentary on Daniel, he clearly states that the military weakness of the Empire revealed that the end of Roman hegemony had arrived.¹⁰ In his sixtieth letter Jerome recounts the tragic history of the emperors from Constantius to the usurper Eugenius and, after describing the chaos caused by the barbarian invasions, adds: *Romanus orbis ruit et tamen cervix nostra erecta non flectitur.*¹¹ Thirteen years later, in 409, learning that Alaric and his Gothic host were approaching the walls of Rome, Jerome was filled with just and gloomy apprehension. *O lugenda res*

---

⁹ Letter 106. 1. On the identity of Sunnia and Fretela see J. Zeiler, "St. Jérôme et les Goths," in *Miscellanea Geronimiana* (Rome, 1920), 123–130. He accepts the identification of the two with the editors of the Latin-Gothic Bible, the *Codex Brixianus*. He also identifies Fretela with a Gothic bishop of Thracian Heraclea of that name, but Cavallera (I, 292, n. 1) demurs. De Bruyne believes the circumstances of the letter to be completely fictitious, *Zeitschr. für neutest. Wiss.*, XXVIII (1929), 1–13.

¹⁰ *PL* 25, 504A. See J.-R. Palanque, "St. Jerome and the Barbarians," in *A Monument to St. Jerome* (New York, 1952), 173–199. Also, E. Demougeot, "St. Jérôme les Oracles Sibyllins et Stilicho," *Rev. des Et. Anciennes*, LIV (1952), 83–92, who gives an account of other contemporary predictions of the end of the Roman Empire.

¹¹ Letter 60. 16. H. Levy has demonstrated that this passage was influenced by Claudian's *In Rufinum*: see "Claudian's *In Rufinum* and an Epistle of St. Jerome," *Am. Journ. Philol.*, LXIX (1948), 62–68.

publica, he exclaims, as he describes in detail the lands of the Empire lost to the barbarians. Then, citing Lucan, Jerome declares: *Potentiam Romanae urbis ardens poeta describens ait:* quid satis est, si Roma parum est? *Quod nos alio mutemus elogio: quid salvum est, si Roma perit?*[12]

We see then that in spite of several expressions of optimism on the improvement of society effected by the advance of Christianity, St. Jerome was thrown into deep gloom by the political events of his day. Yet his real dissatisfaction with the world in which he lived was not the result of political affairs but sprang rather from his disapproval of the moral state of society. Jerome could not fail to observe that Christianity's external victories had not wrought any significant reform of social mores. Indeed, he directly attributes the distracted state of the Empire to the wickedness of the age. In his description of the barbarian incursions he exclaims, "Through our sins are the barbarians strong, through our vices is the Roman army defeated."[13] Let us now follow chronologically, through each category of Jerome's writings, his satiric expression of disgust with the condition of his age.

Letters

Many of the letters written during Jerome's second sojourn in Rome (382–385) contain satiric references to the faults of contemporary society. In his thirty-third letter Jerome draws up catalogues of the enormous scholarly output of Varro and of

---

[12] Letter 123. 15 and 16. Cf. Lucan v. 274. Jerome's reaction to the capture of Rome is expressed in Letter 127. 12. For St. Augustine's first reaction, see his sermon *De urbis excidio*, ii. 3 (PL 40, 718): *Horrenda nobis nuntiata sunt; strages facta, incendia, rapinae, interfectiones, excruciationes hominum. Verum est, multa audivimus, omnia gemuimus, saepe flevimus, vix consolati sumus; non abnuo, non nego multa nos audisse, multa in illa urbe esse commissa.* For a summary of contemporary views on the collapse of the Roman world, see H. Daniel-Rops, *The Church in the Dark Ages*, tr. by A. Butler (London, 1959), 76–79.

[13] Letter 60. 17.

Origen the Adamantine.[14] These catalogues reveal, says Jerome, that we in our own day are sleeping the sleep of Epimenides and that the labor expended by Varro and Origen on literature we use in gathering riches.[15] To be sure we too have learned men in our day:

Sciuntque pisces in quo gurgite nati sint, quae concha in quo litore creverit. De turdorum salivis non ambigimus. Paxamus et Apicius semper in manibus; oculi ad hereditates, sensus ad patinas, et si quis de philosophis, vel de Christianis qui vere philosophi sunt, trito pallio et sordida tunica lectioni vacaverit, quasi vesanus exploditur.[16]

In this passage Jerome suggests that excessive interest in food was a vice peculiar to his own age. And yet gluttony had always been grist to the satirist's mill. Lucilius, Varro, Horace, Persius, Petronius, and Juvenal had ridiculed the Roman passion for delicacies of the table.[17] Among later writers Tertullian comments satirically on the refined voracity of the Romans, and

---

[14] So called after Didymus Chalcenterus, of whom Origen is the Christian equivalent. Jerome says of him, *Tanto in sanctarum scripturarum commentariis sudore laboravit, ut iuste adamantis nomen acceperit* (Letter 33. 4).

[15] It is noteworthy that Jerome here (Letter 33. 1) chides his contemporaries for their lack of interest in *secular* letters, since throughout his biblical commentaries he constantly derides heretics and pagans for their devotion to *saecularis sapientia* (see below, Chapter V). This incongruity is of singular importance in Jerome's life and career. Jerome again lampoons the ignorance of his age in Letter 43. 2.

[16] Letter 33. 3. The date is probably 385. See Cavallera, II, 26. There are very similar passages in Letter 27. 1 and 52. 6. See also S. Dill, *Roman Society in the Last Century of the Western Empire* (London, 1899), 130–131.

[17] Lucilius iv, 167; viii, 308–318; ix, 327–329; xiii, 140, in Marx's edition. Varro had treated the subject in his Menippean satire Περὶ ἐδεσμάτων (Schanz-Hosius I⁴, 558); Horace in *Sat.* ii. 2 and 4. For a list of satiric passages on gluttony (many of them similar to Jerome's attack) in Seneca and Juvenal, see Carl Schneider, *Juvenal und Seneca* (Würzburg, 1930), 27–28. For the Greek background of this topic, see G. Fiske, *Lucilius and Horace* (Madison, 1920), 398–405.

Ammianus Marcellinus describes the host at a banquet calling for scales to weigh the fish, fowl, and dormice.[18] In satirizing the corruption of Rome, Ammianus mentions only by *praeter-itio* the "abyss of dinner-table luxury and the varying ways of arousing pleasure," since the full exposition of these topics would be excessively long.[19] Subsequently in a tone very much like that of Jerome, Ammianus ridicules supposedly educated contemporaries for their greater interest in food than in books: "And if in the circle of the learned the name of an ancient author is dropped, they think it is a foreign name for a fish or a canape."[20]

Thus in attacking the gluttony of his age Jerome is working well within the satiric tradition. Even the diction of his remarks shows the influence of pagan satire. We may compare Jerome's words, *de turdorum salivis non ambigimus,* with Persius' expression, *turdarum nosse salivas.*[21] Moreover, the sense of the ridicule of gluttony cited above has a close parallel in Juvenal:

> Nulli maior fuit usus edendi
> tempestate mea: Circeis nata forent an
> Lucrinum ad saxum Rutupinove edita fundo
> ostrea callebat primo deprendere morsu,
> et semel aspecti litus dicebat echini.[22]

Furthermore in mentioning Apicius, Jerome recalls a standard pagan prototype of gluttony. Juvenal uses Apicius as a symbol of voracity twice and Martial three times.[23]

[18] Tertullian *De Pallio* v. 6; Amm. Marc. xxviii. 4. 13.

[19] Amm. Marc. xiv. 6. 16.

[20] *Ibid.,* xxx. 4. 17.

[21] Persius 6. 24.

[22] Juvenal 4. 139–143. Cf. *Sat.* 14. 8–10, Juvenal's description of the education of a youthful glutton who:

> "Boletum condire et eodem iure natantis
> mergere ficedulas didicit nebulone parente
> et cana monstrante gula. . . ."

[23] Juvenal 4. 23 and 11. 1; Martial ii. 69. 3; ii. 89. 5; iii. 2. 1. On Paxamus, see Morel in Pauly-Wissowa-Kroll, 36³, 2436.

Jerome touches briefly in this passage upon another fault which he considers characteristic of his age, the longing for legacies. So conspicuous is legacy hunting in the picture of society drawn by the classical satirists that one might perhaps suspect that Jerome, in his desire to attack his age, hits upon a failing which was no longer common but which he had learned of from his reading.[24] Yet the testimony of Ammianus Marcellinus shows that legacy hunting was still a widespread practice in the Roman society of the fourth century.[25] The edict of the emperor Valentinian in 370 which prohibited legacy hunting among ecclesiastics shows how common this fault was among the clergy.[26] Indeed, St. Jerome himself has been accused of legacy hunting as a result of his numerous invitations to wealthy Romans to join him in Bethlehem.[27]

Jerome concludes his letter by comparing the men of contemporary Rome to Aristippus and Epicurus, that is, lovers of luxury and sloth.[28] This theme of the worldliness and sensuality of Babylon, as Jerome calls Rome, is ubiquitous in his letters of the years 382–385.[29] Writing to the wealthy and noble Marcella in 384, Jerome describes Rome as "[a city] of pomp, of lewdness, of pleasures, a city in which to be humble is to be wretched."[30] The Christian poet Prudentius, a contemporary of St. Jerome, agrees with him. He envisages *Luxuria*, who *pervigilem ructabat marcida cenam*, arising on the western bounds of

---

[24] Horace *Sat.* ii. 5 is devoted to legacy hunting. Also Juvenal 1. 37–44; 5. 137–145; 12. 93–130. See in addition, Horace *Epist.* i. 1. 78–79, Cicero *Paradoxa Stoic.* 5. 2. 39, Seneca *De ben.* vi. 38 and *Ad Marc.* 19. 2.

[25] Amm. Marc. xxviii. 4. 22.

[26] See *Codex Theodosianus* 16. 2. 20, and *Novels of Valentinian*, III. 21. 3.

[27] Grützmacher, II, 223.

[28] Letter 33. 6.

[29] For Rome as Babylon, see Letter 45. 6. Cf. *Praefat. trans. libri Didymi de Spiritu Sancto*, PL 23, 107A: *Cum in Babylone versarer: et purpuratae meretricis essem colonus.*

[30] Letter 24. 5.

the world.[31] This has been interpreted to mean that Rome is regarded as the original home of sensuality.[32]

The luxury and materialism of the city stifle the life of the spirit, says Jerome. In his forty-third letter he again contrasts the learned diligence of the great Origen with the typical scholar of his own day. If the latter reads for as much as two hours, he yawns, rubs his face with his hand, tries to restrain his desire for food, and after so much intellectual labor returns to worldly occupations.[33] This brief caricature is but the beginning of an attack on the life of Babylon. Gluttony is briefly touched upon: *Praetermitto prandia, quibus onerata mens premitur*, says Jerome. Social life, he claims, consists of an endless round of meaningless visits dominated by malicious gossip: *Deinceps itur in verba . . . vita aliena describitur et mordentes invicem consumimur ab invicem.*[34] In this sentence the master of the biting insult inveighs against the art at which he was so adept. He then touches lightly upon the luxuriousness of clothing and passes to a satiric picture of the businessman:

Ubicumque conpendium est, velocior pes, citus sermo, auris adtentior; si damnum, ut saepe in re familiari accidere solet, fuerit nuntiatum, vultus maerore deprimitur. Laetamur ad nummum, obolo contristamur.[35]

Jerome proceeds to compare the changing countenance of a businessman with the masks of an actor who plays now Hercules, now Venus. In his careful construction of this passage, Jerome is trying to achieve the greatest possible vividness. He chooses three details to highlight, *pes, sermo,* and *auris,* using these as the subjects of brief successive clauses. With these three quick

[31] *Psychomachia*, 310–343.
[32] By T. R. Glover, *Life and Letters in the Fourth Century* (Cambridge, 1901), 264.
[33] Letter 43. 2. Cf. Letter 33.
[34] Letter 43. 2.
[35] *Ibid.*

strokes he immediately draws the sarcastic picture of greedy profit seekers. The asyndeton of the three clauses and the omission of the verbs also aim at swiftness.[36] Satiric contrast is achieved by chiasmus: *Laetamur ad nummum, obolo contristamur.*

Jerome concludes with a general statement of disgust with the worldliness of Rome: *Habeat sibi Roma suos tumultus, harena saeviat, circus insaniat, theatra luxurient et, quia de nostris dicendum est, matronarum cotidie visitetur senatus.*[37] The passage demonstrates that Jerome did not hesitate to castigate faults of which he himself was guilty. In speaking of *nostri* who visit *matronarum senatus*, he is presumably referring to those clergymen who were closely attached to noble patronesses, a type of ecclesiastic whom Jerome bitterly satirizes as foppish and hypocritical in his twenty-second letter.[38] Yet it must be remembered that Jerome's entire life at Rome revolved around aristocratic and pious ladies such as Marcella, her mother Albina, her companion Asella, and, of course, the famous Paula, who was to be

[36] Asyndeton as a device for creating vividness is common in Juvenal. See I. G. Scott, *The Grand Style in the Satires of Juvenal*, in "Smith College Classical Studies" (Northampton, 1927), 26; also William S. Anderson, "Juvenal and Quintilian," *Yale Classical Studies*, XVII (1961), 84. For asyndeton in Jerome, see J. N. Hritzu, *The Style of the Letters of St. Jerome* (*Cath. U. of Am. Patristic Studies*, LX), 48.

[37] Letter 43. 3.

[38] Letter 22. 16 and 28. It seems not previously to have been noticed that the expression *matronarum senatus* is probably derived from Porphyry's lost work on chastity in which he made bitter remarks on women and marriage. In his commentary on Isaiah, *PL* 24, 67C, Jerome says that Porphyry had spoken of *mulieres* and *matronae* as a *senatus*. E. Bickel has brilliantly succeeded in reconstructing Porphyry's work on chastity and has shown that Jerome was thoroughly acquainted with it and used it in writing *Adversus Iovinianum.* See Bickel's *Diatribe in Senecae Philosophi fragmenta* (Leipzig, 1915), 195–204. Since the phrase *matronarum senatus* does not seem to be derived from any of Porphyry's extant works (Luebeck did not attribute it to any known work), it is probable that it was derived from this work, in which Porphyry made bitter references to women.

the closest friend and support of Jerome's later life. It is just such a *matronarum senatus* which Jerome in this letter dismisses as one of the most unpleasant aspects of the worldly life of Babylon. The remark seems to be in particularly poor taste in a letter addressed to the very Marcella who was the center of Jerome's social circle.

Jerome's tone of disgust with the tumult of Rome, its arena, circus, and theater closely resembles in spirit those passages of Horace and Juvenal in which the satirists reject the inconvenience and confusion of Rome in favor of the peace of the countryside.[39] The resemblance is heightened when Jerome juxtaposes to his caustic portrayal of Rome an idyllic description of country life with its cheap and simple diet, its leaves and flowers, and its chirping birds.

Quam primum licet quasi quendam portum secreta ruris intremus. Ibi cibarius panis et holus nostris manibus inrigatum, lac, deliciae rusticanae, viles quidem sed innocentes cibos praebeant. . . . Si aestas est, secretum arboris umbra praebebit; si autumnus ipsa aeris temperies et strata subter folia locum quietis ostendit. Vere ager floribus depingitur, et inter querulas aves psalmi dulcius decantabuntur.[40]

Yet this description decidedly lacks the odor of reality. It appears to be rather a rhetorical exercise in drawing the traditional contrast between the city and country life. We know from Quintilian that the question *Rusticane vita an urbana potior?* was a standard rhetorical thesis.[41] Surely when a monk who is an ascetic zealot and a secretary to the pope suggests to a noble Roman widow, *secreta ruris intremus*, the invitation cannot be seriously meant.

---

[39] Horace *Sat.* ii. 6. 17–58, and Juvenal *Sat.* 3 and 11. 183–208. Cf. Jerome Letter 125. 8: *Mihi oppidum carcer est, et solitudo paradisus. Quid desideramus urbium frequentiam, qui de singularitate censemur?*

[40] Letter 43. 3. Cf. the praise of country life as an aid to asceticism in *Adv. Iovin., PL* 23, 311C–312A.

[41] Quintilian ii. 4. 24.

And yet even if the invitation was not meant to be accepted literally, it reflected Jerome's profound and passionate desire for escape from the endless troubles and grief which he had brought upon himself during his stay in Rome. His longing praise of country life is contained in one of the last letters that he wrote before his final departure from the city.[42] The death of Jerome's powerful patron, Pope Damasus, on December 11, 384, removed the great dam which had long held back a sea of enmity.[43] Jerome's letters reveal his increasingly difficult position. His attacks on the luxury of the city had not been well received. "We who refuse to wear silken garments," complains Jerome, "to get drunk, to part our lips in raucous laughter are called gloomy monks. If our tunic is not gleaming white we are pointed out at the street corner and called 'imposter and Greek.' "[44] Jerome concludes this letter with a brief but penetrating sketch of his accusers: *Cavillentur vafriora licet, et pingui aqualiculo farsos circumferant homines.*[45] In these words of ridicule the influence of pagan satire is clearly visible. Persius uses the word *aqualiculus*, which literally signifies "the maw of a pig," to mean "belly." Jerome's phrase *pinguis aqualiculus* is taken from Persius 1. 57:

> Pinguis aqualiculus protenso sesquipede extet.[46]

Thus Jerome relies upon the Stoic satirist to supply the most

[42] Chronology in Cavallera, II, 26.

[43] On the relationship between Jerome and Damasus see esp. A. Penna, *S. Girolamo* (Rome and Turin, 1949), 64–74, and E. Caspar, *Geschichte des Papstums* (Tübingen, 1930), I, 246–256. Jerome claims to have been the Pope's mouthpiece, Letter 45. 3. The extremely unfavorable opinion of Damasus found in Amm. Marc. xxvii. 3. 12. and in the *Libellus precum* (*PL* 13, 81–112, and *CSEL*, XXXV, ed. O. Guenther) is reflected nowhere in Jerome's writings.

[44] Letter 38. 5. The sentiment is repeated in Letter 54. 5.

[45] Letter 38. 5.

[46] Cf. Letter 107. 10. There are open references to this line of Persius in *Adv. Iovin.* 329C and *Comm. in Jer.*, PL 24, 794C; *CSEL*, LIX, 164. Con-

striking phrase in his description of the profligate enemies of Christian asceticism.

Jerome's thirty-ninth letter, the *epitaphium* of Blesilla, clearly reveals how much hostility his ascetic propaganda had aroused. Blesilla, the young daughter of the noble Paula, had been converted to the ascetic life by Jerome. When she died suddenly, her death was attributed to the ascetic rigors imposed upon her by Jerome. At her funeral the hostility of the mob broke forth, as the people murmured, "How long before this detestable class of monks will be driven from the city, crushed with stones, tossed into the waves?"[47] And yet Jerome's propaganda for reform was only partially responsible for the enmity of the city of Rome toward him. In his parting letter to Rome (No. 45), he catalogues the charges brought against him, "I am infamous, I am tricky and slippery, I am a liar and deceive with satanic art."[48] It is absolutely clear from this letter that it was Jerome's ambitious and bitter personality which drove him from Rome, the city which, he claimed, had once considered him worthy of the papacy itself.[49] In this letter, written at the very moment of his departure, Jerome delivers himself of some Parthian shots against the sensuality of the city. Addressing Rome in general he says:

Tibi placet lavare cotidie, alius has munditias sordes putat; tu attagenam ructuas et de comeso acipensere gloriaris, ego faba ventrem inpleo; te delectant cachinnantium greges, Paulam Malaniumque plangentium; tu aliena desideras, illae contemnunt sua; te delibuta melle vina delectant, illae potant aquam frigidam suaviorem; tu te

---

ington in his edition of Persius refers to the scholiast's comments on this line and to Isidore of Seville *Orig.* xi. 1. 136. for the original meaning of *aqualiculus.* Conington suggests that Persius was the first to apply the word to the human paunch.

[47] Letter 39. 3.

[48] Letter 45. 2.

[49] Letter 45. 3. It is not known whether Jerome had any reasonable grounds for this claim. See E. Caspar, *Geschichte des Papstums*, I, 257.

perdere aestimas quidquid in praesenti non hauseris, comederis, devoraris. . . . Bono tuo crassus sis, me macies delectat et pallor; tu tales miseros arbitraris, nos te miseriorem putamus: Par pari refertur sententia; invicem nobis videmur insani.[50]

In the month of August, 385, when the Etesian winds were blowing, St. Jerome set sail from Rome, never to return.[51] At Cyprus he was joined by Paula and her daughter Eustochium, who had rejected the pleas of their relatives and with great courage and religious fervor abandoned forever the evil life of Babylon. In company with these ladies Jerome made an extensive tour of the Holy Land and Egypt, piously visiting a large number of biblical sites.[52] Finally in the summer of 386 they settled in Bethlehem with the intention of building two cloisters, one for men under Jerome's direction and a convent for women to be headed by Paula.

Some years after his settlement in the East, Jerome dispatched to Marcella an invitation to join him in Bethlehem.[53] This letter purports to have been written by Paula and Eustochium, but it is generally agreed that it came from the hand of Jerome.[54] In this document Jerome's old hatred for the evils of decadent Rome again blazes forth. The quiet piety of Bethlehem is contrasted to the luxury of the city:

Procul luxuria, procul voluptas. . . . Ubi sunt latae porticus? ubi aurata laquearia? ubi domus miserorum poenis et damnatorum labore vestitae? ubi ad instar palatii opibus privatorum extructae basilicae, ut vile corpusculum hominis pretiosius inambulet et, quasi mundo

---

[50] Letter 45. 5.

[51] *Contra Ruf.* iii. 22 (*PL* 23, 494C).

[52] This whole tour is described in detail in Letter 108.

[53] Letter 46. Although Jerome's relations with Rome were broken for about seven years after his departure, the favorable view of the spiritual life of the Holy Land expressed in this letter suggests that it was written not too long after Jerome's settlement there. See Cavallera, II, 43; the year 392 is a probable date.

[54] Cavallera, I, 165.

quicquam possit esse ornatius, tecta sua magis velit aspicere quam caelum?[55]

This attack on the Roman passion for grandiose buildings recalls a traditional moralistic theme. Seneca attacked luxury in building, using *laquearia* as a symbol of wanton magnificence.[56] Juvenal satirized the Roman love of *latas porticus*.[57] One might suspect that Jerome's denunciation of building is more a rhetorical commonplace which belongs by tradition in a castigation of urban vices than an honest expression of moral outrage. Indeed, elsewhere in his writings we can see how his denunciation of the passion for building was guided more by tradition than by present reality. As early as 376 Jerome had written from the desert of Chalcis a letter in which he contrasted the piously ascetic life of the desert with Roman luxury. Addressing Heliodorus, a friend of his school days, he says, *Et tu amplas porticus et ingentia spatia metaris?*[58] Since Jerome certainly knew that his friend was a monk and hence in no position at all to construct magnificent porticoes, we must assume that he was speaking in a traditional and rhetorical manner. This opinion is strengthened when it is discovered that Jerome's words contain a reminiscence of Horace's praise of old-time frugality (*Carmen* ii. 15. 15):

> Nulla decempedis
> metata privatis opacam
> porticus excipiebat Arcton.

We have in fact striking confirmation from Jerome himself of the derivative nature of his critique of city life in the letter to Heliodorus. About twenty years after that letter, he wrote to Heliodorus' nephew Nepotianus, admitting:

---

[55] Letter 46. 10 and 11.

[56] *Ep.* 90. 42. *Laquearia* are used with the same moral significance in *Ep.* 90. 15.

[57] *Sat.* 7. 178. Cf. *Sat.* 4. 6 and 14. 85–95.

[58] Letter 14. 6.

Dum essem adulescens, immo paene puer, et primos impetus lasci-
vientis aetatis heremi duritia refrenarem, scripsi ad avunculum tuum
sanctum Heliodorum exhortatoriam epistulam plenam lacrimis
querimoniisque, et quae deserti sodalis monstraret affectum. Sed in
illo opere pro aetate tunc lusimus, et calentibus adhuc rhetorum
studiis atque doctrinis, quaedam scolastico flore depinximus.[59]

This admission should give us serious pause. If Jerome can
describe his censure of urban luxury as rhetorical play, it is
probable that other aspects of his satire were heavily influenced
by inherited declamatory moralism. We will have to face this
problem frequently in the course of this study.

Although Jerome's denunciation of the passion for building
is influenced by traditional pagan moralism, his remarks do in
fact represent a theme found in other Christian writers of his
time. Thus John Chrysostom, whose strictures on the wantonness of Antioch and Constantinople parallel in many ways
Jerome's attacks on Roman luxury, writes:

Τί δέ, ὅταν οἰκίας οἰκοδομῶμεν λαμπρὰς καὶ μεγάλας, καὶ κίοσι καὶ μαρμάροις καὶ
στοαῖς καὶ περιπάτοις ταύτας κατακοσμῶμεν, εἴδωλα πανταχοῦ καὶ ξόανα
ἱστῶντες; . . . τί βούλεται καὶ ὁ χρυσοῦς ὄροφος; οὐχὶ τὴν αὐτὴν τῷ μετὰ
συμμετρίας οἰκίαν ἔχοντι παρέχεται τὴν χρῆσιν; Ἀλλ' ἔχει, φησί, τέρψιν πολλήν.
Ἀλλ' μέχρις ἡμέρας μιᾶς καὶ δευτέρας, λοιπὸν δὲ οὐκέτι.[60]

We find, then, that the emphasis in pagan moralism on simplicity and frugality is continued in Christianity. It is precisely this
continuity of ethical commonplaces which permits St. Jerome to
borrow repeatedly from those representatives of pagan moralism
with whom he was so well acquainted, the satiric poets.

John Chrysostom confines his attack on the luxury of building

---

[59] Letter 52. 1, dated 394. With Jerome's use here of the word *lusimus*
may be compared Horace's references to his writing of satire as *ludere*
and *illudere* (*Sat.* i. 10. 37 and i. 4. 39).

[60] *Comm. in Phil.* x. 3 (*PG* 62, 260). On John Chrysostom as a social
critic, see A. Puech, *St. Jean Chrysostôme et les Moeurs de son Temps*
(Paris, 1891), esp. ch. ii, pp. 46–92. Also L. Meyer, *Chrysostôme Maître
de Perfection Chrétienne* (Paris, 1934) and P. Petit, *Libanius et la Vie
Municipale à Antioche au IV Siècle après J.-C.* (Paris, 1955).

to private edifices. It is curious to see how Jerome's repudiation of luxury in building extends even to churches. We find the ardent champion of Christian orthodoxy attacking the magnificent churches built *ad instar palatii opibus privatorum.*[61] Jerome is fond of contrasting the outward splendor of the contemporary Church with certain inner weaknesses. In his letter of exhortation on the ascetic life addressed to Nepotianus, Jerome writes: *Multi aedificant parietes et columnas ecclesiae subtrahunt; marmora nitent, auro splendent lacunaria, gemmis altare distinguitur et ministrorum Christi nulla electio est.*[62] In another letter of exhortation, to Paulinus of Nola, Jerome asks: *Quae utilitas parietes fulgere gemmis, et Christum in paupere fame mori?*[63] Again, in his letter to the nun Demetrias, Jerome satirizes mildly the builders of luxurious churches:

Alii aedificent ecclesias, vestiant parietes marmorum crustis, columnarum moles advehant, earumque deaurent capita pretiosum ornatum non sentientia, ebore argentoque valvas et gemmis aurea vel aurata distinguant altaria—non reprehendo, non abnuo.[64]

Jerome's mocking purpose is shown in his use of the highly ironic phrase *capita pretiosum ornatum non sentientia.* Grützmacher, who has in general a very low opinion of Jerome's character and motives, suggests that he had "persönliche Absichten" in his advice to Demetrias. Jerome preferred that Demetrias send money to his own monastery, which at the

---

[61] Letter 46. 11.

[62] Letter 52. 10. Jerome is referring here, of course, to the corruption of the clergy.

[63] Letter 58. 7.

[64] Letter 130. 14. Cf. *Comm. in Zach.*, PL 25, 1467B, where the language describing the outward luxury of churches is very similar but where the tone is much less disapproving, since there Jerome is trying to use these outward signs as proof of the progress of Christianity. On the "marble crusts" mentioned by Jerome cf. Ulpian's legal principle that when a building is sold, *Quae tabulae pictae pro tectorio includuntur itemque crustae marmoreae aedium sunt.* See *Digest* 19, 1, 17, 3; *Corpus iuris civilis*, I (Berlin, 1954), 280.

time of this letter (A.D. 414) was in serious financial difficulty, rather than spend it on showy basilicas.[65] But Grützmacher's opinion cannot be maintained in view of Jerome's frequently expressed scorn for glorious churches.[66]

Even after he took up permanent settlement in the East, Jerome did not cease to lampoon the failings of his age in general and of the city of Rome in particular. In his invitation to Marcella to join him in the East (Letter 46), Jerome, after comparing Rome to *mulier purpurata Babylonis*, proceeds to the following satiric description:

Sed ipsa ambitio, potentia, magnitudo urbis, videri et videre, salutari et salutare, laudare et detrahere, audire vel proloqui et tantam frequentiam hominum saltim invitum pati, a proposito monachorum et quiete aliena sunt. Aut enim videmus ad nos venientes et silentium perdimus, aut non videmus et superbiae arguimur. Interdumque, ut visitantibus reddamus vicem, ad superbas fores pergimus et inter linguas rodentium ministrorum postes ingredimur auratos.[67]

This unpleasant description again illustrates a remarkable aspect of Jerome's moralizing: his readiness to attack faults of which he too was guilty. We have already seen this tendency at work in Letters 43 and 44. In the present list of the objectionable aspects of Roman social life Jerome includes backbiting and the *linguas rodentium ministrorum*, although he specifically claims for himself the right *laudare et carpere* and was well aware that

---

[65] Grützmacher, III, 256. The letter is attributed to the year 414 by N. Pronberger, *Beiträge zur Chronologie der Briefe des hl. Hieronymus* (Amberg, 1913), 95.

[66] It is possible that the disapproval of ornate churches expressed in the spurious Letter 148. 19 influenced its erroneous attribution to Jerome. Vallarsi (*PL* 22, 1204, Note D) attributed the letter to Sulpicius Severus. As a leader of the monastic movement, Sulpicius, like Jerome, would probably have felt the ascetic's dislike of elaborate churches. For Jerome's attitude toward the plastic arts in general, see Eiswirth, *Hieronymus' Stellung*, 53–72.

[67] Letter 46. 12.

his own evil tongue was a major cause of his enforced retirement from Rome.[68]

Jerome's tendency to see only the faults of others is exemplified by another letter written in the early years of his settlement in Bethlehem. We have seen that in his forty-third epistle, written while he was still in Rome, Jerome had charged that the age in which he lived was unlettered and unscholarly. His removal to Bethlehem had not changed this view at all. Writing to Paulinus of Nola, Jerome again attacks the ignorance of the day. "Today how many men, imagining that they understand literature, hold in their hands a sealed book which they cannot open, unless He shall unlock it 'who has the key of David, who opens and no man closes, who closes and no man opens.' "[69] The idealization of an age long past, so common in satire, is implied by the contrast with "today." Jerome then calls upon Horace to reinforce his strictures:

> Quod medicorum est,
> promittunt medici, tractant fabrilia fabri.

Sola scripturarum ars est, quam sibi omnes passim vindicent:

> Scribimus indocti doctique poemata passim.

Hanc garrula anus, hanc delirus senex, hanc soloescista verbosus, hanc universi praesumunt, lacerant, docent, antequam discant.[70]

---

[68] Jerome insists (Letter 24. 1), *Nemo reprehendat quod in epistulis aliquos aut laudamus aut carpimus, cum et in arguendis malis sit correptio ceterorum et in optimis praedicandis bonorum ad virtutem studia concitentur.* Jerome well knew the effect his satire was creating. Writing to Marcella, he says, *Scio te cum ista legeris rugare frontem, et libertatem rursum seminarium timere rixarum, ac meum, si fieri potest, os digito velle comprimere, ne audeam dicere quae alii facere non erubescunt* (Letter 27. 2).

[69] Letter 53. 3; Revelation 3:7.

[70] Letter 53. 7. The quotation is from Horace, *Epist.* ii. 1. 115–117. P. Courcelle believes that these barbs are directed specifically against Vigilantius. See his "Paulin de Nole et Saint Jérôme," in *Revue des Etudes Latines*, XXV (1947), 263, n. 4.

A mocking description of these pseudo scholars is then given:

Alii adducto supercilio grandia verba trutinantes inter mulierculas de sacris litteris philosophantur, alii discunt—pro pudor!—a feminis quod viros doceant, et, ne parum hoc sit, quadam facilitate verborum, immo audacia disserunt aliis quod ipsi non intellegunt.[71]

This portrayal is highly effective, with its detail of the haughtily raised eyebrow of the pompous and ignorant weigher of words. The passage again illustrates Jerome's habit of satirizing faults of which he himself was guilty. What had been his major occupation during his years in Rome if not *inter mulierculas de sacris litteris philosophari?* He himself admits that at Rome, "a great crowd of maidens frequently surrounded me; to some I explained the divine books, according to my ability."[72] Jerome was well aware that his relationships with women were the source of considerable scandal.[73] His attack in the letter to Paulinus of Nola on those who explain scripture to women reveals the inconsistency in his moralizing which led Eiswirth to declare that, "Hieronymus war ein sehr sensibiler Charakter, der stark von der Augenblickstimmung abhängig war."[74] In his wish to convert Paulinus of Nola to the life of perfect asceticism Jerome shoots his arrows broadcast at the vices of the age, meanwhile quite unaware that he is hitting some of the faults of which contemporaries thought him guilty.

A much more important and puzzling example of Jerome's inconsistency is discovered when his Letters 46 and 53 are compared with Letter 58. In his invitation to Marcella (Letter 46) Jerome had strongly contrasted the debauchery of Rome with the quiet piety of Bethlehem. In Letter 53 Jerome invites Paulinus to come to Bethlehem in order, like Paul, to sit at the feet

[71] Letter 53. 7. Cf. Persius 3. 82, from which Jerome has borrowed some descriptive details.
[72] Letter 45. 2.
[73] Letter 45. 3.
[74] Eiswirth, *Hieronymus' Stellung*, 43.

of Gamaliel and be armed with spiritual weapons. But suddenly and unexpectedly we find Jerome in another letter (58) urging Paulinus by no means to voyage to the East if he wishes to maintain the ascetic life: Jerusalem had suddenly become the old painted woman of Babylon, as Jerome launches into a satiric attack on the Holy City:

Si crucis et resurrectionis loca non essent in urbe celeberrima, in qua curia, in qua ala militum, in qua scorta, mimi, scurrae et omnia sunt quae solent esse in ceteris urbibus, vel si monachorum solummodo turbis frequentaretur, expetendum revera huiusce modi cunctis monachis esset habitaculum; nunc vero summae stultitiae est renuntiare saeculo, dimittere patriam, urbes deserere, monachum profiteri, et inter maiores populus peregre vivere quam eras victurus in patria. De toto huc orbe concurritur; plena est civitas universi generis hominibus, et tanta utriusque sexus constipatio, ut quod alibi ex parte fugiebas hic totum sustinere cogaris.[75]

The puzzlement aroused among modern scholars by this sudden attack on the life of Jerusalem and its environs and the withdrawal of the invitation to Paulinus was largely the result of a chronological difficulty: which letter was earlier, the invitation in Letter 53 or its withdrawal in Letter 58? In the manuscripts Letter 58 is placed before 53, but Vallarsi reversed the order because of the phrase *in principio amicitiarum* in Letter 53. 1. On the basis of this reversed order Grützmacher built the theory that Jerome withdrew the invitation when he realized that the strong-minded Paulinus would never be subject to his own direction. Furthermore, Jerome feared, claims Grützmacher, that Paulinus might take sides against him in the incipient quar-

---

[75] Letter 58. 4. Apparently Paulinus took Jerome's portrayal of Jerusalem seriously. In his Letter XXXI. 3 (*CSEL*, XXIX, 270), Paulinus repeats part of Jerome's description. See the work of Courcelle cited above (n. 70), p. 254, n. 1. Jerome's inconsistency is clearly revealed when Letter 58, in which Jerusalem is described as another Rome, is compared with Letter 127. 8, where Rome is hailed as a new Jerusalem.

rel with Bishop John of Jerusalem.[76] More recent scholarly opinion, however, has restored the original order of the letters, placing the letter now numbered 58 before 53.[77] Grützmacher's theory, so unfavorable to Jerome's character, is no longer tenable if this order of the two letters is accepted, for now the satiric attack on Jerusalem precedes rather than follows the invitation to Paulinus. The solution to this chronological problem significantly affects our view of Jerome's attacks on the age. Grützmacher's theory implies that Jerome wrote his satiric description of the busy life of Jerusalem solely for personal reasons: to prevent the arrival in the East of a distinguished and strong-minded cleric who might question his own authority. But Cavallera seems right in maintaining that Jerome's invitation to Paulinus is only comprehensible if it was made after an exchange of letters had drawn the two men closer together and after Jerome had become concerned for Paulinus' spiritual well-being.[78] On this theory the unfavorable picture of Jerusalem would have been painted in Jerome's first letter to Paulinus and thus would have been the free expression of his wrath at the moral delinquencies of the Holy City. It is then reasonable to conclude that Jerome was truly shocked, at Jerusalem as at Rome, by the contrast between an ideal of Christian behavior and the reality of a society nominally Christian but still tainted by many vestiges of pagan immorality. We may then say that, like the satiric pictures of pagan society found in earlier Latin

[76] Grützmacher, II, 228.

[77] Cavallera, II, 89; Labourt's edition of the Letters, III, 235; Eiswirth, *Hieronymus' Stellung*, 73–96. Courcelle's brilliant reconstruction of Paulinus' letters to Jerome requires Letter 58 to precede Letter 53. See above, n. 70.

[78] Cavallera, II, 90. Even if Cavallera's reasonable view is accepted, the truth of the following remark of Grützmacher cannot be denied: "Dem vielgewandten Hieronymus ist es natürlich ebenso gut möglich, für die Wallfahrt nach Jerusalem, wenn er sie wünscht, wie gegen eine solche, wenn er sie nicht wünscht, eine Fülle von Argumenten beizubringen" (II, 228).

Fathers, Jerome's satire arose from his moral indignation and from his consequent desire to reveal before society the vices which to his mind implied the failure of a Christian ideal.

As the years passed and Jerome's memories of Rome faded, his anger and indignation at that city appear to have cooled. In 397 he wrote a letter to the aristocratic, wealthy Roman senator Pammachius. In this document the former satiric attacks on Rome have been transformed into a paean to the Eternal City as the capital of Christian asceticism. Jerome's satire now refers only to the past. The present merits unqualified praise. *Tunc rari sapientes, potentes, nobiles christiani, nunc multi monachi sapientes, potentes, nobiles.*[79] With this sentiment we may compare Letter 33. 3, a passage written about twelve years earlier: *At e contrario nostra saecula habent homines eruditos, sciuntque pisces in quo gurgite nati sint.*[80] In his later epistle Jerome proceeds to praise the disappearance of luxury from the city:

Ardentes gemmae, quibus ante collum et facies ornabatur, egentium ventres saturant; vestes sericae et aurum in fila lentescens in mollia lanarum vestimenta mutata sunt, quibus repellatur frigus, non quibus nudetur ambitio; deliciarum quondam supellectilem virtus insumit.[81]

Only twelve years earlier Jerome had spoken of *vestes sericae, nitentes gemmae, picta facies, auri ambitio* as characteristic elements in the life of the city.[82] Now, however, he applies his satire only to failings already corrected. *Fores quae prius salutantium turbas vomebant nunc a miseris obsidentur.*[83] Jerome's earlier views on Roman social life may be compared: *Sed ipsa ambitio, potentia, magnitudo urbis, videre et videri, salutari et salutare . . . a proposito monachorum et quiete aliena sunt.*[84]

[79] Letter 66. 4.
[80] Discussed above, p. 24.
[81] Letter 66. 5.
[82] Letter 45. 3.
[83] Letter 66. 5. This passage may recall Vergil *Georgics* ii. 461–462.
[84] Letter 46. 12.

To what cause may Jerome's reversal of opinion on Rome be attributed? It is difficult to suppose that Jerome suddenly began to think of Rome as the holiest city on earth. A consideration of the nature of the letter in which his new opinion is contained may be helpful. The immensely wealthy senator Pammachius, to whom the letter in question was addressed, had been married to Paulina, the second daughter of Jerome's companion Paula.[85] Upon Paulina's death in 398, Jerome addressed to Pammachius an *epitaphium*, which is the letter under consideration. The *epitaphium*, however, occupies only the beginning of the letter, which quickly becomes a highly exaggerated panegyric of Pammachius. At his wife's death Pammachius had adopted the ascetic life and had dared to enter the senate house in the dun-colored garb of a monk.[86] Jerome was well aware how mean-ingful was the adherence of a rich and noble senator to the cause of asceticism. The enemies of the monastic movement had been mounting strong attacks.[87] Jerome had already been forced to reply in his polemical tracts *Adversus Helvidium* and *Adversus Iovinianum*. Moreover, the Origenist controversy was currently raging hotly. In both these quarrels Pammachius was a powerful ally in Rome. By flattering Pammachius through excessive praise of the improvements his conversion to asceticism had wrought in the moral life of Rome, Jerome hoped to make him even more favorable to the monastic cause. Hence the glowing portrayal of Rome, for in the description of the city's transformation, Pammachius is glorified as *magnus in magnis, primus in primis,* ἀρχιστρατηγὸς *monachorum*.[88] The artificiality of the letter is revealed by the turgid rhetoric of its diction:

[85] On this important aristocrat, who played a considerable role in many of the religious controversies of the later fourth century, see W. Ensslin in Pauly-Wissowa-Kroll, 36², 296–298.

[86] Letter 66. 6.

[87] On the opposition to monasticism see Fliche and Martin, *Histoire de l'Eglise* (Paris, 1950), III, 358–364.

[88] Letter 66. 4.

Nobis post dormitionem somnumque Paulinae Pammachium monachum ecclesia peperit postumum, declares Jerome.[89] This artificiality reaches its height in Jerome's description of a mute mendicant: *Alius elinguis et mutus, et ne hoc quidem habens unde roget, magis rogat quia rogare non potest.*[90]

Jerome's picture of a Rome transformed, a picture in which satire is used to contrast a decadent past with an improved present cannot be accepted as the true expression of an optimistic view of the morals of the day. The passage of time had probably softened the old anger, and the desire to flatter Pammachius had dictated Jerome's praise of the new Rome. Yet in the very same letter the indignation of earlier years flares up briefly once again. Inconsistently Jerome turns to satirize the profligacy of the city:

Ubi videris fumare patinas et Phasides aves lentis vaporibus discoqui, ubi argenti pondus, ferventes mannos, comatulos pueros, pretiosas vestes, picta tapetia, ubi ditior est largitore cui largiendum est, pars sacrilegii est rem pauperum dare non pauperibus.[91]

Jerome's return here to his more usual view of the moral state of Rome strongly supports the theory that he had ulterior motives in praising the city to Pammachius. Again he emphasizes gluttony and luxury, delivering a slap *en passant* at the wealth of certain worldly clergymen who might be the unworthy recipients of Pammachius' bounty. Jerome's mockery of *comptos pueros* recalls Juvenal's disdain for dandified slave boys (*Sat.* 11. 149–151) and his preference for servants who have:

> tonsi rectique capilli
> atque hodie tantum propter convivia pexi.

His mention above of pheasants (*Phasides aves*) recalls Juvenal's use of *Scythicae volucres,* the same bird under another name,

[89] *Ibid.*
[90] Letter 66. 5.
[91] Letter 66. 8.

as a symbol of overrefined eating habits.⁹² Jerome again uses these traditional "birds of Phasis" as a symbol of gluttony in one of his later letters, and pheasants also appear in one of John Chrysostom's attacks on luxury of the table:

Ἴδωμεν τὰς ἐκ τῆς τρυφῆς ἐπιθυμίας τὰς ἐκ τῶν ὀψοποιῶν, τῶν μαγείρων, τῶν τραπεζοποιῶν, τῶν πλακουντοποιῶν. Ἀισχύνομαι μὲν γὰρ πάντα διηγούμενος. Πλὴν ἀλλ᾽ ὁμῶς ἐρῶ τὰς ὄρνεις ἀπὸ Φάσιδος, τοὺς ζωμοὺς, τοὺς χύδην μιγνυμένους, τὰ ὑγρὰ, τὰ ξηρὰ ἐδέσματα τοὺς περὶ τούτων κειμένους νόμους.⁹³

Jerome now proceeds, with a monk's scorn for the ways of the world, to characterize the eating habits of laymen: *Saecularis homo in quadragesima ventris ingluviem decoquit, et in coclearum morem suo victitans suco, futuris dapibus ac saginae aqualiculum parat.*⁹⁴ In these few words Jerome demonstrates his use of ridiculing description as a means of ascetic propaganda. His aim is plainly to arouse the disgust of the reader for the behavior of the *saecularis homo.* Thus his choice of the word *ingluvies*, which is literally the maw of an animal, to mean gluttony. The word *ingluvies* is used in the same scornful way by Horace:

---

⁹² Juvenal 11. 139. Petronius too uses the birds of Phasis in his satiric references to gluttony, *Satyricon* 119, lines 36–37.

⁹³ Jerome Letter 107. 10. John Chrysostom *In Matthaeum homilia*, LXX, 4 (*PG* 58, pt. ii, 659–660). There is another attack on gluttony *ibid.*, 494. In the pastoral letter of Theophilus, Bishop of Alexandria, which was translated by Jerome and is included in his correspondence as Letter 100, there is a description of gluttony which is so like passages on this subject in Jerome's own works that it is hard to believe that Jerome merely translated and did not elaborate the original passage: *Neque fasides aves sollicito labore perquirere, et garrulas volucres, earumque pinguedinem hianti ingerere gulae; nec investigare magni pretii cocos . . .* (Letter 100. 6). Unfortunately the Greek original of Theophilus' letter is not extant, so that it must remain uncertain whether Jerome added to it. For another example of *Phasides aves* in Jerome's writings, see *Comm. in Zach., PL* 25, 1529C.

⁹⁴ Letter 107. 10.

Hunc si perconteris, avi cur atque parentis
praeclaram ingrata stringat malus *ingluvie* rem.[95]

Furthermore, Jerome in this passage again uses *aqualiculus*, as did Persius, with a strongly pejorative meaning, in satiric reference to gluttony.[96] This description is meant, then, to be a brief but effective exposé of the sensuality of the worldly life.

Jerome's later letters reveal deepening despair over the state of the world. This despair was in part the result of the catastrophic political events of the first decade of the fifth century. Although a recluse and ascetic, Jerome could hardly avoid a feeling of profound shock and grief at the terrible incursions of the barbarians into the western part of the Empire. *Aruerant vetustate lacrimae,* he exclaims.[97] In such times one can hardly hope for more than merely to stay alive: "But in view of the miseries of the time and the savagery of the swords everywhere raging, he is rich enough who is not in need of bread, he is excessively powerful, who is not compelled to be a slave."[98] Yet the tragic events of those days did not quiet Jerome's enthusiasm for moral reform. On the contrary, they but strengthened his appeal for the rejection of worldly evils. The world collapses about us, *et solliciti sumus, quid manducemus aut quid bibamus?*[99] In spite of his old hatred of Rome, the news of the city's capture by Alaric in 410 filled him with gloom. In meditating on this dark event, Jerome turns to a consideration of the worldly vices which he had always associated with the fallen city:

Pro nefas, orbis terrarum ruit et in nobis peccata non corruunt. Urbs inclita et Romani imperii caput uno hausta est incendio. Nulla regio, quae non exules eius habeat. In cineres et favillas sacrae quon-

---

[95] *Sat.* i. 2. 8. Cf. Tertullian *De ieiunio* i. 1 for a similar use of *ingluvies.*
[96] Persius 1. 57. Cf. Letter 38. 5 and *Adv. Iovin., PL* 23, 329C.
[97] Letter 123. 16.
[98] Letter 125. 20.
[99] Letter 123. 14.

dam ecclesiae conciderunt et tamen studemus avaritiae. Vivimus quasi altera die morituri et aedificamus quasi semper in hoc victuri saeculo. Auro parietes, auro laquearia, auro fulgent capita columnarum et nudus atque esuriens ante fores nostras in paupere Christus moritur.[100]

The satirist's censure of his society gains new significance when that society is in very fact proved to be in a state of total collapse.

In reviewing now the passages of St. Jerome's letters in which he condemns the age in which he lived, one can see the special qualities which fitted him for his satiric role: the power keenly to observe the minute details of human behavior, the ability so to describe these details that their absurd elements are much exaggerated, and a certain lack of sympathy for human failings. It is a much more difficult task to try to evaluate the motives for his satire. The powerful influence of Jerome's rhetorical education which is so apparent in many passages suggests that his satire is at times based more on traditional ethical commonplaces than on his own immediate observations. Thus when he addresses to a simple monk a warning against building a luxurious home, the complete inappropriateness of the exhortation in its context makes it plain that Jerome is drawing on a traditional moralizing theme dear to the heart of satirists.[101] In contrasting in a letter to Marcella the hatefulness of the city and the pleasantness of the simple country life, he recalls, without much reference to reality, a theme on which the sixth satire of Horace's second book and the third and eleventh satires of Juvenal are built.[102] Yet there is no necessary conflict between a fully sincere disapproval of the faults of one's age and a somewhat artificial method of castigating those faults. Jerome's ardent championship

---

[100] Letter 128. 5. Cf. Letter 23. 15. Cf. also Tertullian *Apologeticum* xxxix. 14: *De nobis scilicet Diogenis dictum est: "Megarenses obsonant quasi crastina die morituri, aedificant vero quasi numquam morituri"* (*CSEL*, LXIX, 94).

[101] Letter 14. 6.   [102] Letter 43. 3.

This description of luxury is not entirely original. The phrase *gemma bibitis* comes from Vergil's satiric denunciation of urban luxury at the end of the second book of the *Georgics*.[108] The scornful reference to necklaces as "estates and country houses sewn on one thread" is derived from a writer who spiritually was closely akin to Jerome. Tertullian, in an attack on luxury, says of necklaces, *Uno lino decies sestertium inseritur*.[109] Jerome's scorn and distaste are even more ardent than Tertullian's. Later in the passage, however, Jerome is clothing in Christian garb a traditional piece of pagan moralism when, turning to the silk-clad men who do not even know how much money they have, who dress their homes in marble and drink from jeweled cups, he says that in spite of their sculptured tombs they are doomed to burn in hell, wealth and all. We may compare Horace, *Carmen* ii. 14. 5–12:

> Non, si trecenis, quotquot eunt dies,
>   amice, places illacrimabilem
> Plutona tauris, qui ter amplum
>   Geryonen Tityonque tristi
>
> compescit unda, scilicet omnibus,
> quicumque terrae munere vescimur,
>   enaviganda, sive reges
>   sive inopes erimus coloni.

Jerome's reference to burning in hell adds a superficially Christian color to his invective against luxury. Nonetheless, the tra-

---

sepultura Domini, ambitio divitum condemnatur, qui ne in tumulis quidem possunt carere divitiis.

[108] *Georgics* ii, 506. The phrase *gemma bibere* is also used in Letter 30. 13. This phrase is also found in Ambrose's satiric denunciation of female luxury: *Illa tibi inponet sumptuum necessitatem, ut gemma bibat, in ostro dormiat, in argentea sponda recumbat. . . . De Nabuthae*, 5, 25–26. Quoted by Weston, 80.

[109] *De cultu feminarum* I, 9; *CSEL*, LXX, 70. The interpretation of *uno filo villarum insuunt pretia* here given follows Vallarsi's note on the passage. For *pretia* Vallarsi prints *praedia*, which cannot be correct.

ditional spirit of this passage is plain. Jerome's remarks are in
fact a Christian version of the attacks on luxury found in Stoic
literature and epecially in Seneca.[110]

The *Life of Malchus* belongs to a later period of Jerome's life,
the early years of his settlement in Bethlehem.[111] His view of
society had scarcely improved in the years which separated the
biography of Paul from that of Malchus. On the contrary, his
opinions had grown far more critical in that he came to see the
level of human civilization in general as having sunk to a new
low. The Church too had shared in this decline. A separate
chapter will be devoted to Jerome's bitter remarks on the corrupt
state of the Church. Here, however, a passage must be pointed
out in which the deterioration of the Church appears to be
mentioned as part of the larger decline of human society as a
whole. In his introduction to the *Life of Malchus*, Jerome declares that he is planning to write a complete history of the
Church,

ab adventu Salvatoris usque ad nostram aetatem, id est, ab apostolis
usque ad nostri temporis faecem, quomodo et per quos Christi ecclesia nata sit, et adulta, persecutionibus creverit, et martyriis coro-
nata sit; et postquam ad Christianos principes venerit, potentia
quidem et divitiis maior, sed virtutibus minor facta sit.[112]

The reference to *faecem nostri temporis* implies that society has
been steadily declining until the bottom has been reached in
Jerome's own day.[113] We have seen above that such a view is

[110] E.g., *Naturales quaestiones* i. *praef.* 8: *Non potest* [animus] *ante
contemnere porticus et lacunaria ebore fulgentia et tonsiles silvas et de-
rivata in domos flumina quam totum circumit mundum et, terrarum orbem
superne despiciens.* . . . Cf. *ibid.*, i. xvii and iii. xviii.

[111] Cavallera, II, 27.   [112] *PL* 23, 55A–B.

[113] It is possible that *faecem nostri temporis* refers only to the condition
of the Church. It is much more probable however that Jerome here is
speaking of the decline of civilization in general, for he expresses this
pessimistic view of the world elsewhere. Cf. *Comm. in Eccles., PL* 23,
1090B: *Nunc vero pro saeculorum quotidie in peius labentium vitio.*

common to moralists and especially to satiric moralists. But as a Christian critic of his times Jerome sees the Church as having taken part in this decline. The sentence in which the stages of the Church's deterioration are expressed bears a remarkable similarity to a passage in which Gibbon outlines the early history of Christianity: "The indissoluble connexion of civil and ecclesiastical affairs has compelled and encouraged me to relate the progress, the persecutions, the establishment, the divisions, the final triumph, and the gradual corruption of Christianity."[114] Since the chapter of Gibbon in which the sentence is found is replete with references to Jerome's works in general and to the *Life of Malchus* in particular, it is possible that Gibbon was recalling here the passage in which Jerome described the decline of Christianity.[115] It would be indeed ironic if the great critic of Christianity were borrowing the words of the most ardent champion of orthodoxy to sketch the Church's gradual corruption.

Polemical Works

The works written by Jerome expressly to crush his personal enemies and those of the Church are, as might be expected, filled with the bitterest kind of satiric references to individual persons. They are not, however, entirely devoid of caustic remarks on larger and more general themes, the vices of society as a whole.

One of Jerome's most acid polemical works is his pamphlet against Jovinianus. This "Urprotestant" held, among other heterodox opinions, the view that fasting was no more holy than moderate eating *cum actione gratiarum*. This opinion gave Jerome the opportunity to describe and lampoon gluttony in two highly colored passages:

---

[114] *Decline and Fall*, IV, 62.

[115] For references to the *Vita Malchi*, see Gibbon, ch. xxxvii, n. 17 and 34.

Propter brevem gulae voluptatem, terrae lustrantur et maria; et ut mulsum vinum pretiosusque cibus fauces nostras transeat, totius vitae opera desudamus.[116]

Then again:

Cum variis nidoribus fumant patinae, ad esum sui, expleta esurie, quasi captivos trahunt. Unde et morbi ex saturitate nimia concitantur; multique impatientiam gulae vomitu remediantur; et quod turpiter ingesserunt, turpius egerunt. . . . Noli timere ne, si carnes non comederis, aucupes, et venatores frustra artificia didicerint.[117]

Suddenly Jerome appears to realize the kinship between his theme and the ridicule on sensuality in pagan satire, for into this specifically Christian attack on an enemy of fasting, he introduces Horace:

Irridet Horatius appetitum ciborum, qui consumpti reliquerunt poenitentiam:

> Sperne voluptates, nocet empta dolore voluptas.

Et cum in amoenissimo agro in morsum voluptuosorum hominum se crassum pinguemque describeret, lusit his versibus:

> Me pinguem et nitidum, bene curata cute, vises,
> cum ridere voles, Epicuri de grege porcum.[118]

Jerome then returns to a more specifically Christian tone, as in a vivid passage he warns those who eat even simple foods to avoid excess:

Nothing so overwhelms the mind as a full and boiling belly which turns every which way and releases itself with a blast in belching and breaking wind. What kind of fasting is it . . . when we are swollen with yesterday's banquets and our throat becomes merely a waiting room for the latrine? And while we wish to acquire a reputation for prolonged abstinence, we eat so much that the next night

---

[116] *PL* 23, 311A.   [117] *PL* 23, 313B and 315A.

[118] *PL* 23, 315B; Horace *Epist.* i. 2. 55, and i. 4. 15. On Porphyry's influence, see Luebeck, 70.

will hardly see it digested. Accordingly, this ought not be called fasting so much as drunkenness and stinking indigestion.[119]

This detailed description of the effects of overeating reveals Jerome as an extremely vigorous and effective ridiculer of human behavior, but as one who did not always bother to adhere to the highest standards of taste.

Turning now to a much later controversial work, the *Dialogus contra Pelagianos*, in which an orthodox Catholic and a follower of the Pelagian heresy discuss the problem of free will, we find Jerome satirizing a defect which was characteristic of a Christian society and for which there was no pagan counterpart—hypocrisy in the giving of alms. Nevertheless the orthodox interlocutor is probably quoting classical satire when he addresses the heretic and declares that the Gospel injunction to love one's enemies is hard to fulfill: *Forsitan in vestro coetu invenitur, apud nos rara avis est.*[120] The orthodox speaker then draws a brief picture of brotherly love as he has seen it:

Ad largiendum frustum panis et binos nummulos praeco conducitur, et extendentes manum, huc illucque circumspicimus, quae si nullus viderit, contractior fit. Esto, unus de mille inveniatur, qui ista non faciat.[121]

Here again we see Jerome using satire to expose the failure of a Christian ideal. One characteristic feature of satiric diction which

---

[119] *PL* 23, 315C.

[120] *PL* 23, 572A–B. It is impossible to determine whether the expression *rara avis* here refers to Persius 1. 46, Juvenal 6. 165, or to the general body of proverbial expressions about *aves* of which other examples are given by A. Otto, *Die Sprichwörter der Römer* (Leipzig, 1890), 51–52. Luebeck, 195, n. 4, attributes the phrase, without giving any authority, to Persius.

[121] *PL* 23, 572A–B. Cf. *Anecdot. Mared.*, III, 2, 256. (CC 88, 278): *Invenias aliquos de Christianis ideo dare elemosinam, ut laudentur a populo. Si quando pauper rogat, huc illucque circumspiciunt; et nisi testem viderint, pecuniam non dant. Si solus fuerit, manus contractior est, non dat libenter.*

occurs often in Jerome's passages of ridicule is the use of scornful diminutives (e.g. *nummulos*), a device favored also by Juvenal.[122]

Exegetical Works

In studying St. Jerome's contributions to biblical exegesis, the most voluminous category of his writings, one must deal with works of a highly derivative nature, for Jerome is largely dependent on the long traditions of Jewish and Christian exegesis and especially on the works of Origen and the Alexandrian school.[123] Nonetheless, these writings are extremely rich sources for comments on the contemporary world, for time and time again we find Jerome applying the moral strictures of the Old Testament to his own day and embroidering these strictures in a highly picturesque manner.

The earliest of Jerome's commentaries, that on Ecclesiastes, is full of satiric descriptions of the gatherers of worldly wealth. Thus, expounding Ecclesiastes 2:24, *Non est bonum homini, nisi quod comedat, et bibat,* . . . he writes: *Quid enim boni est, aut quale Dei munus, vel suis opibus inhiare, et quasi fugientem praecerpere voluptatem, vel alienum laborem in proprias delicias vertere?*[124] With the vivid image *opibus inhiare* we may compare *opibus incubare,* used by Jerome elsewhere in this commentary.[125] With both these images may be compared Horace's

> congestis undique saccis
>   indormis inhians.[126]

---

[122] E.g. 1. 11 *pelliculae;* 1. 40 *unciolam;* 7. 119 *petasunculus;* 13. 40 *virguncula.* On Jerome's use of diminutives, see H. Goelzer, *Etude Lexicographique et Grammaticale de la Latinité de Saint Jérôme* (Paris, 1884), 121–130.

[123] See esp. A. Penna, *Principi e caratere dell' esegesi di S. Girolamo* (Rome, 1950), and L. N. Hartmann, "St. Jerome as an Exegete," in *A Monument to St. Jerome,* ed. F. X. Murphy (New York, 1952), 37–81.

[124] PL 23, 1085C; CC 72, 272.

[125] PL 23, 1100B. Also *Comm. in Jer.,* PL 24 742D; *Comm. in Ezech.,* PL 25, 290B and 316C.

[126] *Sat.* i. 1. 70–71.

It is possible, though of course uncertain, that Jerome had Horace's first satire in mind when he used these two images, for elsewhere in this commentary he makes clear and abundant use of Horace's ridicule of worldly pursuits.[127]

The words of the Preacher, "a time to cast away stones, and a time to gather stones," rouse Jerome to an attack on the worldly passion for building:

Alii congregent lapides ad aedificia construenda, alii quae exstructa sunt destruant, secundum illud Horatianum:

> Diruit, aedificat, mutat quadrata rotundis.
> Aestuat et vitae disconvenit ordine toto.[128]

Jerome here takes up a theme often discussed in his letters, using the words of a pagan satirist to support the Old Testament moralist.[129]

We find exactly the same procedure when Ecclesiastes speaks against the lovers of gold.[130] Jerome calls upon Horace to support the strictures:

Flacci quoque super hoc concordante sententia, qui ait:

> Semper avarus eget. . . .

Quanto enim maior fuerit substantia, tanto plures ministros habebit, qui opes devorent congregatas. Ille autem videat tantum quod habet, et plus quam unius hominis cibum capere non possit.[131]

---

[127] *Sat.* i. 10. 72 is quoted immediately above *opibus inhiare, PL* 23, 1085A. The image of brooding upon wealth may be a reminiscence of Vergil *Aeneid* vi. 610:
> "aut qui divitiis soli incubuere repertis."
Cf. *Georgics* ii, 463 and 507 and see also Sulpicius Severus' attack on the clergy: *inhiant possessionibus . . . auro incubant (Chron.* i. 23).

[128] *PL* 23, 1088C. Horace *Epist.* i. 1. 99–100. The reversed order in which Jerome cites these lines suggests that he was quoting from memory.

[129] See above, p. 33.   [130] *Eccles.* 5: 10.

[131] *PL* 23, 1109A–B; Horace *Epist.* i. 1. 56. The remarks on the *ministri* who devour the gathered wealth are reminiscent of Horace *Sat.* i. 1. 77–78:

The last sentence may be an oblique reference to Horace's

Non tuus hoc capiet venter plus ac meus.[132]

Jerome's description of a typical rich man in this commentary is pure satire:

Dives vero distentus dapibus, et cogitationibus in diversa laceratus, dormire non [valet], redundante crapula, et incocto cibo in stomachi angustiis aestuante.[133]

In contrast to the corruption and degeneracy here portrayed, Jerome pictures the ascetic ideal of a poor man walking the straight and narrow path which leads to eternal life.[134]

After commenting on Ecclesiastes, Jerome turned his attention to the New Testament, expounding Paul's letters to Philemon, the Galatians, Titus, and the Ephesians. The first three of these works are virtually devoid of satiric remarks on the contemporary world, except for some caustic descriptions of clerical hypocrisy, a discussion of which may be deferred until we turn to Jerome's satire on the decline of the Church.[135] However, in expounding the Epistle to the Ephesians, Jerome delivers a curious attack on various forms of secular activity:

Nonne vobis videtur in vanitate sensus et obscuritate mentis ingredi, qui diebus ac noctibus in dialectica arte torquetur: qui physicus perscrutator oculos trans coelum levat, et ultra profundum terrarum et abyssi quoddam inane demergit, qui iambum struit, qui tantam metrorum silvam in suo studiosus corde distinguit et congerit; et (ut in alteram partem transeam) qui divitias per fas et nefas quaerit. Qui adulatur regibus, haereditates captat alienas, et opes congregat, quas in momento cui sit relicturus, ignorat?[136]

"Formidare malos fures, incendia, servos,
ne te compilent fugientes, hoc iuvat?"
For the thought cf. Juvenal 14. 303–331.
[132] *Sat.* i. 1. 46. [133] *PL* 23, 1109B–C. CC 72, 295.
[134] *PL* 23, 1113B. CC 72, 299.
[135] *PL* 23, 452B–C. Below, Chapter IV. [136] *PL* 26, 536D–537A.

Jerome's disapproval of *dialectica ars* is not surprising, for he frequently expresses dislike of subtle argumentation, connecting it with the treachery of heretics.[137] More puzzling is the attack on physical scientists and on poets. In view of the age in which Jerome lived, an age which could never be justly criticized for excessive love of science or poetry, these words of strong disapproval seem highly artificial. Yet Jerome does display a theoretical dislike of scientific speculation by twice quoting sympathetically the line of Aristophanes in which the poet mocks the physical speculations of Socrates:

$$\text{'Αεροβατῶ καὶ περιφρονῶ τὸν ἥλιον.}^{138}$$

Since Jerome's attack on intellectual endeavor is accompanied by deprecatory remarks on the gathering of wealth and on legacy hunting, the words of disapproval should probably be considered to reflect a monkish rejection of all forms of worldly activity, including intellectual labor. This same attitude is reflected in other passages in this commentary where Jerome rails against those "who dispute about physical things, claim they can count the sands of the shore and the drops in the ocean, who, drunk with thoughts of this world, vomit, go mad, and fall headlong."[139] It is of course highly incongruous for St. Jerome to express such violent disapproval of worldly knowledge, since, as we have seen, he elsewhere (Letters 33, 43, and 53) points to the lack of interest in secular learning as an indication of the degeneracy of the age. Jerome was never able to reconcile in his own mind his love of worldly knowledge and his feeling that such knowledge was fundamentally unchristian.

After his exposition of the Pauline Epistles, Jerome returned to the Old Testament and began his series of commentaries on the twelve minor Hebrew prophets. In interpreting Micah, he mentions in passing the lovers of *villas istius saeculi*, a phrase in

137 E.g. *PL* 25, 863D, 927A, 1025A, and 1044B.
138 *PL* 24, 544B, and *PL* 26, 625C; *Clouds*, 225.
139 *PL* 26, 552B; cf. 561B.

which the image of a large and noble home is significantly used to represent worldliness.[140] Then in his commentary on Zephaniah, Jerome delivers a brief but effective attack on effeminacy, an onslaught which in the bitterness of its ridicule recalls Juvenal's second satire: *Peribit qui in femineo languore mollitus comam nutrit, vellit pilos, cutem polit, et ad speculum comitur, quae proprie passio et insania feminarum est.*[141] We have no indication that Jerome is here referring to a particular individual. Apparently the words are aimed at a widespread vice of the age.

The commentary on Zechariah belongs to a later period of Jerome's life, the opening years of the fifth century.[142] Taking his cue from the words of the prophet, *Quis enim despexit dies parvos?* Jerome lampoons the worldly splendor of the rich: *Cum viderimus potentes saeculi fulgere auro, purpura, gemmis rutilare, circumdari exercitu, dicamus in nobis: quis, putas, despicit dies parvos?*[143] The satiric element in this passage lies in two words, *rutilare* and *exercitu*. These are the two brush strokes which transform a simple drawing into a caricature of arrogant pomp. Jerome achieves his aim of exposure and ridicule by a subtle use of two exaggerated descriptive details.

In the commentary on Amos, too, Jerome lashes out at the rich and powerful. Explicating Amos 6:1, "Woe to them that are at ease in Zion," he says:

Isti sunt capita populorum, qui confidunt in divitiis, et opulenti sunt in Sion. . . . Et ingrediuntur pompatice domum Israel, ut tumorem animi corpus ostendat, et pomparum ferculis similes esse videantur.[144]

This passage reveals Jerome as a mosaic artist setting into his works highly colored extracts from pagan literature. The satiric description of a haughty manner of walking borrows from Cicero's warning: *Cavendum autem est, ne . . . tarditatibus*

---

[140] *PL* 25, 1167B.   [141] *PL* 25, 1350C.
[142] Cavallera, II, 51–52.   [143] *PL* 25, 1444C.
[144] *PL* 25, 1058A.

utamur in ingressu mollioribus, ut pomparum ferculis similes esse videamur.[145] Jerome the *Ciceronianus* cannot repress a reminiscence of his beloved author even in a commentary on an Old Testament prophet. Evidently the phrase *pomparum ferculis similes* struck Jerome as an apt portrayal of arrogance, for he uses the expression on several occasions.[146]

The detailed commentaries on the three major prophets, Isaiah, Jeremiah, and Ezekiel, were composed by Jerome toward the close of his life. They belong to the years 408–416. The earliest of them, that on Isaiah, contains several bitter references to the faults of the age. It is an age of ignorance in which men's ears are scornful of the products of hard intellectual labor but are delighted by showy eloquence. We become nauseated by the effort required for the understanding of Sacred Scripture.[147] This theme recalls Jerome's attacks on the ignorance of his age in his letters written from Rome.[148] Furthermore, claims Jerome, it is an age in which the rich are flattered but the poor despised, in which the rich taste all the sensual delights of luxurious banquets in houses whose ceilings are gilded, whose walls are clothed in crusts of marble and are agleam with cut ivory, while the poor, without the meanest shelter, freeze to death.[149] This attack on current society is elicited by Isaiah's apocalyptic vision of the destruction of the earthly city. It clearly demonstrates Jerome's use of biblical exhortations as the starting point for his expression of anger at the elements in contemporary society which he considered corrupt and unchristian.

Two of Jerome's attacks on the vices of society in the commentary on Isaiah show the influence of Horace. The first example is obvious and certain: Isaiah's attack on avarice recalls the remark of Horace, *Semper avarus eget.*[150] The second in-

---

[145] *De off.* i. 36. 131.   [146] Cf. Letter 3. 6 and 125. 16.
[147] *PL* 24, 22A and 289D.   [148] Cf. Letters 33. 3; 43. 2; and 53. 5.
[149] *PL* 24, 293A–B.   [150] *PL* 24, 49A; Horace *Epist.* i. 2. 56.

stance is less definite. Jerome describes the dissatisfaction of men with their place in life:

Saepe videmus in saeculo quosdam de alio proposito transire ad aliud. Verbi gratia, ut qui militiam male experti sunt, transeunt ad negotiationem. Rursumque causidicos bellatorum arma corripere. Mutant industriam, ut mutent infelicitatem.[151]

The sentiment of this passage is highly reminiscent of the opening lines of the first satire of Horace's first book, in which the longing of businessmen, soldiers, and lawyers to change their role in life is described. Although there is no verbal similarity between Jerome and Horace, it is possible that Jerome is here drawing upon the pagan satirist or at least upon the same moralistic material which Horace used in composing Satire I. 1.

The commentary on Ezekiel belongs to the years 410–412 and is strongly marked by the tragic political events of those years. The fate of the Roman nobility in Alaric's capture of the city is reflected in the remark that the rich, whose lives were passed amid silk, gems, and the weight of gold and silver, end their days as beggars.[152] Those who belched with their fullness, who did not even know the extent of their wealth, are now in need of food, clothing, and shelter.[153] In spite of the formerly dissipated lives of such people, Jerome gazes upon their fate with tears and groans. And yet he must admit that their spirits have been but little softened by their chastening. On the contrary, they seek gold even in their captivity. Some of the rich have gone so far as to pretend by their vile clothing that they are

---

[151] *PL* 24, 288A. The same sense of the weary uselessness of earthly activity is found in Jerome's exposition of the text *Anni nostri sicut aranea meditabuntur.* The psalmist, says Jerome, *nihil pulchrius potuit dicere quam ut humanam vitam et omnem sollicitudinem nostram studiaque describeret, quibus huc illucque discurrimus et opes praeparamus, divitias quaerimus, aedificamus domos, liberos procreamus; et videte cui rei comparantur. Anni nostri sicut aranea meditabuntur (Anecdot. Mared.,* II, 3. 65; CC 78, 418).

[152] *PL* 25, 71D.   [153] *PL* 25, 175B and 199B.

poor, though they "lie upon the wealth of Croesus."[154] In spite of Jerome's brief attempt to be sympathetic to the plight of the rich, his more usual attitude returns as he attacks their hyprocrisy and secret avarice. Indeed, his view of the rich is only partially and temporarily governed by the actuality of their sad fate at the time he is writing, for sometimes his words recall an earlier period of dissipation before the disastrous events of the Gothic invasion. Thus he suggests that the rich do not dress to keep out the cold but rather choose garments *quae tenuitate sui, corpora nuda demonstrent.*[155]

Conclusion

St. Jerome's sense of the decline of civilization and his disgust with the vices of "the world" form an important theme in all categories of his writings, from the letters written in the desert of Chalcis when he was a young man to his late exegetical and homiletic works. Every opportunity offered by a biblical text to mount an attack upon contemporary failings is immediately seized upon, with the result that these invectives sometimes appear as leitmotivs automatically recalled whenever the context of a passage suggests worldly sin. Jerome can rarely mention the contemporary world without adding a portrayal of silken garments, gluttonous banquets, and marble-encrusted buildings. In Jerome's mind the disastrous political events of the day are the result of the decline of morals.

To be sure, disdain for the contemporary world and its standards is an attitude to be expected in the writings of an ascetic enthusiast such as Jerome. Moreover, it should be considered neither surprising nor coincidental that the manner in which Jerome expresses his disdain closely resembles in thought and diction passages in such pagan writers as Horace, Persius, Seneca, and Juvenal. All these writers were influenced to a greater or lesser extent by Stoicism, and between the ethics of

[154] *PL* 25, 231C–D.   [155] *PL* 24, 432C. Cf. Letter 127. 3.

the Stoa and those of ascetic Christianity were many points of contact.[156] Jerome himself refers to *Stoici, qui nostro dogmati in plerisque concordant*.[157] Certainly the Stoic doctrine that virtue is the only source of happiness led to a repudiation of commonly accepted standards of behavior. There is a powerful note of asceticism in later Stoicism.[158] Zeller compares the Stoic sense of the depth and extent of human depravity as expressed, for instance, by Seneca to the attitude of the early Christian theologians.[159] The forged correspondence between Seneca and St. Paul implies that the early Christians sensed in Seneca a kindred spirit. St. Jerome includes Seneca in his catalogue of illustrious Christians.[160] But Jerome's realization of the similarity of his own moral outlook to that of certain pagan writers extended beyond an appreciation of Seneca alone. As a scholar whose mind was deeply imbued with pagan Latin letters, Jerome seized upon those passages in pagan writers in which contemporary standards were lampooned and in which he found adumbrated his feelings toward his own society. The richest source of such passages were the satiric poets.

However, in addition to Jerome's ascetic outlook on the world and his acquaintance with pagan Latin letters, the element of personal animus should not be overlooked in investigating the hostilities of this harsh and bitter man. Jerome had had his worldly ambitions, the complete failure of which filled him with bitterness toward the society that had refused to recognize his

[156] On the influence of Stoicism on Roman Satire see Duff, *Roman Satire*, 116; for Horace and the Stoa, 78 and 80–81; for Juvenal, 162. Also De Decker, *Juvenalis declamans*, 19–20, and R. Schütze, *Juvenalis ethicus* (Greifswald, 1905). G. Highet, "The Philosophy of Juvenal," *TAPA*, LXXX (1949), 254–270, sees Juvenal as an Epicurean late in life.

[157] *Comm. in Isa.*, XI, 6–9 (PL 24, 151B).

[158] See E. Hatch, *The Influence of Greek Ideas on Christianity* (Hibbert Lectures, 1888; reprinted, New York, 1957).

[159] E. Zeller, *Outlines of the History of Greek Philosophy*, tr. by L. R. Palmer (13th ed.; London, 1955), 221.

[160] *De vir. ill.* XII (PL 23, 662A).

claims and that had driven him into the comparative retirement of his Bethlehem monastery.

Yet it is too simple to see in Jerome's attacks on society merely the propaganda of a leader of the monastic movement or the petulant anger of a disappointed recluse. The ideals which lay behind his satiric attacks were higher. We find them expressed in a passage in his commentary on Jonah: "It is difficult for powerful men and noble men and rich men, and much more difficult for eloquent men, to believe in God. For their mind is blinded by riches and wealth and luxury, so that, surrounded by vices, they cannot see the virtue and simplicity of Holy Scripture."[161] Again, in the commentary on Ezekiel: "Pride, satiety of food, abundance of possessions, leisure and pleasure are the sins of Sodom and on account of them forgetfulness of God follows, that forgetfulness which imagines that present goods will last forever and that the necessities of life will never be needed."[162] Jerome's feeling that contemporary morals had reached a new depth of debasement was, then, the same sense of the failure of Christianity to reform society completely which kindled the growth of the monastic movement in the latter part of the fourth century. To be sure, the highest ideal of the ascetic was complete indifference to the affairs of the world: *Nos quoque eos, qui ad saeculi mala et bona vel contristantur vel exultant, mulieres appellemus, molli et effeminato animo.*[163] But St. Jerome, unable by nature to achieve this ideal, returns again and again *ad saeculi mala.* His caustic personality and his keen and penetrating powers of observation precluded his merely denouncing the social evils which he perceived. Rather he portrays them with an exactness and an amplitude whose obvious aim is to lampoon and ridicule. Even in his monk's cell at

[161] *PL* 25, 1143C. We may contrast the Stoic position as phrased by Seneca: *Hanc praecedentem causam divitiae habent: inflant animos, superbiam pariunt, invidiam contrahunt, et usque eo mentem alienant, ut fama pecuniae nos etiam nocitura delectet* (*Epist.* 87. 31). Cf. Matt. 19:23.

[162] *PL* 25, 155A.   [163] *PL* 25, 83A.

Bethlehem his mind ranged over the faults and failings of the Worldly City, and he could truthfully say in a passage in which his devotion to Christian scholarship and to the ascetic life is strikingly blended with his concern for the fate of the world: *Totum me huic trado studio, et quasi in quadam specula constitutus, mundi huius turbines atque naufragia, non absque gemitu et dolore contemplor.*[164]

[164] *PL* 24, 195B.

CHAPTER III

The Church and the Clergy

ST. JEROME'S repudiation of the society of his age was largely the expression of his opposition to the wanton debauchery of city life. In his view, the tone of urban society was still determined by a tenacious paganism of morality. Out of his disgust for contemporary standards of behavior in general grew a thorough disenchantment with the condition of the Church and the clergy. Jerome believed that the Church, whose task had been to purify by its doctrines the whole mass of society, had instead been corrupted by its rise to wealth and power until it stood no higher than the surrounding paganism. This view is manifest in the preface to the *Life of Malchus*, in which Jerome, sketching his projected history of Christianity, outlines the development of the Church from its origins through its dissemination by the apostles and its glorification by persecutions and martyrdoms until, "after it passed under Christian emperors, it became greater indeed in power and riches, but weaker in virtues."[1]

Evidence to support Jerome's view of the deleterious effects

[1] *PL* 23, 55B. In the *Dial. contra Luciferianos,* however, Jerome combats the extreme and heretical view, *factum de Ecclesia lupanar* (*PL* 23, 163A).

of worldly victory on the Church is found in many writers of the fourth century. Ammianus Marcellinus, a fair-minded pagan, describes the gory battle for the papal throne between Damasus and Ursinus in 366 and comments that he can hardly blame the zeal of men to achieve a position which would afford them rich opportunity for wanton luxury.[2] This ironic remark gains support when Jerome relates that Vettius Agorius Praetextatus, the leader of the pagan party at Rome, had told Damasus that he would straightway become a Christian if he might experience the sensual delights enjoyed by the occupant of the papal throne.[3] Yet it was not the higher clergy alone who had felt the corrupting effects of success. The lower ranks had become so worldly that on July 30, 370, the Emperor Valentinian was forced to forbid priests to enter the houses of wealthy women in search of legacies.[4] Gregory Nazianzen, Jerome's mentor, was enraged at the worldly splendor of the secular clergy.[5] An anonymous writer of the late fourth century, the author of the apocryphal *Apocalypse of Paul*, envisages special torments in hell for clergymen devoted to sensual pleasure.[6] Sulpicius Severus, a leader of the ascetic movement, attacks the cupidity of the clergy in satiric terms: *Inhiant possessionibus, praedia excolunt, auro excubant, emunt venduntque, quaestui per omnia student.*[7] Elsewhere too Sulpicius expatiates in vitriolic terms on clerical corruption but

---

[2] Amm. Marc. xxvii. 3. 14.   [3] *Contra Joannem* 8, PL 23, 361C.

[4] *Codex Theodosianus* 16. 2. 20 (*Novels of Valentinian*, III, 21, 3): "We decree, further, that the aforesaid clerics shall be able to obtain nothing whatsoever, through any act of liberality or by a last will of those women to whom they have attached themselves privately under the pretext of religion" (*The Theodosian Code*, tr. by C. Pharr [Princeton, 1952], p. 444).

[5] *Orat.* XLII, xxiv (*PG* 36, 488A).

[6] M. R. James, *The Apocryphal New Testament* (Oxford, 1924; reprinted 1945), 543.

[7] *Chron.* i. 23. Cf. Jerome, *Comm. in Eccles.*, PL 23, 1085C; CC 72, 272: *Quid enim boni est, aut quale Dei munus, vel suis opibus inhiare, et quasi fugientem praecepere voluptatem.* See above, p. 54.

concludes his remark with the words, *Verum haec describenda mordacius beato Hieronymo relinquamus.*[8]

The monastic movement, which experienced a phenomenal growth in the fourth century, arose in part as a powerful protest against the declining moral standards of the secular clergy. The development of asceticism was a direct challenge to the novel theory of the Church as a *corpus permixtum* including both saint and sinner, a theory which in the fourth century was swiftly replacing the older view of the Church as the community of the holy.[9] Yet even the ascetic movement was unable to maintain the high standards it had originally championed. The protection afforded by the monastic life against the crushing economic burdens and the dangerous barbarian raids which were very real hazards to survival in the fourth century naturally attracted to monasticism some adherents whose motives were impure. The author of the *Apocalypse of Paul* sees aflame in hell those clerics "that seemed to renounce the world, wearing our garb, but the snares of the world made them to be miserable."[10] The difficulty of enforcing true renunciation on the monks is succinctly expressed by Jerome: *Nec erubescimus, paupertatem vili palliolo praeferentes, Croesi opibus incubare.*[11] Jerome gives an example of the unworthy motives which pro-

---

[8] *Dial.* i. 21. It thus seems that Jerome was well known even in his own day as a satirizer of the clergy. Cf. also *Dial.* i. 8, where Jerome's attack on the clergy in his Letter 22 is mentioned.

[9] See E. Hatch, *The Influence of Greek Ideas on Christianity*, 165; also H. Bitterman, "The Beginning of the Struggle between the Regular and Secular Clergy," *Medieval and Historical Essays in Honor of J. W. Westfall* (Chicago, 1938), 19–26. On the development of monasticism, see A.-J. Festugière, O.P., *Les Moines d'Orient* (Paris, 1961), and Carl Schneider, *Geistesgeschichte des Antiken Christentums* (Munich, 1954), I, 523–530. See also *Dictionnaire d'Archéologie Chrétienne et de Liturgie*, the articles of H. Leclercq on "Monachisme," XI (1934), col. 1774 ff., esp. 1847 ff., and "Cénobitisme," II (1925), col. 3047 ff., esp. 3175 ff.

[10] M. R. James ed., p. 546. [11] *Comm. in Ezech.*, PL 25, 231C.

moted the growth of monasticism when he says that parents
were wont to dedicate to the Church their deformed and ugly
daughters who could not have found husbands.[12] Under such
circumstances rapid decline of the monastic ideal was inevitable.
Although St. Jerome was the most vigorous champion of the
ascetic movement of his day, he directed his great powers of
satiric ridicule toward exposing the corruption then rife in
monasticism. Our task now will be to examine Jerome's attempts
to correct by satiric exposure the fallen state of the Church and
of the clergy, both the secular and the regular.

Letters

Caustic remarks on the clergy begin early in Jerome's correspondence. In his seventh letter, written from the desert of
Chalcis about 375, Jerome denounces the moral state of Stridon,
his native town: *In mea patria rusticitatis vernacula deus venter
est et de die vivitur: sanctior est ille qui ditior.*[13] To this pot, says,
Jerome, the town priest is the suitable cover, for, in the words of
Lucilius, *Similem habent labra lactucam asino cardus comedente.*[14]

---

[12] Letter 130. 6. The stimulus given to the ascetic movement by Alaric's
capture of Rome is evident in this letter, beneath the thick layer of un-
merited praise for Demetrias' contribution to the popularity of monasticism.

[13] Letter 7. 5. The expression *deus venter est,* often used by Jerome to
describe gluttony, is derived from Phil. 3:19. It is used in the same sense
by Tertullian, *De virg. vel.* 14. Cf. *Jerome, Comm. in Isa.,* PL 24, 125B,
and *Comm. in Jer.,* PL 24, 813A.

[14] Marx, 1299. The text of this saying has never been restored with
certitude. Cf. the same quotation in Letter 130. 13 and *Adv. Ruf.* i. 30,
PL 23, 441B. Whence Jerome derived his knowledge of this line is un-
clear, since there is no evidence that he had read Lucilius. Jerome says
that it was this line which made Crassus laugh for once in his life. The
story of Crassus' laughing only once is told by Cicero (*De. Fin.* v. xxx.
92 and *Tusc.* iii. xv. 31) and by Pliny (*N.H.* vii. xix. 79), but they do
not quote the line of Lucilius. There is, however, a remarkable similarity
between the words of Jerome and Cicero. Cicero says, *M. Crasso, quem
semel ait in vita risisse Lucilius.* Jerome's words are, *de quo semel in vita*

Jerome thus explains this obscure remark: *ut . . . talis sit rector quales illi qui reguntur*. Although the precise meaning of Lucilius' words has never been fully explained, their general import is obvious: the local priest had no higher sense of morality than the rest of the town. Hence he too was a gluttonous boor and a lover of wealth. It has been suggested that Jerome's anger in this passage was not so much the result of the priest's moral turpitude as of this cleric's irrepressible dislike for monks.[15] The importance of the passage for our study is that it reveals how early Jerome was registering his disapproval of the secular clergy and how he expresses this hostility by borrowing from the pagan satiric tradition.

Jerome's return to Rome from the East in 382 gave him an opportunity to view the activities of the secular clergy at closer range. Not long after his arrival he addressed to Pope Damasus an exegetical letter on the parable of the prodigal son, in the course of which he found an opportunity to castigate the attachment of the clergy to secular literature:

At nunc etiam sacerdotes Dei omissis evangeliis et prophetis videmus comoedias legere, amatoria bucolicorum versuum verba cantare, tenere Vergilium, et id quod in pueris necessitatis est crimen in se facere voluntatis.[16]

The outrageous unfairness of this attack hardly requires comment. In these words Jerome seems to be soothing the pangs of his conscience over his own unchristian fondness for pagan let-

---

Crassum ait risisse Lucilius. It certainly looks as if Jerome had Cicero's words in mind but was adding the actual words of Lucilius from another source. Cavallera has suggested (I, 22, n. 3) that the priest ridiculed in this passage was really the local bishop.

[15] By F. A. Wright in the Loeb edition of the Letters (Harvard, 1954), p. 24, n. 3.

[16] Letter 21. 13. The date of the letter is suggested by Jerome's listing it among the early works of his second stay at Rome in his autobiographical entry in *De viris illustribus* (PL 23, 758A).

ters by mocking the same weakness in others.[17] Jerome demonstrates in this passage the zeal of the recent convert to the attitude of rejecting pagan literature. As so often, he allows his powers of description to carry him away as, in an effort to ridicule the clergy, he portrays them perusing comedies, reciting erotic poems, and tightly gripping copies of Vergil in their hands. A malicious and sardonic note was already threatening to dominate the tone of Jerome's relations with the Roman clergy.

The strains of ridicule and exposure become thunderously loud in Jerome's twenty-second letter. This *libellus* is Jerome's best-known work of his second sojourn in Rome. It is a powerful and even violent defense of the ascetic life. At the time it was written, its bitterly censorious attitude toward the failings of society and its exaggerated statement of the virtues of the cloistered life appear to have shocked Roman public opinion and to have aroused considerable enmity against Jerome. Since the work was meant to be a source of guidance and encouragement to Paula's daughter Eustochium, then a girl of some fourteen years, the scurrilous language in which Jerome exposes some of the faults of the times appears highly injudicious. This malevolent document is crammed with references to the corruption of the clergy. Thus Jerome draws the following mocking picture of worldliness:

Plena adulatoribus domus, plena convivis. Clerici ipsi, quos et magisterio esse oportuerat et timori, osculantur capita patronarum et extenta manu, ut benedicere eos putes velle, si nescias, pretium accipiunt salutandi.[18]

These are the words of a man whose own relationships with noble patronesses has led one scholar to say that he gives the

---

[17] In his *Apology*, Rufinus takes Jerome to task for his continued attachment to pagan letters in violation of his dream oath (*PL* 21, 588C–590B and 591C–592A).

[18] Letter 22. 16. Cf. Amm. Marc. xxvii. 3. 14 on the enrichment of the pope by the offerings of *matronae*.

impression "eines Salonbeichtvaters im Stile der Abbés des Zeitalters Ludwigs des XIV."[19] Later in this letter Jerome brings his heavy artillery of scorn, irony, and ridicule to bear upon the lustful clergy, whom he divides into two major classes, the grim and filthy hypocrites and the dandified fops. These two types are united in their desire to seduce women. The hypocrites are satirized first:

Sed ne tantum videar disputare de feminis, viros quoque fuge, quos videris catenatos, quibus feminei contra apostolum crines, hircorum barba, nigrum pallium et nudi in patientiam frigoris pedes. Haec omnia argumenta sunt diaboli. Talem olim Antimum, talem nuper Sophronium Roma congemuit. Qui postquam nobilium introierint domos et deceperint mulierculas . . . tristitiam simulant et quasi longa ieiunia furtivis noctium cibis protrahunt; pudet reliqua dicere, ne videar invehi potius quam monere.[20]

Jerome proceeds then to the second category of clergymen, the description of whom hardly supports his insistent claim that he is interested in edification, not invective:

Sunt alii—de mei ordinis hominibus loquor—qui ideo ad presbyterium et diaconatum ambiunt, ut mulieres licentius videant. Omnis his cura de vestibus, si bene oleant, si pes laxa pelle non folleat. Crines calamistri vestigio rotantur, digiti de anulis radiant et, ne plantas umidior via spargat, vix inprimunt summa vestigia. Tales cum videris, sponsos magis aestimato quam clericos.

It may be added that Jerome's own patron, Pope Damasus, was in the view of his contemporaries guilty of one of the faults here lampooned: he was popularly known as *matronarum auriscalpius*, the ladies' ear-scratcher.[21]

As Jerome's letter continues, his description becomes more elaborate and detailed:

Quidam in hoc omne studium vitamque posuerunt ut matronarum nomina, domos moresque cognoscant. E quibus unum qui huius artis

---

[19] Grützmacher, I, 262. [20] Letter 22. 28.
[21] *CSEL*, XXXV, 4.

est princeps breviter strictimque describam, quo facilius magistro cognito discipulos recognoscas. Cum sole festinus exsurgit; salutandi ei ordo disponitur; viarum conpendia requiruntur, et paene usque ad cubilia dormientium senex inportunus ingreditur. Si pulvillum viderit, si mantele elegans, si aliquid domesticae supellectilis, laudat, miratur, adtrectat, et se his indigere conquerens non tam inpetrat quam extorquet, quia singulae metuunt veredarium urbis offendere. Huic inimica castitas, inimica ieiunia; prandium nidoribus probat et "altilis," γέρων vulgo ποππύζων nominatur. Os barbarum et procax et in convicia semper armatum. Quocumque te verteris, primus in facie est. Quidquid novum insonuerit, aut auctor aut exaggerator est famae. Equi per horarum momenta mutantur tam nitidi, tam feroces, ut illum Thracii regis putes esse germanum.[22]

Thus St. Jerome summons all his mordant powers of invective to attack decadent priests, one of whose failings is *os barbarum et procax et in convicia semper armatum!*

Wilhelm Süss has propounded the theory that Jerome's model in this critique of the clergy was Cicero's scurrilous polemic against the debauched and effeminate Piso and his colleague Gabinius.[23] To be sure Jerome's words *Crines calamistri vestigio rotantur* are a recollection of Cicero's description of Gabinius' *frons calamistri notata vestigiis* (*Post red. in senat.* 16), but for the most part Jerome's portrayal is original. Some of his touches are brilliant: the picture of the foppish priest walking on his

---

[22] Letter 22. 28.

[23] "Der heil. Hieron. und die Formen seiner Polemik," *Giessener Beiträge zur deutschen Philologie*, LX (1938), 237. H. Reich, *Der Mimus* (Berlin, 1903), 764–767, points out the influence of the character drawing of the mime on this passage. The officious, grasping priest is the descendant of the Ardalio figure of Philistion's mime. Reich sees striking confirmation of this in the curious fact that, although Jerome begins by describing a young man, he later calls him a *senex inportunus*. Reich sees this as the result of the traditional portrayal of Ardalio as an old man. But the similarity of Jerome's satiric portraits to those of the mime is more easily explained as the result of the great influence of the character drawing of the mime and of Theophrastus on pagan satire. See G. C. Fiske, *Lucilius and Horace* (Madison, 1920), 168–175.

tiptoes to avoid wetting the soles of his feet and the description of the profit-seeking cleric rushing at dawn through short cuts to the bedrooms of the rich reveal a truly rich gift for satiric portraiture.

However, Jerome had not yet expressed the fullness of his choler. He finds an opportunity in this letter to depict the disgraceful behavior of the class of monks known as *remmuoth* who lived completely without discipline in groups of two and three:

Inter hos saepe sunt iurgia, quia suo viventes cibo non patiuntur se alicui esse subiectos. Re vera solent certare ieiuniis et rem secreti victoriae faciunt. Apud hos affectata sunt omnia: laxae manicae, caligae follicantes, vestis grossior, crebra suspiria, visitatio virginum, detractatio clericorum, et si quando festior dies venerit saturantur ad vomitum.[24]

Later in this same letter Jerome castigates the finicky voracity of the clergy of his day by showing ecclesiastics at dinner in a vivid scene:

Si cibus insulsior fuerit, contristamur et putamus nos Deo praestare beneficium; cum aquatius bibimus, calix frangitur, mensa subvertitur, verbera sonant et aqua tepidior sanguine vindicatur.[25]

Jerome implies that such scenes were daily occurrences. It is thus hardly to be wondered at that Rufinus of Aquileia, Jerome's great enemy, charged in later years that this *libellus* gave aid and comfort to the enemies of Christianity and of God by not only repeating but even exaggerating the charges brought against the Church by the pagans.[26]

[24] Letter 22. 34.

[25] Letter 22. 40. It is clear that Jerome is here describing the clergy, for he is contrasting the trials of Paul with the luxury of *nostri*, a comparison which only makes sense if the clergy is meant.

[26] *Apol.*, PL 21, 587A. Even Cavallera, who rarely finds faults in Jerome, admits (I, 108, n. 2), "il y a des exagérations intolérables," in the satiric passage of this letter. Cf. Letter 52. 17. for Jerome's defense of the outrageous character of the *libellus*.

No small part of St. Jerome's difficulties as an apostle of the monastic movement in Rome was the necessity of doing battle on two fronts, first, against the large body of opinion which opposed the introduction of asceticism and, secondly, against those clergymen who had indeed adopted the ascetic life, but merely as a cloak for their vices and as a source of arrogant pride. Thus in Letters 38 and 39 Jerome lashes out at those enemies who hated the monks as the gloomy destroyers of natural human feelings.[27] Yet almost in the same breath he is forced to combat the monks in whom *humilitas vestium . . . tumentes animos arguebat.*[28] He complains that there are but few monks who can avoid the sin of pride, a failing which Jerome, recalling a line of Horatian satire, compares to the ugliness of moles scattered over a fair body.[29] Elsewhere, in answering a group of *homunculi* who had objected both to his scholarly work and to his bitter tongue, Jerome lets fall a phrase which strongly implies that clergymen who had adhered to the ascetic movement were among his attackers: in defending himself he asks the ironic question, *Numquid ex mendicis divites fieri dolui?*[30] He thus implies that such false and corrupt monks were among the gathering host of his enemies. And yet in the letter written at the time of his departure from Rome he claims that the vanguard of his enemies was composed of worldly women only nominally Christian who *lacerant sanctum propositum*, that is, were bitterly opposed to the spread of the monastic movement.[31] Hard pressed by this double attack of the opponents and perverters of the monastic movement, Jerome abandoned Rome.

But Jerome had by no means abandoned his idealistic campaign for clerical reform, a campaign in which his major weapon was

[27] Letter 38. 5 and 39. 6.

[28] Letter 39. 1. Cf. Letter 22. 27, where Jerome bitterly exposes the hypocrisy of nuns.

[29] Letter 22. 27. See Horace *Sat.* i. 6. 65–67. This is one of Jerome's favorite lines of Horace. See below, p. 112.

[30] Letter 27. 2.   [31] Letter 45. 4.

satire. Ten years after his *libellus* addressed to Eustochium,
Jerome had a new opportunity to preach reform by lacerating
current ecclesiastical decadence. Heliodorus, a friend of his
childhood and now bishop of Altinum, had approached Jerome
with a request that he compose for his young nephew Nepotianus
a manual on the proper conduct of the ascetic life. In acceding
to this request, Jerome drew up a caustic tract which was evidently meant for a larger audience than Nepotianus alone, for
in his later epitaph for Nepotianus he arrogantly refers to this
manual, claiming, "In a brief tract I consecrated our friendship
to the memory of the ages."[32] Mindful of the storm of abuse
aroused by his earlier *libellus*, Jerome insists that his strong remarks are not intended to injure but to improve. He is writing
not an invective against sin but a warning to sinners.[33] Nonetheless, Jerome's method of exhortation is chiefly negative. His
appeal for moral behavior consists largely of acid descriptions
of immorality. Thus, early in the manual, Jerome preaches
against the use of the ascetic profession as a source of riches and
arrogance:

Negotiatorem clericum, et ex inope divitem et ex ignobili gloriosum,
quasi quandam pestem fuge. . . . Tu aurum contemnis, alius diligit;
tu calcas opes, ille sectatur; tibi cordi est silentium, mansuetudo,
secretum, illi verbositas, adtrita frons, fora placent et plateae ac
medicorum tabernae.[34]

A. S. Pease has tentatively suggested that the use of *adtrita frons*
here to mean a shameless countenance is a recollection of Juvenal
13. 242:

> Quando recepit
> eiectum semel adtrita de fronte ruborem?[35]

It would be highly characteristic of Jerome to recall Juvenal,

---

[32] Letter 60. 11.   [33] Letter 52. 17.
[34] Letter 52. 5.
[35] See *TAPA*, XII (1919), 166, n. 117. Cf. Letter 52. 8 for *adtrita frons*.

consciously or unconsciously, in such a passage of *saeva indignatio*.

The relationship of clerics to women also occupies Jerome in his manual for Nepotianus:

Crebra munuscula et orariola et fasciolas et vestes ori adplicatas et degustatos cibos, blandasque et dulces litterulas, sanctus amor non habet. "Mel meum, lumen meum meumque desiderium" et ceteras ineptias amatorum, omnes delicias et lepores et risu dignas urbanitates in comoediis erubescimus, in saeculi hominibus detestamur: quanto magis in clericis et in clericis monachis.[36]

The repeated use of diminutives (*munuscula, orariola, fasciolas, litterulas*) is meant to give an impression of lisping effeminacy and thus to add vividness to the mocking description. It is perhaps doing St. Jerome no injustice to recall in the context of this passage that whilst at Rome he had flirted lightly and gallantly with Eustochium and Marcella in thanking them for such *munuscula* as bracelets, doves, stuff for a garment, candles, chairs, and cups, although he later has the audacity to say in defense of his relations with women, *Munera vel parva vel magna non sprevi?*[37]

Jerome's treatment of the theme of legacy hunting among the clergy places the reader back in the world of pagan satire. He begins by bewailing the edict of Valentinian which forbade the bequeathing of legacies to ecclesiastics. Jerome complains not of the law itself but of the behavior which made the law so necessary. For the sake of effect Jerome distorts the truth by claiming that this legislation did not apply to pagan priests, actors, and prostitutes.[38] Yet for Christians, he claims, even this law is in-

---

[36] Letter 52. 5.

[37] See Letters 33 and 44 for Jerome's thank-you notes for gifts and Letter 45. 2. for his denial that he had accepted them.

[38] Letter 52. 6. We know that Jerome is not telling the whole truth,

effective, since priests avoid it by legal tricks. Then Jerome proceeds to satirize legacy hunting in the following scene:

Audio praeterea in senes et anus absque liberis quorundam turpe servitium. Ipsi apponunt mattulam, obsident lectum, et purulentias stomachi et phlegmata pulmonis manu propria suscipiunt. Pavent ad introitum medici trementibusque labiis, an commodius habeat sciscitantur et, si paululum senex vegetior fuerit, periclitantur ac simulata laetitia mens intrinsecus avara torquetur. Timent enim ne perdant ministerium, et vivacem senem Mathusalae annis conparant. O quanta apud Dominum merces, si in praesenti pretium non speraret! quantis sudoribus hereditas cassa expetitur! minori labore margaritum Christi emi poterat.[39]

The scene is at once brilliant, vitriolic, disgusting, and amusing, the true and sincere expression of *saeva indignatio*. Jerome reveals his descriptive gifts as he penetrates the crafty and greedy motives of the legacy hunter. The portrayal of the minute and disgusting details of the sickroom are patently products of Jerome's vivid imagination. Extreme irony is expressed by the use of the word *ministerium*, which had become associated with churchly offices, to describe the attendance of obsequious clergymen at a rich man's sickbed.

To this revolting study Jerome juxtaposes another satiric portrait—that of the cleric as glutton and gourmet. The portrayal takes the form of a brief monologue:

Natus in paupere domo et in tugurio rusticano, qui vix milio et cibario pane rugientem saturare ventrem poteram, nunc similam et mella fastidio; novi et genera et nomina piscium, in quo litore conca

---

for Symmachus in his address to Valentinian II complains that the Vestal Virgins and the priests of the mysteries were excluded from rights of inheritance. See Symmachus *Relatio* iii. 13.

[39] Letter 52. 6. With the phrase *apponunt mattulam* compare Letter 117. 8, the description of the obsequious priests who go so far as to *portare mattulam*.

lecta sit calleo, saporibus avium discerno provincias, et ciborum me raritas ac novissime damna ipsa delectant.[40]

This literary technique of introducing the representative of a characteristic to be satirized and allowing him to reveal his objectionable traits in his own words is found also in Juvenal. Into his first satire Juvenal introduces the pushy Syrian freedman at the distribution of the *sportula:*

> Sed libertinus prior est. "prior" inquit "ego adsum.
> Cur timeam dubitemve locum defendere, quamvis
> natus ad Euphraten, molles quod in aure fenestrae
> arguerint, licet ipse negem. . . ."[41]

The spirit of classical satire which breathes through Jerome's vitriolic descriptions cannot have been unconscious or accidental. Jerome was using pagan satire as the model for the expression of his reforming zeal. Indeed he may have had Petronius specifically in mind when he wrote the words *damna ipsa delectant.* We may compare the words of Petronius satirizing gluttony:

> Siculo scaurus aequore mersus
> ad mensam vivus perducitur, atque Lucrinis
> eruta litoribus vendunt choncylia cenas,
> ut renovent per damna famem.[42]

There is perhaps no better testimony to the cultural force of the Roman satiric tradition than St. Jerome's invoking its spirit for the purpose of lacerating, ridiculing, and reforming a society centuries removed in time and in character very different from the society in which the satire was originally conceived.

To return to Jerome's manual for Nepotianus, clerical gluttony and worldliness are repeatedly satirized in this work. It is disgraceful, says Jerome, for a priest to invite high provincial offi-

---

[40] Letter 52. 6. Cf. the very similar passage in Letter 33. 3.

[41] *Sat.* 1. 102–105. Exactly the same technique is used throughout the dialogue in *Sat.* 9.

[42] Petronius 119. 33–36. The parallel is suggested by Labourt in his edition of Jerome's *Letters*, ad loc.

cials to dinner, and, while lictors and soldiers proper to a consul's estate stand guard outside, a more brilliant dinner is served than one could find in a palace.[43] Jerome succinctly caps his exhortations against voracity by translating a Greek proverb: *Pinguis venter non gignit sensum tenuem.*[44] But then, when the reader thinks Jerome has finally ended his diatribe, he returns yet again to a description of clerical gluttony:

Caricae, piper, nuces, palmarum fructus, simila, mel, pistatia, tota hortorum cultura vexatur ut cibario non vescamur pane. Audio praeterea quosdam contra rerum hominumque naturam aquam non bibere nec vesci pane, sed sorbitiunculas delicatas et contrita holera betarumque sucum non calice sorbere sed conca. Pro pudor, non erubescimus istiusmodi ineptiis, nec taedet superstitionis![45]

Here Jerome again adapts a standard theme of pagan satire, the ridiculing of gluttony, to a specifically Christian purpose, the reformation of the clergy.

It was, however, not only the open indulgence in actual sensuality which Jerome found widespread among the clergy but also the pious pretense of a holiness which masked hidden vice. The exposure of hypocrisy plays a large part in Jerome's exhortations to Nepotianus. He announces his theme with the words, *Delicatus magister est, qui pleno ventre de ieiuniis disputat; accusare avaritiam et latro potest.*[46] To be sure, in satirizing hypocrisy, as in so many other themes of his invective, Jerome was continuing a common topic of pagan satire. One need think only of the opening of Juvenal's second satire, in which the poet

---

[43] Letter 52. 11. Cf. sec. 15, Jerome's remarks on clerics as guests in wealthy houses.

[44] Letter 52. 11. Cf. Kock, *Com. Att. frag.*, p. 163, frag. 1234. Evidently this line had become part of the moralistic and satiric tradition. The scholiast claims it as the original of Persius 3. 56. Cf. also Horace, *Sat.* ii. 2. 77 and A. Otto, *Die Sprichwörter und sprichwörtlichen Redensarten der Römer* (Leipzig, 1890), 363.

[45] Letter 52. 12.   [46] Letter 52. 7. Cf. Letter 58. 2.

expresses his preference for those men who openly admit their
sexual failings over those who skillfully try to cloak them. Indeed, in warning Paulinus of Nola against hypocrisy, Jerome
supports his argument with a phrase of Persius (3. 30), *ego te
intus et in cute novi.*[47] Yet in ridiculing the voluptuary ascetic,
a specifically Christian type of hypocrite, Jerome would have
little opportunity to call upon his knowledge of pagan satire.[48]
His references to hypocrisy are cast in a specifically Christian
mold: *Alioquin ridiculum et plenum dedecoris referto marsuppio
quod sudarium orariumque non habeas gloriari.*[49] Evangelical
poverty is often the cloak under which seekers of wealth pursue
their ends:

Sunt, qui pauperibus parum tribuunt, ut amplius accipiant, et sub
praetextu elemosynae quaerunt divitias: quae magis venatio appel-
landa est quam elemosyna. Sic bestiae, sic aves, sic capiuntur et
pisces: modica in hamo esca ponitur, ut matronarum in eo sacculi
protrahantur.[50]

As in many of his expressions of moral indignation, Jerome here
carefully uses alliteration to achieve satiric contrast: *Pauperibus
parum, amplius accipiant.*

Subsequently in this letter Jerome draws a somewhat stylized
picture of the Pharisaical cleric:

Nolo te orare in angulis platearum, ne rectum iter precum tuarum
frangat aura popularis; nolo te dilatare fimbrias et ostentui habere

---

[47] Letter 58. 7. For Juvenal's anger at hypocrisy, see esp. his remark on
effeminates, 2. 14–17:
  "Rarus sermo illis et magna libido tacendi
  atque supercilio brevior coma. verius ergo
  et magis ingenue Peribomius; hunc ego fatis
  imputo, qui vultu morbum incessuque fatetur."
[48] Of course Jerome might have recalled Lucian's ceaseless satire of
hypocritical philosophers, e.g. *Icaromenippus* 16 and 28. Also *Hermotimus*
9. However, there is no evidence that St. Jerome was acquainted with
Lucian.
[49] Letter 52. 9.   [50] *Ibid.*

φυλακτήρια, et conscientia repugnante pharisaeica ambitione circumdari.[51]

In this passage Jerome does not ridicule by painting in exaggerated detail a scene based on autopsy. Rather by adroitly referring to Jewish religious practices (fringes and phylacteries), he suggests that hypocritical clergymen are no better than the hated Jews.

Unfortunately, Nepotianus was not fated to benefit from these warnings, for a few months after Jerome's letter he died. Jerome uses the opportunity offered by his *epitaphium* on the youth, addressed to his uncle Heliodorus, to satirize the clergy in now familiar terms:

Alii nummum addant nummo, et marsuppium suffocantes matronarum opes venentur obsequiis, sint ditiores monachi quam fuerant saeculares; possideant opes sub Christo paupere quas sub locuplete diabolo non habuerant, et suspiret eos ecclesia divites quos tenuit mundus ante mendicos.[52]

The satiric tone of exposure and ridicule which pervades Jerome's remarks on the clergy reveals the basis of Grützmacher's comment that, "Hieronymus kennt die Menschen zwar nur von einer Seite, nämlich von der schlechten."[53] There seems indeed to be no end to Jerome's laceration of the clergy's decadent and fraudulent behavior. Thus, writing to Paulinus of Nola, he contrasts the sincere religiosity of his correspondent with the current standard: You change your state of mind along with your clothing, writes Jerome, and you do not aim at filth as a source for boasting while your moneybag is full. We, crammed full of gold, follow a poor Christ, and under the pretext of charity we brood over the wealth of which we should have divested ourselves.[54]

As a propagandist for the regular clergy, Jerome had special

[51] Letter 52. 13. [52] Letter 60. 11.
[53] Grützmacher, II, 210. [54] Letter 58. 2.

barbs for the secular clergy of the cities: *Si episcopatus te vel opus vel honos forte delectat,* he writes, *vive in urbibus et castellis, et aliorum salutem fac lucrum animae tuae.*[55] This is surely an ironic allusion to the venality of the city clergy. It was particularly galling to Jerome that the city priests, who should have been the great counterpoise to the voluptuousness of the age, had instead absorbed the world's sins. The bitterness of his feelings against them sometimes leads Jerome to exceed the bounds of good taste. Thus attacking the gluttony of the city clergy he writes to Paulinus, *Qui Christum desiderat et illo pane vescitur, non quaerit magnopere quam de pretiosis cibis stercus conficiat.*[56]

Like the pagan satirists, Jerome had cause to be concerned over hostile reactions to his mordant comments. His fear of stirring up even greater hatred than he already had aroused by his attacks on the clergy is obvious in a letter written from Bethlehem near the close of the fourth century.[57] He proposes to the Roman aristocrat Oceanus to describe the behavior of the perfect bishop, but he prefaces his remarks with an assurance that such an ideal portrait is not meant as a reflection on the morality of the contemporary clergy, any more than Cicero's description of the perfect orator is intended as an insult to Demosthenes.[58] Even if Jerome's promise was sincerely made, he was unable to keep it. Feeling as he did about the clergy, his picture of their ideal virtues naturally and insensibly became an attack on their actual vices. He begins mildly enough: the possession of a bishopric should be a source of humility and not of swollen pride. A bishop should have wisdom and not the simplicity under the guise of which clerical stupidity is excused.[59] A note of reality here creeps into the idealistic description. As Jerome proceeds, the note gradually becomes louder:

[55] Letter 58. 5.   [56] Letter 58. 6.

[57] Letter 69. Cavallera (II, 46) dates it between 395 and 401. By 403 or 404, when Sulpicius Severus published his *Dialogus,* Jerome was already famous as a satirist of decadent clergy. See above, n. 8.

[58] Letter 69. 8.   [59] *Ibid.*

Sunt enim quidam ignorantes mensuram suam, et tantae stoliditatis ac vecordiae, ut et in motu et in incessu et in habitu et in sermone communi risum spectantibus tribuant, et quasi intelligentes quid sit ornatus, comant se vestibus et munditiis corporis, et lautioris mensae epulas parent, cum omnis istius modi ornatus et cultus sordibus foedior sit.[60]

Jerome's primarily negative approach leads him to expose present vices rather than to idealize future virtues. He passes from the description of worldliness to the castigation of the petty quarrelsomeness of the clergy: "There is nothing more insolent than the arrogance of the boors who believe garrulity to be a sign of prestige, who are always ready for disputes, who thunder with swollen words against the flock subject to them."[61] Thus Jerome, whose whole life was a series of violent altercations and whose writings are replete with the most bitter personal vituperation, scornfully describes clergymen given to verbal battles. His inconsistency is exposed in this very letter, for when he gives a caustic description of those bishops who are suddenly transferred from a catechumen's estate to a bishop's throne, he is delivering an intentional slap at the great Ambrose, whom Jerome disliked intensely: *Heri catechumenus, hodie pontifex; heri in amphitheatro, hodie in ecclesia; vespere in circo, mane in altari; dudum fautor histrionum, nunc virginum consecrator.*[62]

Jerome's pretense of avoiding any derogatory comment on the present state of the clergy is completely dropped toward the end of the letter: *At nunc plerosque cernimus vel favorem populi in aurigarum modum pretio redimere, vel tanto omnium hominum odio vivere, ut non extorqueant pecunia quod mimi inpetrant gestibus.*[63] Jerome is unable to repress his bile as he claims to have seen with his own eyes debased clergymen trying, like

---

[60] *Ibid.*   [61] Letter 69. 9.

[62] *Ibid.* Grützmacher (II, 194) believes that Ambrose is meant here. See below, Chapter VI.

[63] Letter 69. 9. Cf. Letters 77. 2 and 78. 42.

circus charioteers who hire a claque, to purchase popular favor, but even so unable to overcome the hatred which they so richly deserve.

St. Jerome did not use merely the occasional opportunity afforded by his manifold writings on various subjects to denounce the fallen state of the clergy. Rather, he saw himself in the role of a reformer and corrector of morals. Therefore he actively sought opportunities for using his linguistic skill and rhetorical training to inculcate higher moral standards. This can be shown by an examination of his Letter 117. This document purports to be addressed to the mother and sister of a Gallic priest who was concerned for the spiritual wellbeing of his relatives. The two women had refused to live together, each having chosen a clergyman with whom to set up a separate ménage. The request of the Gallic priest that Jerome castigate such behavior and thus reconcile the two women provided the perfect occasion for Jerome to paint a caustically satiric picture of the corrupt habits to which the ascetic life sometimes gives rise. Indeed, the occasion was too perfect to be true. We have evidence that Jerome had in fact no actual case of moral delinquency to combat but was rather composing a rhetorical declamation of a moralizing nature. The evidence for this is found in Jerome's polemical tract against Vigilantius. In that work Jerome assures the reader that in attacking Vigilantius he will quote the heretic's actual words:

Fieri enim potest, ut rursum malignus interpres dicat fictam a me materiam, cui rhetorica declamatione respondeam: sicut illam quam scripsi ad Gallias, matris et filiae inter se discordantium.[64]

Jerome here refers in somewhat ambiguous terms to his Letter 117. The *sicut* clause can be interpreted in two ways, either as part of the charge brought by the *malignus interpres,* or as a separate and independent remark, that is, Jerome's admission

[64] *PL* 23, 356B.

that the letter was in fact a rhetorical declamation. The second interpretation is certainly the more natural one, especially since Jerome uses the indicative *scripsi*. If the letter had indeed *not* been the product of a fictitious situation but Jerome's enemies had falsely charged that it was, Jerome would certainly have answered the accusation in unambiguous words. We must assume then, in examining Jerome's remarks on the clergy in this letter, that he has gone out of his way to gather condemnatory evidence of clerical misbehavior and then to work this into a vitriolic and highly effective, but basically fictitious, literary document.[65]

Jerome announces his satiric purpose in clarion tones at the outset of the letter. He describes a conversation with the Gallic priest in which he expresses his reluctance to take up the task of reconciling the two women and then has the priest protest: *Nimium . . . formidolosus. Ubi illa quondam constantia, in qua multo sale orbem defricans, Lucilianum quippiam rettulisti?*[66] Since this remark was almost surely an invention of Jerome himself, it is a clear statement that in using satire to expose and correct the evils of the day Jerome considered himself heir to the tradition of Lucilius and Horace. He proves himself in this letter worthy of their mantle. In a brilliant scene of parody he describes the foppish clergyman who has taken over the woman's household and the consequent annoyance of the woman's servants:

Iuvenem non quidem comatum, non vestium sericarum, sed trossulum et in sordibus delicatum qui ipse sacculum signet, textrinum teneat, pensa distribuat, regat familiam, emat quidquid de publico necessarium est. Dispensator et dominus, et praeveniens officia servu-

---

[65] Cavallera (I, 308), who is at pains to place all of Jerome's actions in the best light, naturally refuses to admit outright that the letter is a rhetorical exercise. Labourt (V, 76, n. 1) does not doubt its fictitious nature.

[66] Letter 117. 1. Cf. Horace *Sat.* i. 10. 3–4. Note that Jerome has enlarged Horace's *urbem defricuit* to *orbem defricans*! But Hilberg reads *urbem* here. Cf. below, p. 256.

lorum, quem omnes rodant famuli. . . . Ipsum iactant adsidere lectulo, obstetrices adhibere languenti, portare mattulam, calefacere lintea, plicare fasciolas.[67]

Jerome here gives free rein to his lively imagination in order to create a fictitious account of an effeminate monk, dandified amidst his rags, a type of cleric described elsewhere in this letter as *adulescentem necdum bene barbatulum* and *formosulus*.[68] Jerome employs asyndeton to heighten the irony of his portrait. Alliteration is used with the same purpose: *sacculum signet, textrinum teneat*.[69] The word *trossulus*, meaning literally a cavalryman, is a traditional satiric term for dandy. It is used in this sense by Persius and Seneca.[70]

One of Jerome's longest and most thorough satires on the clergy is contained in a letter written toward the end of his life to the Gallic monk Rusticus.[71] In this document Jerome again offers, in answer to a request by Rusticus, a detailed picture of the proper life to be led by a monk. But Jerome was again unable to rise above the unpleasant reality of clerical behavior as it was in his day and thus to describe the true monastic life as a difficult but attainable ideal. Rather, his disquisition consists largely of mocking descriptions of the faults he observed in contemporary monastic life. Early in the letter, in an attempt to disarm the opposition which he knows must follow from his satiric critique, Jerome says, *Ego enim neminem nominabo nec veteris comoediae*

---

[67] Letter 117. 8.

[68] Letter 117. 10. Note the diminutives, meant to suggest delicate effeminacy.

[69] On the studied arrangement of the cola in this passage, see G. Harenzda, *De oratorio genere dicendi, quo Hieron. in epistulis usus sit* (Bratislava, 1905), 58.

[70] Persius 1. 82; Seneca *Epist.* 76. 2 and 87. 9.

[71] Letter 125. Grützmacher (III, 245, n. 1) and Cavallera (I, 320) identify Rusticus with the Bishop of Narbonne at the time of Leo the Great. The letter is dated 409 by Pronberger, *Chronologie*, 95, and after 411 by Cavallera (II, 54).

licentia certas personas eligam atque perstringam.[72] This is probably a reference to Horace's description of Lucilius, who in his satires attacked individuals with the freedom of old comedy.[73] It is a subtle admission by Jerome that he is writing in the tradition of pagan satire. Yet later in the letter Jerome has the boldness to preface his attack on the clergy with the statement: *Non est humilitatis meae neque mensurae iudicare de ceteris et de ministris ecclesiarum sinistrum quippiam dicere.*[74] After this profession of humility, Jerome presents his opinion of the behavior of a typical solitary ascetic:

Quod gula poposcerit, porrigit manus; dormit quantum voluerit, facit, quod voluerit; nullum veretur, omnes se inferiores putat crebriusque in urbibus quam in cellula est et inter fratres simulat verecundiam, qui platearum turbis conliditur.[75]

This castigation of the eremitic clergy is later expanded into an attack on the ascetic clergy in general. When they renounce the world, they change nothing but their clothes and their title; their behavior they alter not at all. Their worldly property is not only not diminished but is even increased. Their lives are filled with wantonness:

Eadem ministeria servulorum, idem apparatus convivii; in vitro et patella fictili aurum comeditur et inter turbas et examina ministrorum nomen sibi vindicant solitarii.[76]

Those who really do give up their property are in consequence filled with ignorant pride:

Qui vero pauperes sunt et tenui substantiola videnturque sibi scioli, pomparum ferculis similes procedunt ad publicum, ut caninam exerceant facundiam.[77]

---

[72] Letter 125. 5.
[73] Hagendahl, *Latin Fathers*, 155, refers to Horace *Sat.* i. 4. 1–6.
[74] Letter 125. 8.
[75] Letter 125. 9. Cf. Letter 130. 17 on the unbearable arrogance of the solitary ascetics.
[76] Letter 125. 16.   [77] *Ibid.*

Jerome here, as in other satiric passages, makes abundant use of diminutives to enhance the mocking tone of his description: *servulorum, substantiola, scioli.* The comparison of arrogance walking abroad to *pomparum ferculis,* an image borrowed from Cicero, is found elsewhere in Jerome's satiric descriptions.[78] The expression *caninam facundiam,* meaning doglike backbiting, is traditional. It is first found in Sallust's *Histories* (Maurenbrecher, IV, 54), and later in Quintilian and Lactantius.[79] Jerome evidently thought this expression effective, for he used it often to satirize the raucous and meaningless talk of his enemies.[80]

Jerome's parody of clerical arrogance in his letter to Rusticus continues in even more bitter terms:

Alii sublatis in altum humeris et inter se nescio quid cornicantes stupentibus in terram oculis tumentia verba trutinantur, ut, si praeconem addideris, putes incedere praefecturam.[81]

This description was not written without the help of pagan satire. The rare verb *cornicare,* "to caw like a crow," recalls Persius 5. 12:

Nescio quid tecum grave cornicaris inepte.[82]

Furthermore, the details of the eyes solemnly fixed on the ground and the image of the arrogant words carefully weighed as if in a balance are derived from a ridiculing description of philosophers put by Persius into the mouth of a grizzly centurion:

Obstipo capite et figentes lumine terram . . .
atque exporrecto trutinantur verba labello. . . .[83]

[78] Cf. Letter 3. 6; *Adv. Iovin.* i. 34 (*PL* 23, 269B).

[79] Quintilian xii. 9. 9; and Lactantius *Div. inst.* vi. 18. 26. For other examples, see Otto, *Sprichwörter,* s.v. *canis* 3.

[80] Cf. Letters 119. 1 and 134. 1; *Dial. contra Luc.* (*PL* 23, 163A); *Adv. Helvid.* 22 (*PL* 23, 216B).

[81] Letter 125. 16.　　[82] Cf. Hagendahl, *Latin Fathers,* 255.

[83] Persius 3. 80 and 82. Cf. Letters 46. 14 and 40. 2. Also *Comm. in Eph.* (*PL* 25, 525C) and *Adv. Iovin.* i. 40 (*PL* 23, 280A).

Certain monks, continues Jerome, are driven to melancholia by the dampness of their cells, by their immoderate fasting, by the boredom of solitude, and by their excessive reading. For such unfortunates Jerome has no sympathy. He simply states that they require the fomentations of Hippocrates more than his exhortations. Other clerics are businessmen in disguise. At least before they took the habit their activities were under the supervision of aediles. Now their mad rapacity is uncontrolled.[84] The ascetic's rags are merely a veil to conceal ill-gotten wealth: "Stretching out our hands in public, we conceal gold beneath rags, and we who have lived like poor men die rich with our money bags filled, although no one is aware of this."[85] The same theme of riches concealed by hypocritical rags is introduced into several other letters of the later years of Jerome's life: "He who is swollen with the wealth of Croesus," says Jerome, "and while wearing a cheap little cloak battles against the moths living in his silken garments vainly preaches poverty with his tongue and teaches charity."[86] Because of the catastrophes of the times, he claims, the nobles are forced to sell their ancestral estates, but, Jerome complains, these are immediately snatched up by *omnis ecclesiastici ministerii gradus et cassa nomina monachorum.*[87]

It is to be noted that Jerome's attacks on clerical hypocrisy increase in frequency as the political condition of the Empire deteriorates. Letters 69, 77, 78, 117, 120, 125, 127, and 130, all of which contain portraits of wealthy ascetics who hide their luxury under clerical garb, belong to the years 397–414, years of disastrous barbarian ravages.[88] These were the years of Alaric's

---

[84] Cf. Letter 120. 11, where Jerome describes the difficulty of finding clerics who do not *quaestum putant esse pietatem et turpis lucri gratia omnia faciunt.*

[85] Letter 125. 16.

[86] Letter 127. 4. Cf. Letter 22. 32 on women: *At nunc plerasque videas . . . tunicas mutare cotidie et tamen tineas non posse superare.*

[87] Letter 130. 7.

[88] Chronology of letters in Pronberger, 94–95.

devastation of Illyria and of his invasion of Italy (401). On December 31, 406, the frozen Rhine was crossed by hordes of Vandals, Quadi, Gepidae, Heruli, Alemanni, Burgundians, and Saxons, whose depredations spread over Gaul and as far as Spain in the west and into Pannonia in the east. In 410 the civilized world was shaken by Alaric's entry into Rome. Under these unhappy conditions it must have become common for the wealthy to hide from barbarian rapacity beneath a monk's cowl. The protection afforded by the Church against the savagery of the Christianized Goths attracted into the clergy many who were unsuited to the ecclesiastical life.[89] We have evidence in Jerome's writings that the Goths were wont to consider the ascetic garb a device for hiding riches. When in the course of the sack of Rome the barbarians came to the house of the aristocratic nun Marcella, in spite of her protestations of poverty, *non tamen fecit fidem voluntariae paupertatis.* The Goths were probably basing their incredulity on past experience. It is likely, then, that St. Jerome had excellent grounds for the satiric references in his letters to the essential worldliness of the clergy. Our task now is to investigate how St. Jerome's satire in his other works also sought to expose that decline in the moral level of the clergy which was inevitable when the ecclesiastical life began to offer greater material rewards and more security than the worldly life.

Polemical Works

St. Jerome rages but rarely against the current condition of the Church in his controversial works. This is not surprising. In attacking individual heretics by insisting on their moral corruption, Jerome would hardly wish to point out by his own testimony that the morality of the orthodox clergy was hardly

[89] On the respect of the Goths for the churches, see Letter 127. 13, where Jerome describes the barbarians escorting Marcella to the protection of the Basilica of Paul.

better. Yet sometimes the requirements of Jerome's argument forced him to portray the corruption which he could see in the Church. Thus, when in his polemic against Jovinianus he defends the orthodox insistence on clerical celibacy, Jerome is obliged to explain why a married man is sometimes advanced in the Church over an unmarried one. At times the celibate candidate has other disqualifications:

Evenit interdum ut tristior vultus, adductum supercilium, incessus pomparum ferculis similis, offendat populum, et quia nihil habet quod reprehendat in vita, habitum solum oderit et incessum.[90]

In this lively description Jerome brings up to the battle line some well-used artillery pieces. *Pomparum ferculis similis* is, as we have seen, an important descriptive phrase in Jerome's vocabulary of ridicule.[91] *Adductum supercilium* also is used elsewhere to portray hypocritical solemnity.[92] It appears that Jerome was particularly sensitive on the subject of clerical advancement, for once he has brought up the subject in order to answer the arguments of Jovinianus, he seems unable to drop it. He launches into an attack on methods of ecclesiastical promotion which has little relationship to the purpose of his tract. Unworthy motives determine the selection of clerics. The priests with clever tongues are chosen over the morally pure. Innocence and lack of sophistication are considered disqualifying attributes. Nepotism is rife. A priest has to have powerful relatives in order to advance. The rich dictate the distribution of ecclesiastical offices. But worse than this, high officials of the Church hand out positions only when they are "smeared with obsequiousness" (*obsequiis*

[90] *Adv. Iovin.* i. 34 (*PL* 23, 269B). It is possible that Jerome is thinking of his own failure to achieve high ecclesiastical position. We may compare what Jerome says of himself in Letter 45. 2: *Alius incessum meum calumniabatur et risum, ille voltui detrahebat, haec in simplicitate aliud suspicetur.*

[91] See above, p. 59.

[92] Letter 53. 7, and 125. 18. Also *Comm. in Ezech.*, PL 25, 331B.

deliniti).[93] One must remember in reading such denunciations that for personal reasons Jerome, who had never become a bishop, had no reason to be pleased with the current system of distributing church offices.

In a later polemical work, the tract against Vigilantius, Jerome is called upon to defend the desert hermits who flee from moral battles (a type of monk he elsewhere attacks).[94] His argument forces him to point out certain characteristic dangers of the cenobitic life. He makes ironic reference to an aspect of monasticism which must have caused severe consternation to those concerned with standards of ecclesiastical behavior:

Matres vocamus sorores et filias, et non erubescimus vitiis nostris nomina pietatis obtendere. Quid facit monachus in cellulis feminarum? quid sibi volunt sola et privata colloquia, et arbitros fugientes oculi? Sanctus amor impatientiam non habet.[95]

Testimony in Jerome's writings shows that he had excellent grounds for fearing that the monastic life might serve as a concealment for clandestine love affairs. Letter 147 is addressed to a deacon who had seduced a nun by leaving love notes in the Bethlehem church, where she would be sure to find them. Jerome's wrath is expressed in a mocking recollection of this scene:

Tu inter ostia quondam praesepis domini, nunc altaris amatorias epistulas fulciebas, quas postea illa miserabilis quasi flexo adoratura

---

[93] For this phrase applied to ecclesiastical elections, cf. *Comm. in Titum*, *PL* 26, 596D. Cf. *PL* 23, 589B.

[94] Letters 125. 9 and 130. 17.

[95] *Adv. Vig.* 16, *PL* 23, 368A. John Chrysostom in his sermon *Contra eos qui subintroductas habent virgines* pictures vividly the immorality which the early monasteries frequently concealed. See *PG* 47, 495–514. On the *virgines subintroductae* see M. Viller and K. Rahner, *Askese und Mystik in der Väterzeit* (Freiburg im Breisgau, 1939), 48–49 with bibliography.

genu inveniret et legeret; stabas deinceps in choro psallentium et inpudicis nutibus loquebaris.[96]

This description, which reads like the plot of a romance, cannot fail to bring a smile to the lips of the modern reader. Jerome himself compares the incident to a scene from an Atellan farce, although he was probably full of wrath when he recounted it.[97] It is possible that Jerome is alluding to this very event in the passage cited above from *Contra Vigilantium*, since that tract is dated 407 and the letter in question belongs certainly to the period after 406 and possibly to the year 407.[98]

Homiletic Works

We pass now from works by which the ascetic recluse of Bethlehem maintained his relationships with the outer world to those which were the product of his position as head of a monastery. In his capacity as priest of the church of Bethlehem, Jerome delivered a large number of homilies. These were taken down by his auditors and published, along with the numerous errors inevitable to such a method of recording.[99] These homilies were in a state of great confusion and disarray until all was set aright by Dom G. Morin in his edition of the works.[100]

Of all Jerome's manifold writings, his homilies alone were not

[96] Letter 147. 4. Pagans too were wont to use their temples as trysting places. See Juvenal 6. 489 and 9. 22. Also Minucius Felix 25. 11.

[97] Letter 147. 5: *repertum est facinus, quod nec mimus fingere nec scurra ludere nec Atellanus possit effari.*

[98] Pronberger dates it 407–408. Cavallera (II, 192) refuses to commit himself on a date. De Bruyne, *Zeitschr. für Neutest. Wiss.*, XXVIII (1929), 1–13, believes that the occasion and circumstances of the letter were invented by Jerome.

[99] Cavallera, I, 185.

[100] *Anecdot. Mared.*, III. 1. 2, and 3 (1895, 1897, 1903). For a full discussion of these works see Dom G. Morin, *Etudes, Textes, Découvertes*, I, 221–293. Also A. S. Pease, "Notes on Jerome's Tractates," *Journ. of Biblical Lit.*, XXVI (1907), 107–131.

addressed to the world at large.[101] They were aimed rather at a small group of monks of no particular learning or sophistication gathered in the Bethlehem church. It is, therefore, not surprising that these works contain less rhetoric, fewer references to pagan literature, and less rancor and bitterness toward society. The simple style of the homilies befits Jerome's pastoral role; the mitigation of his moral fulminations and the infrequency of acidly satiric allusions suggest Jerome's realization that these religious gatherings were not the proper place to vent personal pique. Nonetheless, Jerome's distaste for the secular clergy and his desire to strengthen the brothers in their rejection of the world were so strong that he could not at times avoid referring with vitriolic words to secular ecclesiastics. On one occasion he speaks of priests as *lupi*.[102] The piety of the monastic life is contrasted with the corrupt and worldly behavior of secular clerics: *Utique alius ad domum ire festinat, alius ad circum, alius in ecclesia de usuris cogitat*.[103] The debauchery of secular clergymen is satirized in coarse terms: *Et ecce video multos vacare ebrietatibus, ructare vinum, et inter epulas exorcizare et clamare*.[104] Jerome comments bitterly on secular clerics who turn the church into a place of business, *qui heri pauper, hodie dives, et dives in domo Dei*.[105]

But Jerome's caustic comments were not directed solely at those clergymen who lived in "the world." As the spiritual leader of a monastic community, Jerome undertook the task of castigating the moral lapses of the brothers. Since his most usual means of exhortation was ridicule, we occasionally find in his homilies satiric pictures of monastic behavior. Some of his most vividly descriptive passages give rare and valuable glimpses of life inside

---

[101] Very few of Jerome's letters are of a strictly private nature. His inclusion of the letters among the literary works listed in *De vir. ill.* (PL 23, 755C) suggests that many of them were meant for a wider audience than the actual addressees.

[102] *Anecdot. Mared.*, III. 2, 75–76.   [103] *Ibid.*, 246.

[104] *Ibid.*, 335.   [105] *Ibid.*, 364.

an early monastic community. The brothers are quarrelsome and uncooperative. We have given up the life of the world, complains Jerome, merely

ut propter rem levem, fribolam, rixam cum fratribus faciamus in monasterio. Dimisimus possessionem, dimisimus patriam, dimisimus saeculum: et propter calamum rixam facimus in monasterio. Si verbum amarum audiero, ferre non possum, est in corde meo, inscribitur in medullis diebus decem aut quindecim, non potest tolli de corde meo, loquor fratri meo qui mihi iniuriam fecerat, et pacem labiis promitto, et corde venenum teneo.[106]

Monks are given to backbiting. Their habit is *circumire cellas, aliis detrahere.*[107] They have an altogether worldly zeal for competing with each other in knowledge of Scripture: *Solent et viri, solent et monachi, solent et mulierculae hoc inter se habere certamen, ut plus ediscant scripturas.*[108] The tone of exposure and ridicule, although clearly audible in these passages directed against the faults of the brothers, is much less harsh than in the exhortations aimed at the secular clergy.

Exegetical Works

Clerical corruption is a theme on which Jerome often expatiates in his exegetical works. The concept of the multiple sense of Scripture which Origen had introduced into Christianity, and which was to dominate exegesis throughout the Middle Ages, allowed the interpreter to apply biblical moral strictures to the iniquity he saw in his own society.[109] Like other exegetes who employed the four senses of interpretation, Jerome held that tropological or moralistic interpretations of Scripture formed the lofty tower of the fortress of exegesis, built upon a strong foundation of literal and historical explanation and roofed

---

[106] *Ibid.*, 231.   [107] *Ibid.*, 225.
[108] *Ibid.*, 257.
[109] See B. Smalley, *The Study of the Bible in the Middle Ages* (2d ed.; Oxford, 1952), 1–13, and H. Caplan in *Speculum*, IV (1929), 282–290.

with the beams of anagoge and mysticism.[110] In accordance with this view of the central importance of tropological exegesis, Jerome's biblical commentaries are filled with invective against contemporary failings, especially those of the clergy.

In one of his earliest exegetical works, the commentary on Ecclesiastes, written during the first years of his permanent settlement in the East, we find many biblical passages stimulating Jerome to comment malevolently on the clergy. Clerics are unwilling to spend any labor on learning. They teach in churches but are themselves ignorant. In their preaching they seek only to excite the applause of the mob.[111] They flatter and deceive when they should castigate and exhort.[112] Bishops are corrupt, but no one is willing to bring them to justice.[113] Jerome feels a very personal anger against powerful churchmen:

Videas enim in Ecclesia imperitissimos quosque florere: et quia nutrierunt frontis audaciam, et volubilitatem linguae consecuti sunt, dum non recogitant quid loquantur, prudentes se et eruditos arbitrantur: maxime si favorem vulgi habuerint, qui magis dictis levioribus delectatur et commovetur. Et e contrario eruditum virum latere in obscuro, persecutiones pati: et non solum in populo gratiam non habere, sed inopia et egestate tabescere.[114]

It is doing Jerome no injustice to see such an attack not only as the expression of the incipient hostility between regular and secular clergy but also as a reflection of his personal feelings of dissatisfaction at his failure to achieve high position in the Church. It must be remembered that the commentary on Ecclesiastes was written most probably in 386, the year after Jerome's enforced

---

[110] So Jerome expresses himself in *Comm. in Abdiam.*, PL 25, 1103C. Cf. PL 25, 147C–D and 1123C.

[111] PL 23, 1070B and 1090B; CC 72, 256 and 276.

[112] PL 23, 1115C; CC 72, 301–302.

[113] PL 23, 1132A; CC 72, 318.   [114] PL 23, 1142C; CC 72, 329.

retirement from Rome. His anger was still burning hotly, and it leaves its mark throughout this work:

Quemcumque in Ecclesia videris declamatorem et cum quodam leno-cinio ac venustate verborum excitare plausus, risus excutere, audientes in affectus laetitiae concitare: scito signum esse insipientiae, tam eius qui loquitur quam eorum qui audiunt.[115]

This is the type of ecclesiastic who in his preaching *peccatores palpet in vitio, et strepitus concitet audientium.*[116]

Elsewhere in this commentary, Jerome describes high ec-clesiastical office as *tumens et superflua dignitas.*[117] When he comes to the interpretation of the biblical passage, *Vidi servos in equis, et principes ambulantes quasi servos super terram,* he applies the words to the exaltation of his enemy Siricius to the papal throne and to his own flight from Rome. *Imprudens quisque* rules the Church, for the devil oppresses the learned and leads the ignorant to power.[118]

The year after the completion of his exposition of Ecclesiastes, Jerome undertook the task of interpreting four Pauline Epistles. His bitter feelings toward the clergy had scarcely abated. He remarks that Paul's words calling the Galatians to humility "strike down the superciliousness of the bishops who, as if stationed on some lofty tower, hardly deign to look upon mortal men and to address their fellow servants."[119] The clergy is filled with ambition and self-seeking; they have turned Holy Scripture into an athletic wrestling pit: *Videas plerosque de Scripturis inter se contendere: et athleticum scamma Dei facere sermonem: invicem provocant, et si victi fuerint, invident: inanis quippe gloriae cupidi sunt.*[120] Jerome probably understood these emo-tions so well because he shared them fully, in spite of his claim

---

[115] *PL* 23, 1145A; *CC* 72, 332.   [116] *PL* 23, 1155B; *CC* 72, 342.
[117] *PL* 23, 1148A; *CC* 72, 335.   [118] *PL* 23, 1148B–C; *CC* 72, 335.
[119] *PL* 26, 406A.   [120] *PL* 26, 453A.

that he wrote nothing for the sake of worldly glory.[121] The full incongruity of his parody of clergymen who battle over Scripture was revealed only fifteen years after this passage was written, when Jerome fell into bitter conflict with Augustine over the latter's disagreement with his scriptural exegesis.

In the commentary on the Epistle to the Ephesians, the arrogant claims of the clergy to erudition are satirized in well-worn phrases:

Nonnulli rugata fronte, demisso supercilio, verbisque trutinatis, auctoritatem sibi doctorum, et iudicium vindicant. Non quo ipsi dignum aliquid arrogantia noverint, sed quo simplices quosque fratrum sui quaedam videant comparatione nescire.[122]

The phrase *verbis trutinatis* recalls that passage of Persius repeatedly used by Jerome to characterize arrogance.[123] The wrinkled forehead and lowered brow are standard details of Jerome's portraits of haughtiness.[124] Compare a description of ignorant churchmen from the commentary on Ezekiel:

Qui cum populo persuaserint vera esse quae fingunt, et in theatralem modum plausus concitaverint et clamores, immemores fiunt imperitiae, et adducto supercilio, libratisque sermonibus, atque trutinatis, magistrorum sibi assumunt auctoritatem.[125]

Another passage of attack on ecclesiastical behavior throws light on a curious social custom of an age in which clerical

[121] *Ibid.* Here Jerome disclaims all desire for glory in future ages. But in *Comm. in Eccles.* (*PL* 23, 1084B–1085A) he expresses concern lest his writings fall into the hands of the unappreciative. Note that in both passages Jerome describes his literary activity with an expression drawn from Horace *Sat.* i. 10. 72, *saepe stilum vertere.*

[122] *PL* 26, 525C.

[123] Persius 3. 82. Though Jerome does not allude specifically to the clergy here, the tone of the passage is so similar to other attacks on clerical arrogance that there can be little doubt as to whom it refers.

[124] Cf. Letter 53. 7 and *Adv. Iovin.* i. 34; *PL* 23, 269B.

[125] *PL* 25, 331B, and cf. 231B, where Jerome seems to be contrasting his own unpretentious language.

celibacy was not yet the rule. Bishops and priests are ambitious for their children. They educate them in pagan literature, have them read comedies, and teach them to sing the filthy verses of mimes. They use the money donated to the Church by a poor virgin or widow to send their children to the school of a pagan *grammaticus*. Thus the Church's funds are dissipated in little presents for the teacher, who in turn spends the money on the *sportula* for the Saturnalia or uses it to purchase the charms of *sordida scorta*, or even contributes it to a pagan temple.[126] Clerics who thus behave are among the *pseudoapostoli et pseudo-prophetae et pseudoevangelistae et pseudopastores et pseudo-magistri* who, Jerome says, abound in the Church. [127] The glow of Jerome's righteous anger pales a bit when we recall that Rufinus felt justified in chiding him for educating the young boys entrusted to his care in pagan authors, among whom, says Rufinus, the comic poets figure prominently.[128]

The commentary on the Epistle to the Ephesians, also written soon after Jerome's establishment at Bethlehem, exceeds all the other exegetical works in the frequency and virulence of its attacks on the clergy. It is the bishops above all who are the object of Jerome's invective. Bribery, obsequiousness, and even worse are the means of achieving a bishop's throne.[129] Bishops consider their offices one of command (*imperium*) rather than of helpful ministration (*dispensatio*).[130] They are subject to violent outbursts of anger, which Jerome describes in mocking detail:

Ille e diverso torvo vultu, trementibus labiis, rugata fronte, effrenatis conviciis, facie inter pallorem ruboremque variata, clamore per-

---

[126] *PL* 26, 574A. For another attack on the excessive devotion of the clergy to the welfare of their children, cf. *Comm. in Soph., PL* 25, 1398C–D.

[127] *PL* 26, 532C.   [128] *PL* 21, 592A.

[129] *PL* 26, 596–597. One hesitates to imagine what Jerome hints at in saying, *ut deteriora taceam*.

[130] *PL* 26, 600B.

strepat: ut errantes non tam ad bonum retrahat, quam ad malum sua saevitia praecipitet.[131]

The detailed description of the countenance changing rapidly from redness to pallor, the trembling lips and wrinkled brow could only have been written by an astringent personality whose natural harshness was intensified at once by moral outrage and private animus. Jerome does not limit himself to the portrayal of a bishop enraged but goes on to draw a caricature of a bishop under the influence of alcohol.

Quale est autem episcopum videre vinolentum, ut senso occupato, vel exaltet risum contra gravitatis decorem et labiis dissolutis cachinnet: vel si paululum tristis cuiusdam rei fuerit recordatus, inter pocula in singultus prorumpat et lacrymas.[132]

The passage clearly reveals Jerome's keen powers of observation. The meaningless laughter, the pendulous lips, the maudlin tears are all such well-chosen details of inebriation and are so vividly described that this passage may rank as a classic portrayal. How ironic that it was written by a Christian monk about Christian bishops! But Jerome does not stop even here. He is aroused by his indignation to give a highly exaggerated portrayal of a drunken brawl which breaks out among the bishops:

Videas alios pocula in tela vertentes, scyphum in faciem iacere convivae; alios scissis vestibus in vulnera aliena proruere; alios clamare; alios domitare; qui plus biberit fortior computatur; accusationis occasio est, adiuratum per regem, frequentius non bibisse. Vomunt ut bibant, bibunt ut vomant. Digestio ventris et guttur uno occupantur officio. . . . Et ubicumque saturitas atque ebrietas fuerint, ibi libido dominetur. Specta ventrem et genitalia, pro qualitate vitiorum ordo membrorum. Numquam ego ebrium castum putabo, qui et si vino consopitus dormierit, tamen potuit peccare per vinum.[133]

---

[131] *PL* 26, 601A.   [132] *PL* 26, 601B.

[133] *Ibid.* Cf. St. Ambrose's description of drunkenness in *De Helia et leiunio* 12. 43: *De ebrietate ad arma consurgitur, calcibus tela succedunt.*

This is surely a most unusual description to be found in a biblical commentary! The powerful expression *Vomunt ut bibant, bibunt ut vomant* is taken directly from Seneca's social satire. It also recalls Juvenal's description of a disgusting female voluptuary:

> Nam sic, tamquam alta in dolia longus
> deciderit serpens, bibit et vomit. Ergo maritus
> nauseat atque oculis bilem substringit opertis.[134]

One may wonder how much experience Jerome had had with such banquets. That his *saeva indignatio* and love for rhetorical elaboration are here leading him into this violent description is perhaps more probable than that he had actually witnessed such behavior. It is, in fact, possible to show that the description is partly dependent on the Christian satiric tradition. The sentence which begins *Spectra ventrem* is based on a passage in which Tertullian attacks his enemies the sensualists: *Specta corpus et una regio est. Denique pro dispositione membrorum ordo vitiorum.*[135]

One might suppose that in the passage above Jerome had discharged all his venom against the clergy. On the contrary, there seems to be no limit to the accusations which Jerome can bring against them. If bishops and priests see laymen enjoying life, complains St. Jerome, they roar at them and excommunicate them out of sheer envy, *quasi non liceat facere quod episcopus non faciat.*[136] This surprising remark suggests that Jerome's

---

Pro vino sanguis effunditur et ipsum sanguinem vina succedunt. Also *ibid.* 16. 60: *Alii risu solvuntur incondito, alii inconsolabili maerore deplorant, alii inrationabilis cernunt pavores.* See Weston, 73–75. Weston has failed to notice that Ambrose has adapted these descriptions with minor changes from St. Basil's homily *In ebriosos* 449AB (124C–D). See Sister M. J. A. Buck, *S. Ambrosii de Helia et Ieiunio* (*Cath. U. of Am. Patristic Studies*, XIX; Washington, D.C., 1929), 7, 165, 187.

[134] Seneca *Ad Helvid.* 10. 3; Juvenal 6. 431–433. The deprecation of drunkenness is a *topos* of Cynic-Stoic popular philosophy. See Seneca *Epist.* 83. 20 and Juvenal 5. 26 and 6. 314.

[135] *De ieiuniis* i. 2; *CC* 2, 1251. Parallel noted by Vallarsi, *PL* 26, 601D.

[136] *PL* 26, 603A.

hatred of the clergy was stronger than his attachment to asceticism. More than any other churchman of his age, Jerome strove to introduce asceticism into every aspect of Christian life. But if the *amatores bonorum*, the rich and worldly, come into conflict with the hated clergy, it is the former who win Jerome's support.

Jerome's exegetical treatment of the five minor Hebrew prophets (Nahum, Micah, Zephaniah, Haggai, and Habakkuk) followed soon after his interpretation of the four Pauline Epistles.[137] The commentary on Micah contains two mocking exhortations against clerical corruption. Jerome takes the words of the prophet, *Duces populi mei proicientur de domibus suarum*, as applying to the luxurious clerics:

Sed et Ecclesiae quoque principes qui deliciis affluunt, et inter epulas atque lascivias pudicitiam servare se credunt, propheticus sermo describit quod eiciendi sint de spatiosis domibus, lautisque conviviis, et multo labore epulis conquisitis, et eiciendi propter malas cogitationes et opera sua. . . . An non confusio et ignominia est, Jesum crucifixum, magistrum, pauperem atque esurientem fartis praedicare corporibus, ieiuniorumque doctrinam, rubentes buccas, tumentiaque ora proferre?[138]

The passage again illustrates Jerome's fondness for elaborating biblical exhortations with satiric details. The prophetic words contain no hint of the *spatiosae domus* and *lauta convivia* amid which Jerome sets the princes of the Church. Jerome merely uses the scriptural passage as the starting point of a detailed attack in which his own descriptive gifts are used to the full. Thus the stuffed bodies, reddened lips and swelling mouths of the pompous and worldly bishops are elements suggested by Jerome's own satiric imagination and testifying to his thorough hatred of the higher clergy. As in many satiric passages, his imagination seizes the upper hand as he enlarges his canvas enormously,

[137] Cavallera, II, 29–30.   [138] *PL* 25, 1172A.

filling it with grotesque details. He goes on to describe the rich clergy entertaining soldiers and judges at their banquets, while centurions keep guard at the doors:

At nunc non dico pauperes, non dico fratres, et qui rursum invitare non possint (ex quibus excepta gratia, nihil aliud episcopalis speret manus) sed militantes et accinctos gladio, et iudices, excubantibus ante fores suas centurionibus et turmis militum, Christi sacerdos invitat ad prandium. Tota clerici urbe discursant: quaerunt exhibere iudicibus, quae illi in praetoriis suis aut invenire non possunt, aut certe inventa non coemunt.[139]

The exactitude with which Jerome paints this picture suggests that he is enlarging upon scenes which he had actually witnessed at Rome and which had made a deep impression on him.

Another brief exposure of clerical faults in this commentary again reveals the twofold nature of Jerome's dissatisfaction with the Church. On the one hand, as a leader of the regular clergy he inveighs against the worldliness of the secular clergy. On the other hand, he is forced to attack the growing hypocrisy of the adherents of asceticism:

Si autem sub occasione pauperum paucae ditantur domus, et in vitro ac vase fictili aurum comedimus, aut cum thesuaris mutemus et vestes, aut pauper habitus non quaerat divitias senatorum. Quid prodest circa collum ad abstergendos sudores linteolum non habere? Quid iuvat esse μονοχίτωνας et praeferre habitu paupertatem, cum marsuppium nostrum universa pauperum turba suspiret.[140]

The satirist demonstrates his penchant for illustrating exhortations of a general nature with brief but highly detailed vignettes portraying the faults against which he is inveighing. In castigating hypocrisy, Jerome describes a cleric who thinks it a sign of extreme asceticism not to have a handkerchief to wipe away the sweat from his neck.[141]

---

[139] *PL* 25, 1172B.   [140] *PL* 25, 1184C.

[141] For another strong expression of Jerome's rage at clerical hypocrisy, see *Comm. in Gal.*, *PL* 26, 452B–C.

The commentary on Zephaniah contains one of Jerome's longest and sharpest invectives against the clergy. The immediate impulse for this onslaught is provided by the prophet's words, "Woe to her that is filthy and polluted, to the oppressing city! . . . Her princes within her are roaring lions; her judges are evening wolves. . . . Her prophets are light and treacherous persons: her priests have polluted the sanctuary" (Zeph. 3:1–4). Jerome chooses to apply these words to the current state of the Church. The princes of the Church are truly roaring lions and the judges ravenous wolves:

Non ambigimus de rugitu leonum et discursu: quando viderimus principes eius [Ecclesiae] ita in subiectos populos detonare, et voce tyrannica rabidisque conviciis plebem conterere, ut non pastorem in grege, sed leonem inter oviculas putes frendere. Iudices quoque eius quasi lupi Arabiae, occidentes vespere, et nil relinquentes in mane: non aspicientes ad ortum solis, sed morantes semper in tenebris, et possessiunculas Ecclesiae et ea quae in Dei donaria conferuntur, vertentes in lucrum suum, ut non habeant pauperes quod mane comedant, qui quasi in nocte, et nullo vidente, omnia populantur.[142]

But suddenly Jerome stops, realizing that his application of the prophetic passages to the contemporary Church may seem both outrageous and unjustified. But he defends his interpretation as valid by the rules of tropological exegesis. However, in his justification of the parallel he has drawn, he manages to insult the clergy once again. Avaricious clerics are indeed ravenous wolves, he insists, although in saying so he knows he will offend those who believe that the concupiscence of the libidinous elders (*presbyteri*, which means either elders or priests) who sought to violate Susanna does not reflect on the morality of right-living priests (*presbyteros*).[143] This subtle comparison of priests to the elders in the Susanna story, a comparison made again elsewhere in this commentary, is a truly malicious slap at secular clerics.[144]

[142] *PL* 25, 1374B–C.   [143] *PL* 25, 1376B.
[144] Cf. *PL* 25, 1366A.

Jerome concludes his invective by comparing the higher clergy who are enchanted with the dignity of their office to long-necked swans who strive to fly aloft but fail and are perforce demoted to the ranks of ordinary birds.[145]

Jerome's return to New Testament exegesis in the year 398 was occasioned by a request of Eusebius of Cremona, an ardent fighter in the Italian theater of the war against Origen and Rufinus. Eusebius wished a commentary on the first Gospel as a traveling companion on his return journey from the Holy Land to Italy. Since time was pressing, Jerome resolved to limit himself to a purely historical interpretation, leaving the tropological significance aside.[146] Nonetheless, when it happened that a biblical passage could by tropoligical exegesis be interpreted as a slap at the clergy, Jerome was unable to avoid abandoning the original plan of the work in order to denounce clerical iniquity. Thus in expounding the parable of the tares (Matthew 13: 24–30), Jerome explains the men who sleep while the tares are sown as the *magistri Ecclesiarum* who turn away while the Church goes to ruin.[147] The money-changers expelled from the temple are interpreted *secundum mysticos intellectus* as *omnes tam episcopos et presbyteros et diaconos . . . vendentes pariter et ementes.*[148] In the parable of the wise and foolish virgins, the foolish are likened to those, *qui videntur Deo credere, et applaudunt sibi in Scripturis sanctis, tam ecclesiasticos quam Iudaeos atque haereticos.*[149]

Of great interest in this work are Jerome's comments on the famous words, *Et dabo tibi claves regni caelorum. Et quodcumque ligaveris super terram, erit ligatum in caelis. . . .*[150] Jerome is forced *supercilium decutere episcoporum* by refuting

---

[145] *PL* 23, 1377B–C. For another attack on pride in this commentary, cf. *PL* 25, 1344A.

[146] *PL* 26, 20C–21A.   [147] *PL* 26, 96B.

[148] *PL* 26, 157A.   [149] *PL* 26, 191A.

[150] Matt. 16: 19; *PL* 26, 122A–B.

a widely held interpretation of this passage: *Istum locum episcopi et presbyteri non intelligentes, aliquid sibi de Pharisaeorum assumunt supercilio, ut vel damnent innocentes, vel solvere se noxios arbitrentur.*[151] The cause of Jerome's indignation is not far to seek. The bishops, haughty and hypocritical Pharisees, consider as a support for their exalted position a scriptural passage which the popes wished to reserve for their own use, on the theory that it supported the primacy of the Roman See.[152] As an ardent champion of papal claims to supremacy (especially when such claims were made by his patron Pope Damasus), Jerome caustically vents his anger against imperious bishops who seek to undercut papal superiority by arrogantly referring a key scriptural passage to their own position.

In the year 406, Jerome returned to his series of commentaries on the minor Hebrew prophets. In the commentary on Zechariah, dedicated to St. Exuperius of Toulouse, Jerome employs the rhetorical device of *praeteritio* to needle the clergy. In interpreting the prophet's admonitions against evil shepherds (Zechariah 11: 4–5), Jerome declares that the tropological significance is so clear that there is absolutely no need to say that Zechariah refers to the negligent Christian bishops and priests who sell the people entrusted to them, who seek riches from the death of their flock (apparently a reference to legacy hunting), who praise the robbers of the wretched poor and bless the iniquitous. After delivering himself of this tirade, Jerome declares that he has no desire to interpret the passage as applying to the clergy![153]

---

[151] *PL* 26, 122A–B. Jerome elsewhere compares the clergy to a *Senatus Pharisaeorum* (*Praefat. in trans. libri Didymi de S.S., PL* 23, 107A). Vallarsi claims in note *ad loc.* that the phrase is derived from Jerome's mentor Gregory Nazianzen.

[152] Cyprian, *De unitate ecclesiae* 4 (*PL* 4, 513A) had already used the words of Jesus to Peter to justify episcopal power.

[153] *PL* 25, 1500B–C. For direct attacks on the clergy in this commentary, see *PL* 25, 1548D–1549A, and *PL* 25, 1554B.

The exposure of ecclesiastical faults continues in the commentaries on Malachi and Amos. When Malachi inveighs against sorcerers and adulterers, against false swearers, oppressors and deceivers of widows, we are to understand his words, says Jerome, as referring *ad principes Ecclesiarum*.[154] The tropological interpretation of a passage in which the prophet Amos denounces avarice leads to a mocking description of *perversos doctores et principes,*

qui faciunt mensuram minorem atque maiorem, ut pauperibus vel parum, vel nihil, divitibus autem et his, de quibus sectantur lucra, in modum concionatorum loquantur sermone longissimo: et propter pecuniam conterant capita pauperum atque conculcent, et non frumentum Domini . . . sed quisquilias et vilissimum pulverem avidis faucibus ingerant.[155]

The long and elaborate commentaries on the major Hebrew prophets, Isaiah, Ezekiel, and Jeremiah constitute Jerome's final contribution to scriptual exegesis. Written between 408 and 416 under the most trying circumstances of ill health, of grief and dismay at the disastrous course of political events, and of fear for the security of his person from the hostility of the neighboring Pelagian monks, these commentaries show no diminution of Jerome's reforming zeal. His polemic against those clergymen *qui destruunt operibus dignitatem* is as forceful as in his youthful works.[156] However, these works do reveal a certain dimming of Jerome's earlier satiric brilliance. Less attention is devoted to ridiculing the minute and absurd details of conduct upon which Jerome's acute power of observation has seized. Less emphasis is placed on rhetorical elaboration of scriptural denunciations. Exhortation usually takes the form simply of the application of scriptural fulminations to contemporary ecclesiastical society.

Thus in the commentary on Isaiah, when the prophet reproves those "that rise up early in the morning, that they may follow

[154] *PL* 25, 1567D.   [155] *PL* 25, 1081A.
[156] See *PL* 24, 39A.

strong drink," Jerome applies these words to princes of the
Church, *qui de mane consurgunt ad sectandam siceram, et
bibendum usque ad vesperem,* but he does not go on to paint
the expected satiric picture.[157] Elsewhere he denounces the
emptiness of an asceticism whose aim is worldly glory but gives
no such vivid description of this form of hypocrisy as he might
have done in an earlier work.[158]

A common theme in Jerome's invective against the clergy in
the commentary on Isaiah, as in other works, is their flattery of
the rich and oppression of the poor. They praise sinners for the
sake of material rewards.[159] Ecclesiastical offices are in the hands
of the rich and especially of the "senate of matrons and
women."[160] Once the bishops have flattered their way into office,
they crush the common people with the weight of their strictures
but do not utter even a peep (*ne mu quidem*) against the rich,
whose sins are far worse.[161] The plunder which they have ex-
acted from the poor is stored up in their homes. The charitable
contributions which are offered to the Church they either keep
for their own pleasure or distribute to their relatives, *et alienam
inopiam suas suorumque faciunt esse divitias.*[162] Thus, while the
masters of the Church are sleeping, the Church itself goes to
rack and ruin.[163]

In the commentary on Ezekiel Jerome has much to say on the
subject of the evil *quod nonnulli principes Ecclesiarum faciant
in tenebris.*[164] He describes with the following words clerics who
have been reduced to laymen because of their impious crimes but
who make use of ecclesiastical corruption to win their way back
into the clergy: *nunc resupini in pontificali solio sedeant et
ructent nobis simulatae fidei nauseas, immo opertae perfidiae*

---

[157] *PL* 24, 83C.   [158] *PL* 24, 584C and 585A.
[159] *PL* 24, 135C.
[160] *PL* 24, 67C. See above, p. 28. Cf. also *PL* 24, 591A–B.
[161] *PL* 24, 69B.   [162] *Ibid.*
[163] *PL* 24, 226D.   [164] *PL* 25, 82A.

aperta compendia.[165] A similar passage of trenchant ridicule is directed against those time-serving bishops who joined the Arian heresy during the period of persecution but later begged to be readmitted to the ranks of the orthodox:

Audiat hoc sacerdotalis gradus, et Arianae persecutionis ardore superatus ac verae postea fidei, ne opibus careat, potentia colla sub-mittens, sufficere sibi si non expellatur ex templo, si pristini nominis umbram quamdam et imaginem teneat, et non resupinus ructans delicias, quasi immaculatus et purus de excelso throno nobis imperitiae suae, et barbarae garrulitatis ructet nauseam.[166]

The gluttony of the clergy, one of Jerome's standard themes, is also lampooned in the commentary on Ezekiel. The prophet warns that, "the priests shall not eat of any thing that is dead of itself, or torn, whether it be fowl or beast" (Ezekiel 44:31). With these words, says Jerome, Ezekiel *condemnat sacerdotes, qui in turdis, ficedulis, gliribus, et caeteris huiuscemodi, haec aviditate gulae non custodiunt.*[167] This list of luxurious foods consists of standard dishes from the kitchen of pagan satire. *Turdi* are the object of satiric attack in Lucilius, Horace, and Persius; the passion for *ficedulae* is lampooned by Lucilius, Juvenal, and Martial; the eating of *glires* is ridiculed in a highly satiric passage of Ammianus Marcellinus.[168] We would gain valuable insight into Jerome's social critique if we could discover to what extent such an attack was based on personal observation and to what extent on a strong and malevolent imagination strongly assisted by a scholar's knowledge of pagan satire. We can only conjecture that Jerome's long-nourished hostility to

---

[165] *PL* 25, 435C. The adjective *pontificalis* in Jerome's time meant episcopal rather than papal.

[166] *PL* 25, 483C.

[167] *PL* 25, 444B. Cf. *PL* 25, 319A, a description of clerics *deliciis ventrique servientes.*

[168] Lucilius 978 (Marx); Horace *Epist.* i. 15. 41; Persius 6. 24; Juvenal 14. 9; Martial xiii. 5; Amm. Marc. xxviii. 4. 13 (cf. Martial xiii. 59).

the secular clergy may have been fattened by an excessively rich diet of satiric foods.

Most of the usual accusations against the clergy are repeated in the commentary on Jeremiah. Of particular scurrility is a brief description which shows a characteristic mingling of pagan and Christian elements. Interpreting the passage of Jeremiah in which God says, "Behold, I will fill . . . even the kings that sit upon David's throne, and the priests and the prophets . . . with drunkenness" (Jeremiah 13:13), Jerome applies the words to *reges ecclesiarum de stirpe sive filii David, qui sedent resupini et erecta cervice et protento aqualiculo super thronum eius.*[169] The phrase *protento aqualiculo* is a reminiscence of one of Jerome's favorite passages from Persius:

> Nugaris, cum tibi, calve,
> pinguis aqualiculus protenso sesquipede extet.[170]

By thus recalling a line of pagan satire, Jerome is able swiftly to transform the denunciations of an Old Testament prophet into a highly satiric description of luxurious and effeminate (*resupini*) bishops. It is these same bishops who are again lampooned later in the commentary on Jeremiah as *arietes . . . qui principes quidem videntur in populo, sed nihil habent in se doctrinae et sapientiae et per nimiam simplicitatem propemodum stultitiae vicini sunt.*[171] Such clergymen *faciunt stultitiam in Israel.*[172] Aflame with the fires of avarice, they flatter the rich and powerful and by their crimes turn the Church into a den of bandits.[173]

Conclusion

In summary, we may say that Jerome is possessed by unquenchable anger at what he considers the turpitude of the secular clergy in general and of its leaders, the bishops, in par-

---

[169] *PL* 24, 794C; *CSEL*, LIX, 164.   [170] Persius 1. 56–57.
[171] *PL* 24, 875C; *CSEL*, LIX, 319.   [172] *PL* 24, 897A; *CSEL*, LIX, 361.
[173] *PL* 24, 753A; *CSEL*, LIX, 86; and *PL* 24, 759A; *CSEL*, LIX, 97.

ticular. This anger is expressed in ceaseless lampooning of their arrogance, avarice, gluttony, hypocrisy, and ignorance. Such violent hostility must be seen in part as reflecting the rejection by the new monastic movement of that compromise between the Church and "the world" which was the inevitable result of Christianity's political victory. The monastic leaders, with their ideals of a higher type of Christian life than could be lived amid the storm of worldly events, naturally viewed secular clerics, with their pomp and luxury, as little better than pagan priests. This hostility was heartily returned by priests and bishops who considered monks unnatural madmen under the influence of Gnostic extremism. Yet the monastic movement too, as it grew in power, attracted to itself adherents who saw in it a means of escaping hardships beneath a cloak of holiness. Against such enemies within the monastic camp Jerome turned all the force of his incomparable power of ridicule in an effort to maintain the original ideals and standards of asceticism.

It must be recognized, however, that Jerome's motives in satirizing the clergy were not entirely of an idealistic nature. A man of powerful ambitions, Jerome had imagined that through championship of the increasingly influential monastic movement he might win high ecclesiastical position. It is perhaps significant that unlike Ammianus Marcellinus, Jerome never attacks the sensuality of the popes, on whose favor the hopes of an ambitious churchman might depend.[174] But Jerome's hopes, defeated, were swiftly transformed into bile, whose natural object was the clergy which had checked his rise.

Jerome's chief tool in his polemic against the clergy, as in his attack on society as a whole, was his brilliant talent for scurrilous and malevolent description which was based first on penetrating power of observation and then on a profound lack of charity for the weaknesses of human nature. Naturally, pagan models

---

[174] Amm. Marc. xxvii. 3. 14.

had less direct influence on Jerome's satire directed against the clergy than on the lampoons aimed at society in general, for there was no direct parallel to the Christian clergy in the pagan satiric tradition. Nonetheless, when Jerome can recall a passage of pagan satire in which a failing also found among the clergy is ridiculed, he quickly adds it to his stock of satiric ammunition.

Jerome's methods of satire vary very little in different categories of his writings. We may note, however, that in his exegetical works he makes great effort to adapt his invective to the scriptural passage he is interpreting. That he does not really succeed is shown by the constant reappearance of identical attacks on the clergy under the guise of "tropological interpretation" of the most varied biblical passages.

Yet it would be only fair to Jerome to conclude this chapter by showing that he was capable on rare occasions not only of defending the character of the secular clergy but even of employing pagan satire in doing so. In the *Dialogue against the Pelagians*, Jerome has the orthodox speaker refer to Horace in saying of clerical faults, *Quis est . . . qui non quasi in pulchro corpore aut naevum aut verrucam habeat?*[175]

[175] *PL* 23, 538C. Cf. Horace *Sat.* i. 6. 67.

CHAPTER IV

Women and Marriage

IN his mordant attacks on women more than in any other aspect of his satire, St. Jerome was the heir of an age-old literary tradition. Throughout antiquity the question *an vir sapiens ducat uxorem?* was one of the most widely discussed topics of popular ethics. Since the question was usually answered in the negative, its continued treatment produced a large body of antifeminist literature. The roots of the misogynous tradition can be found in Hesiod, who in his tale of Pandora sang of the evils brought forth upon the earth by the creation of woman.[1] The theme is continued in iambic poetry: Semonides of Amorgos expressed his hatred of women by comparing them to various kinds of animals.[2] Euripides bared the darker side of female nature so vividly and explicitly in many of his tragedies that the normally passive women of Athens were shocked and outraged.[3] The women's fury and their merited revenge against Euripides are portrayed with rollicking humor by Aristophanes in his *Thesmophoriazusae*, though Aristophanes himself later went on to

[1] *Works and Days*, 60–105. Cf. *Theogony*, 570–612.
[2] *Anthologia Lyrica Graeca*, ed. E. Diehl (Leipzig, 1952), I³, 52–58.
[3] Euripides himself refers to antifeminism as "an old strain" (*Medea* 421 and *Ion* 1096).

subject the vagaries of female behavior to brilliant mockery in his *Ecclesiazusae*. In the Hellenistic age the virtues and defects of women continued to be the subject of vigorous debate, as was revealed by the discovery of a second-century papyrus florilegium of sentiments, mainly unfavorable, voiced by the poets on the nature of women.[4] At a later period Plutarch wrote his still extant *Praecepta coniugalia*, which is the repository of much antifeminist sentiment.[5]

In Latin literature, misogyny and misogamy are first found in Lucilius, who wrote:

> Homines ipsi hanc sibi molestiam ultro et aerumanam offerunt,
> ducunt uxores, producunt, quibus haec faciant, liberos.[6]

The satiric treatment of women was continued by Varro, who in his Menippean satires expressed strong doubt of the wisdom of marrying.[7] The philosophic discussion of marriage is represented by Seneca's tract *De matrimonio*, which was devoted, at least in part, to painting a black picture of married life. Seneca probably borrowed from a similar work of Theophrastus. Juvenal, whose sixth satire is the fullest statement of misogyny in all ancient literature, may in turn have borrowed some of his antifeminist material from Seneca.[8] However, the hatred of women in its most extreme form was characteristic of the Cynic rather than of the Stoic school, and antifeminism entered Roman satire at least in part by way of the Cynic diatribe.[9]

---

[4] Published by W. Schubart and U. von Wilamowitz in *Berliner Klassikertexte*, V, pt. 2 (Berlin, 1907), 127–130.

[5] For Jerome's use of this work in *Adversus Iovinianum*, see Luebeck, 51–52.

[6] Lucilius, 678–680 (Marx). For other misogamistic opinions cf. *ibid.*, 282–283; 504–505; 990–1007.

[7] Buecheler's 6th ed. (Berlin, 1922), 166–168.

[8] See below, pp. 153–154.

[9] On the philosophic, the rhetorical, and the satiric attack on women and on the complex interrelationship of the three, see K. Praechter,

Misogamy continued into late antiquity; the Neoplatonic philosopher Porphyry is conjectured to have written an attack on marriage in which he made use of Theophrastus' and of Plutarch's works. In the rhetorical schools the pains and pleasures of marriage had long been a standard topic of argumentation among students practicing deliberative oratory.[10] Exactly such a school thesis is set forth in the *Progymnasmata* of Aphthonius, a rhetorician contemporary with Jerome.[11] Thus St. Jerome had a long pagan tradition of antifeminism on which to draw in inveighing against women and marriage. The influence of several of the works mentioned above can be traced in St. Jerome's misogynous satire, and no small part in our task will be to try to discover which pagan sources most influenced Jerome.

One might have expected the unfavorable attitude toward women found so frequently in pagan writers to weaken or vanish in Christianity, for St. Paul had written that "there is neither male nor female; for ye are all one in Christ Jesus."[12] However, it was Paul himself who sowed the fateful seeds of Christian antifeminism when he wrote in his First Epistle to the Corinthians, "It is good for a man not to touch a woman," and, "I say therefore to the unmarried and widows, It is good for them if they abide even as I. But if they cannot contain, let them

---

Hierokles der Stoiker (Leipzig, 1901), 66–90; Schneider, *Juvenal und Seneca*, 34–39; De Decker, *Juvenales declamans*, 24–29; and F. Gauger, *Zeitschilderung und Topik bei Juvenal* (Greifswald, 1936), 33–50. On the relationship of the sexes in general, see J. Vogt, *Von der Gleichwertigkeit der Geschlechter in der bürgerlichen Gesellschaft der Griechen* (Wiesbaden, 1960).

[10] Quintilian ii. 4. 25.

[11] See the translation of Aphthonius by R. E. Nadeau in *Speech Monographs*, XIX (1952), 281.

[12] Gal. 3: 28. St. Augustine expresses a lofty view of the relationship between the sexes when he declares that woman's share of rational intelligence is equal to man's, *Confessions* xiii. 32. 47. Yet even Augustine tempers his opinion by immediately adding that women are by nature subject to men.

marry: for it is better to marry than to burn."[13] These words were picked up and developed by the ascetic movement, whose greatest period of development fell in the later fourth century and of which St. Jerome was the most enthusiastic champion. It is significant that Jerome's severe and lengthy attack on marriage in the first book of his tract *Adversus Iovinianum* is based largely on the very words of St. Paul cited above. Of course asceticism was also subject to many non-Christian influences. The severe ethic of the Stoa and the extreme dualism of the Gnostic world view gave powerful encouragement to the ascetic rejection of the flesh.[14] Proponents of such austere views looked with horror upon women as sensuality incarnate and in their exhortations in behalf of chastity naturally attacked marriage as the destroyer of holiness.

This extreme attitude is found as early as the end of the second century in the apologist Tatian, who was much influenced by Gnosticism and of whom Jerome says, *Non solum nuptias, sed cibos quoque . . . damnat et reprobat.*[15] Tertullian too devoted his caustic genius to inveighing against women and marriage in such works as *De exhortatione castitatis, De cultu feminarum, De monogamis, De pudicitia,* and in the lost tract *Ad amicum philosophum,* which Jerome twice names as a full and severe treatment of the disadvantages of marriage.[16] About a century after Tertullian, the Lycian bishop Methodius composed a curious dialogue modeled on Plato's *Symposium* in which ten virgins deprecated physical love and marriage. We have evidence that St. Jerome had read this work, for he refers to Methodius'

[13] I Cor. 7: 1, 8–9.

[14] See esp. Hatch, *Influence of Greek Ideas,* 139–170.

[15] Jerome specifically but incongruously rejects the extremism of Tatian, Letter 49. 9.

[16] See Letter 22. 22 and *Adv. Iovin.* i. 13 (PL 23, 241A). On Tertullian's work *Ad amicum philosophum,* see E. Bickel, *Diatribe in Sen. Phil. frag.* (Leipzig, 1915), 239–287.

nitidus et compositus sermo.[17] As the ascetic movement grew in strength, louder and more severe grew the voices raised against the corrupting influence of women and marriage. In the fourth century, the author of the *Apocalypse of Paul* envisages women in hell being devoured by serpents. "These are the women," he explains, "that beautified themselves with paint and unguents and went to church to ensnare men."[18] Jerome mentions his teacher Gregory Nazianzen, his patron Pope Damasus, and St. Ambrose as the authors of works directed against women and marriage.[19] The last of these writers, in addition to three specifically misogamous tracts, also incidentally satirized the pride, luxury, and sensuality of women in many of his other works.[20]

We may say then that the tendencies toward misogyny in pagan thought were not only continued but much intensified in Christianity. St. Jerome was the direct heir of these two anti-feminist traditions, and we shall find in his satire of women that curious mingling of pagan and Christian elements which is so characteristic of much of his writing. Before, however, a study of Jerome's misogynous polemic is undertaken, it is essential to examine his actual relationships with women, for our view of the motives of his literary invective must inevitably be influenced by the facts of his behavior.

The biography of Jerome reveals that he was able to evoke

[17] *De vir. ill.* LXXXIII (*PL* 23, 727B). The dialogue is still extant, published in *PG* 18, 27–220.

[18] Ed. M. R. James (Oxford, 1945), 545.

[19] Letter 22. 22; *Adv. Iovin.* i. 13 (*PL* 23, 241A). For Gregory's poem on chastity see *PG* 37, 643.

[20] E.g., *De Nabuthae* 5, 25–26 (*CSEL*, XXXII, 480–481). See Weston, *Latin Sat. Writing*, 80. However, contrary to Weston's assumptions, the description of feminine extravagance in *De Nabuthae* 26 is not original but is adapted from St. Basil's homily *In divites* 288 and 297. See Martin R. P. McGuire, *S. Ambrosii De Nabuthae: A Commentary with an Introduction and Translation* (*Cath. U. of Am. Patristic Studies*, XV; Washington, D.C., 1927), 5 and 137–139.

in women an enthusiasm and devotion which counterbalanced the hostility which men so frequently felt toward him. While he lived in Rome, his life revolved around the aristocratic ladies of the Aventine. In the noble Marcella, Jerome aroused so wonderful a scholarly zeal that he had reason to complain of her excessive ardor.²¹ Paula and her daughters were the completely devoted disciples of Jerome, and we find them his most loyal champions in all the numerous conflicts which beset his life. With these ladies and with numerous others Jerome carried on an extensive correspondence. In the catalogue of his own writings included in *De viris illustribus* Jerome mentions *Ad Marcellam epistolarum unum librum*. He states, however, that his letters to Paula and Eustochium were not collected into a book; *quia quotidie scribuntur, incertus est numerus.*²² A large number of his scholarly works are addressed to women. In two of them, the commentaries on Zephaniah and Isaiah, he feels called upon to defend himself against those enemies who mocked his encouragement of scholarly interests in women. In direct contradiction to views he expresses elsewhere on the proper role of women in the Church, he cites Deborah, Judith, and Esther as examples of women who had advanced the cause of true religion.²³ In many of Jerome's other writings we find evidence that his close relationships with women had, not unnaturally, brought from his enemies charges of improper behavior. However, we have no reason to believe that Jerome's vigorous defense of the purity of his relations does not represent the truth.²⁴ In brief, St. Jerome in

²¹ E.g., Letter 29. 1. This faithful lady tried to save Jerome's career by checking the violence of his tongue, that *seminarium rixarum.* See Letter 27. 2.

²² *De vir. ill.* CXXXV (PL 23, 758A and 759A).

²³ PL 24, 425A, and PL 25, 1337A. Cf. also Letter 127. 5, a defense of the role of women in Christianity, and Letter 130. 7, an apology for his praise of the nun Demetrias. For the opposite view on women, see *Dial. contra Pelag.* 25; PL 23, 542B.

²⁴ Letter 45. 2. Cf. Letter 54. 2, where Jerome reveals that he had been called *seductorem.*

practice not only was not a misogynist but on the contrary maintained close relationships with women, for which he felt called upon to apologize. Our task is now to compare with his actual behavior the literary expression of his attitude toward women.

Letters

The most famous and influential of all St. Jerome's letters, his *libellus* of advice to Eustochium "De virginitate servanda,"[25] may be considered the greatest slander of women since Juvenal's sixth satire. Zeal for his ascetic cause rouses Jerome to paint some of his most extravagantly malicious portraits of women. As a prelude to his attack, he parodies marriage in bitter terms. He begins by denying any intention to describe the *molestias nuptiarum* but immediately juxtaposes exactly such a description: *quomodo uterus intumescat, infans vagiat, cruciet paelex, domus cura sollicitet, et omnia quae putantur bona, mors extrema praecidat. . . .*[26] But this is merely a list of trivial bourgeois inconveniences. The most serious charge brought against marriage is its encouragement of the natural sensuality of women, especially those of the aristocratic kind, who are *semper in deliciis, semper in plumis,* unable to abstain from *vino et esculentioribus cibis.*[27] The natural lewdness of women, unless checked by severe asceticism, leads to corruption. Each woman is an *ardens corpusculum* to which the luxury of marriage and

---

[25] Letter 22.

[26] Letter 22. 2. Cf. Letter 50. 5, *uteros tumescentes, infantum vagitus et lectulos maritorum.* Although later in this *libellus* (Letter 22. 22) Jerome denies that he will attack marriage and refers the reader to Tertullian's works for such severity, his own description is hardly less scurrilous than the following words of Tertullian: *ubera fluitantia et uteros nauseantes et infantes pipiantes* (*De monag.* xvi. 5). Cf. also *De exhortat. cast.* ix. 5: *de nuptiis enim uteri et ubera et infantes.*

[27] Letter 22. 11.

the worldly life merely adds fuel.²⁸ Yet even those women who adopt an ascetic life often fail to maintain their chastity, claims Jerome. Fallen virgins may be divided into three categories: first those who attempt to conceal their sin by pretending to be widows:

Videas plerasque viduas ante quam nuptas infelicem conscientiam mentita tantum vestem protegere, quas nisi tumor uteri et infantum prodiderit vagitus, erecta cervice et ludentibus pedibus incedunt.²⁹

The second category consists of those who *sterilitatem prae-bibunt et necdum sati hominis homicidium faciunt.*³⁰ But some former virgins go even further in an effort to conceal their lust:

Nonnullae, cum se senserint concepisse de scelere, aborti venena meditantur et frequenter etiam ipsae commortuae trium criminum reae ad inferas perducuntur, homicidae sui, Christi adulterae, necdum nati filii parricidae.³¹

Such debased and foul nuns also indulge in other forms of sensuality. They gorge themselves with wine and then, adding blasphemy to drunkenness, they exclaim: *Absit, ut ego me a Christi sanguine abstineam.*³² Here Jerome adopts the satiric

---

²⁸ Letter 22. 8. Jerome's words, *Quid oleum flammae adicimus?* are probably proverbial rather than a reference to Horace *Sat.* ii. 3. 321, *oleum adde camino,* as Luebeck (p. 164) claims.

²⁹ Letter 22. 13. Cf. Letter 64. 21: *O quantae virgines et quantorum sperata pudicita in die iudicii dehonestabitur.*

³⁰ Letter 22. 13.

³¹ *Ibid.* The practice of abortion is attacked by Jerome also in Letter 123. 4 and *Adv. Iovin.* i. 49 (PL 23, 241A). The theme also forms part of Juvenal's satire of women. Cf. *Sat. 6.* 594–597.
    "Sed iacet aurato vix ulla puerpera lecto.
    tantum artes huius, tantum medicamina possunt,
    quae steriles facit atque homines in ventre necandos
    conducit."

³² Letter 22. 13. The word "nun" is used throughout to refer generally to a woman who has dedicated herself from religious motives to a life of virginity, whether she lived in a religious community and was bound by vows or not.

technique of mimicry, allowing the objects of his attack to expose their faults in their own words, but he soon returns to
narrative satire as he brilliantly lampoons licentious nuns:

Hae sunt, quae per publicum notabiliter incedunt et furtivis oculorum
nutibus adulescentium gregem post se trahunt, quae semper audiunt
per prophetam: "Facies meretricis facta est tibi, inpudorata es tu."[33]

What does chastity mean to such women? asks Jerome.

Purpura tantum in veste sit tenuis et laxius, ut crines decidant,
ligatum caput, soccus vilior et per umeros maforte volitans, strictae
manicae bracchiis adhaerentes et solutis genibus fractus incessus: haec
est apud illas tota virginitas. Habeant istiusmodi laudatores suos, et
sub virginali nomine lucrosius pereant.[34]

A comparison of this description, written in the year 384, with
a passage of a letter of 409 will reveal how little Jerome's antifeminist views and his satiric expression of these views varied
with the passage of time.[35] In the later letter Jerome deprecates
second marriages but declares that they are allowable, *ne* [*vidua*]
*oculorum nutibus et hilaritate vultus iuvenum post se greges
trahat, ne aliud verbo, aliud habitu polliceatur.*[36] In yet another
work, the commentary on Isaiah, also written about 409, we find
a portrait of the same lady grown old.

Pulchra mulier quae adulescentium post se trahebat greges . . .
arata fronte contrahitur, et quae prius amori, postea fastidio est.[37]

[33] Letter 22. 13.
[34] *Ibid.* Cf. Ambrose *De Helia et ieiunio* 18, 66: *Illae* [*mulieres*] *in
plateis inverecundos etiam viris sub conspectu adulescentulorum intem-
perantium choros ducunt, iactantes comam, trahentes tunicas, scissae
amictus, nudae lacertos, plaudentes manibus, saltantes pedibus, person-
antes vocibus, inritantes in se iuvenum libidines motu histrionico, petu-
lanti oculo, dedecoroso ludibrio.* (See Weston, *Latin Sat. Writing*, 76.)
This passage of Ambrose is virtually a translation of St. Basil's homily
In ebriosos 445B–D (123A–C). See Buck, *S. Ambrosii*, 193–194.
[35] For chronology, see Cavallera, II, 24 and 52.
[36] Letter 123. 4.   [37] *PL* 24, 417A.

Thus in three works separated by many years, Jerome's desire to ridicule the natural lasciviousness of women evokes satiric descriptions containing similar details. These similarities suggest that in none of these passages was Jerome simply expressing spontaneous moral anger, for it is unlikely that the unhampered overflow of *saeva indignatio* would have produced three such similar descriptions on three separate occasions. The implication is that Jerome was using traditional rhetorical material in these passages. H. Reich has gone so far as to see in the exaggerated detail and extreme vividness of these satiric portraits the direct influence of the mime.[38] If it is objected that Jerome often speaks disapprovingly of the mime, the obvious reply is that such inconsistencies between theory and action are highly characteristic of him.[39] However, Jerome's style of satiric description was probably more influenced by his rhetorical training and by his reading in the pagan satirists and less by his knowledge of the theater than Reich's theories would imply. Indeed Reich himself points out that "in den Rhetorenschulen . . . liebte man die Sujets des Mimus."[40] Yet we do have one piece of evidence, which Reich does not mention, to show that Jerome was aware of the similarity between his own caricatures and the ethology of the Roman mime. In his commentary on Isaiah Jerome lampoons:

Ecclesiae feminas, quae ambulant collo extento, et nutibus loquuntur oculorum, et plaudunt tam manibus quam pedibus, et ut composito incedant gradu, non naturam sequuntur, sed *histriones redimunt praeceptores*.[41]

[38] *Der Mimus*, 762.
[39] For such disapproving remarks see Letters 58. 4 and 79. 9.
[40] Page 762.
[41] *PL* 24, 69D–70A. Some of the details of this portrayal are repeated in *PL* 24, 70C. Jerome's mocking description is directly aroused by a highly satiric picture of worldly women in Isa. 3: 16–23. The prophet attacks the daughters of Zion who are "haughty and walk with stretched forth necks (*collo extento*) and wanton eyes, walking and mincing as

To return now to the *libellus* for Eustochium, we find Jerome satirizing those debauched nuns known as *agapetae* (also called *subintroductae*). These nuns lived in supposedly spiritual unions with men to whom they were not related, even though they had brothers, indeed brothers who had taken religious vows, with whom they might have lived.

Whence has a plague of *agapetae* entered the churches? Whence comes a new kind of unmarried wife? Indeed, whence a novel genus of concubine? I shall add more: whence come monogamous prostitutes? They [a nun and her male companion] live in the same house, in the same bedroom, often in the same bed, and they call us suspicious if we think anything of it. A brother deserts his virgin sister, a virgin scorns her celibate brother and, although they pretend to be devoted to the same ideal, they seek the spiritual solace of outsiders in order that they may at home have carnal relations.[42]

In these bitterly ironic words, Jerome's role as misogynous polemicist is seen to stem directly from his campaign for ecclesiastical reform, as he vents his anger against those nuns *quae nolunt esse virgines, sed videri.*

Just as in his satire on the clergy Jerome was compelled to attack both the open enemies of monasticism and the pseudo monks, so in his misogynous polemic both the worldly women and the corrupt nuns are the objects of his ridicule. The women of the world (*mulierculae*), he exclaims, are inflated by their

---

they go, and making a tinkling with their feet." Such women the Lord will destroy and, "take away the bravery of their tinkling ornaments about their feet, and their cauls, and their round tires like the moon, the chains, and the bracelets, and the mufflers, the bonnets, and the ornaments of the legs, and the headbands, and the tablets, and the earrings, the rings and nose jewels, the changeable suits of apparel, and the mantles, and the wimples, and the crisping pins, the glasses, and the fine linen, and the hoods, and the vails." Jerome adopts the detail *collo extento* into his own satiric language.

[42] Letter 22. 14.

husbands' rank.⁴³ They fence themselves around with a flock of eunuchs. Their garments are ostentatiously interwoven with a metallic thread. The wealthy widows are worst of all:

Praecedit caveas basternarum ordo semivir et rubentibus buccis cutis farsa distenditur, ut eas putes maritos non amisisse sed quaerere. Plena adulatoribus domus, plena convivis. . . . Illae interim quae sacerdotes suo vident indigere praesidio, eriguntur in superbiam, et quia maritorum expertae dominatum viduitatis praeferunt libertatem, castae vocantur et nonnae, et post cenam dubiam apostolos somniant.⁴⁴

Jerome expresses his indignation brilliantly. With a minimum of verbiage he portrays the vast emptiness of the lady's litter, the meretricious elaboration of her toilet, and her revolting sensuality. Jerome may also be suggesting that there is something stupidly bestial about such a woman, since the word *cavea* is frequently used of an animal's den or a bird's cage.⁴⁵ However, the last remark of the passage, a suggestion that female gluttony stimulates lewd dreams, is simply a new application of one of Jerome's oft-repeated ideas.⁴⁶

Later in this letter, Jerome turns back again from excoriating women of the world to an attack on the mundane ascetics. Very few nuns, he complains, are able to avoid seeking fame and glory by their asceticism. Eustochium must avoid those nuns who have indeed ceased to attract notice by their golden robes but seek to do so by their excessive filth, who, when they come into a gathering of brothers and sisters, crouch on a low footstool, pre-

⁴³ On the irrepressible arrogance of wealthy women, cf. *Comm. in Titum*, PL 26, 617A. The apostle urges women to be *subditas viris suis, ne forte divitiis et nobilitate perflatae Dei sententiae non meminerint.*

⁴⁴ Letter 22. 16. For *cena dubia*, cf. Terence *Phormio*, 342. For a similar description, cf. Amm. Marc. xiv. 6. 16: *Matronae complures, opertis capitibus et basternis, per latera civitatis cuncta discurrunt.*

⁴⁵ E.g., Martial ix. 57. 10; ix. 89. 4; xiv. 77.

⁴⁶ This is also his thesis in Letter 22. 8–10, Letter 54. 10, and Letter 55. 2.

tending that they are unworthy, lower their voices as if they are weakened by long fasting, and, feigning the gait of one about to faint, support themselves on another's shoulders. "Indeed," continues Jerome,

there are some who disfigure their faces that they may appear in the eyes of men to be fasting. These women, as soon as they see someone, begin to moan, lower their brow and covering their face, free hardly one eye for seeing: their dress is drab, their girdle of plain material, their hands and feet filthy, while their belly alone is aboil with food, because no one can see it.[47]

But gross hypocrisy seems by comparison only a trivial fault when Jerome comes to warn Eustochium against the debauchery of sybaritic nuns who fall under the influence of voluptuous matrons:

Eas autem virgines viduasque, quae otiosae et curiosae domus circumeunt matronarum, quae rubore frontis adtrito parasitos vicere mimorum, quasi quasdam pestes abice. . . . Nulla illis nisi ventris cura est et quae ventri proxima.[48]

The last remark illustrates how in the heat of his indignation Jerome feels justified in employing the grossness so characteristic of pagan satire, even when he is writing to a young girl. He then turns from straight narrative satire to mimicry:

Istiusmodi hortari solent et dicere: "mi catella, rebus tuis utere et vive, dum vivis," et: "numquid filiis tuis servas?" Vinosae atque

---

[47] Letter 22. 27. That many nuns sought reputation from the practice of extreme asceticism is implied by Jerome's praise of Blesilla: *Humilitas vestium non, ut in plerisque, tumentes animas arguebat* (Letter 39. 1). Cf. also Letter 23. 2, on Lea: *Inculta vestis, vilis cibus, neglectum caput, ita tamen ut cum omnia faceret, ostentationem fugeret singulorum, ne reciperet in praesenti saeculo mercedem suam.* Cf. on the same topic Letter 24. 5.

[48] Letter 22. 29. The reference to *mimi* here may lend some support to Reich's theory of the influence of the mime on Jerome's satire.

lascivae quidvis mali insinuant ac ferreas quoque mentes ad delicias molliunt.[49]

Then Jerome attacks the so-called graces of women in a passage which shows the influence of Persius. He warns Eustochium:

Nec tibi diserta multum velis videri aut lyricis festiva carminibus metro ludere. Non delumbem matronarum salivam delicata secteris, quae nunc strictis dentibus, nunc labiis dissolutis balbutientem linguam in dimidiata verba moderantur, rusticum putantes omne quod nascitur. Adeo illis adulterium etiam linguae placet. . . . Quid facit cum psalterio Horatius? cum evangeliis Maro?[50]

The words in which Jerome ridicules the overrefined speech of women contains a phrase drawn from Persius' attack on the effeminate poetry of his day:

Summa delumbe saliva
hoc natat in labris, et in udo est, Maenas et Attis. . . .[51]

An incongruity highly characteristic of Jerome is the juxtaposition here of a reminiscence from a classical author and an exhortation against the reading of classical authors.[52]

In his *libellus* for Eustochium, Jerome reveals the richness of his satiric gifts by drawing a series of brilliant caricatures in each of which a different feminine failing is mercilessly exposed. In one passage he uses his most vivid colors to stigmatize woman's inborn love of luxury, which is but thinly disguised by studied hypocrisy:

At nunc plerasque videas armaria stipare vestibus, tunicas mutare cotidie et tamen tineas non posse superare. Quae religiosior fuerit unum exterit vestimentum, et plenis arcis pannos trahit. Inficitur

---

[49] Letter 22. 29.

[50] *Ibid.* Cf. Juvenal 6. 434–456, the satirist's attack on "literary" females.

[51] *Sat.* 1. 104–105. The parallel is pointed out by Hagendahl, *Latin Fathers*, 110.

[52] The incongruity is even more remarkable here than elsewhere, for it is at this very point that Jerome introduces the account of his dream oath in order to strengthen his warning against reading the pagans.

membrana colore purpureo, aurum liquescit in litteras, gemmis codices vestiuntur et nudus ante fores earum Christus emoritur. Cum manum porrexerint, bucinant; cum ad agapen vocaverint, praeco conducitur.⁵³

Jerome is well aware that his minutely detailed vignettes of female absurdity are essentially satire, as he reveals in the next sentence of this passage:

Vidi nuper—nomina taceo, ne saturam putes—nobilissimam mulierum Romanarum in basilica beati Petri semiviris antecedentibus, propria manu, quo religiosior putaretur, singulos nummos dispertire pauperibus. Interea—ut usu nosse perfacile est—anus quaedam annis pannisque obsita praecurrit ut alterum nummum acciperet; ad quam cum ordine pervenisset, pugnus porrigitur pro denario, et tanti criminis reus sanguis effunditur.⁵⁴

It would throw a great deal of light on St. Jerome's satiric inventiveness if we could discover whether this sad but amusing tale is in fact the product of his imagination. Although the truth of the story can be neither proved nor disproved, the language in which it is told reveals the influence of Jerome's reading of pagan comedy: the phrase *annis pannisque obsita* is a recollection of Terence's *Eunuchus*, 236:

Video sentum squalidum aegrum, pannis annisque obsitum.⁵⁵

It is hardly surprising that the vitriol with which Jerome described the irrepressible worldliness of Roman women in his long letter to Eustochium aroused indignation in a city which still considered asceticism as a Manichaean and unchristian novelty.⁵⁶ Thirty years after his departure from Rome, Jerome considered this satiric document the chief cause of his unpopu-

---

⁵³ Letter 22. 32.   ⁵⁴ *Ibid.*

⁵⁵ See Hagendahl, 110.

⁵⁶ Cf. Letter 22. 13: The enemies of the nuns were wont to call them Manichaeans. Those who saw in the ascetic movement the influence of Gnosticism were of course correct.

larity.[57] Yet this letter represents but his earliest statement of themes which he was to develop repeatedly in later works. Jerome's refusal to be deterred from his attacks on women by the strong opposition which he knew he was arousing speaks well for the sincerity of his principles and suggests that Grütz-macher's view that in his ascetic propaganda Jerome was serving personal interest is mistaken.[58] Indeed, in a letter he wrote in answer to the critics of his extremism, Jerome returns to the attack with even greater violence and relish. In obvious reference to his letter to Eustochium he exclaims, "Am I not to dare point out the crimes which others do not blush to commit? Wherein has my speech been too free?"

Numquid in lancibus idola caelata descripsi? numquid inter epulas christianas virginalibus oculis Baccharum satyrorumque complexus? num quem amarior sermo pulsavit? numquid ex mendicis divites fieri dolui? numquid reprehendi hereditarias sepulturas? unum miser locutus sum, quod virgines saepius deberent cum mulieribus esse quam cum masculis: totius oculos urbis offendi, cunctorum digitis notor.[59]

This passage implies that in the views of his enemies Jerome's satiric attack on women was the very kernel of his moralistic propaganda.

Jerome's defense here was not calculated as an anodyne to his enemies. No more likely to appease was his final attack on women written from Rome, a satiric piece which forms the central portion of his enthusiastic letter describing the conversion to the ascetic life of Paula's daughter Blesilla (Letter 38). The subject matter of this document was ideal for stimulating Jerome's satiric inventiveness, for his knowledge of rhetoric would suggest that

---

[57] Cf. Letter 130. 19. 4, where Jerome refers to this letter as *qui sermo offendit plurimos*.

[58] Contrast Grützmacher's views (e.g., II, 239) on the selfish motives of Jerome's propaganda.

[59] Letter 27. 2.

he might most effectively eulogize Blesilla's new life by contrasting in vivid colors the life which she had abandoned, the life of corrupt women of the world. The ascetic propagandist calls upon his school-trained powers of description in the following venomous passage:

Illae Christianos oculos potius scandalizent quae purpurisso et quibusdam fucis ora oculosque depingunt, quarum facies gypseae et nimio candore deformes idola mentiuntur, quibus si forte improvidens lacrimarum stilla eruperit, sulco defluit, quas nec numerus annorum potest docere quod vetulae sunt, quae capillis alienis verticem instruunt, et praeteritam iuventutem in rugis anilibus poliunt, quae denique ante nepotum gregem trementes virgunculae componuntur.[60]

Jerome's brilliant powers of observation and description are nowhere better displayed than in this passage. The vignette of the women on whose face an unexpected tear has drawn a furrow is a master stroke. The use of the poetic word *vertex* for head aims at a mock solemnity which heightens the ridicule. The diminutives (*vetulae*, *virgunculae*) are highly ironic. Juvenal employs *virgunculae* in exactly the same scornful and mocking manner.[61] But Jerome has not yet given vent to the fullness of his bile. Looking back on Blesilla's former life, he describes how little maidservants (*ancillulae*) used to arrange her tresses and squeeze her guiltless head (*vertex*) into a headdress filled with curls.[62] Those were the days when Blesilla considered the softness of feathers unbearably hard and could scarcely lie on couches piled with pillows. Such wanton sins must be purged away by knees bent in prayer upon the naked ground and by

---

[60] Letter 38. 3. In the *Comm. in Titum*, written from three to five years after this letter, Jerome repeats the last clause of the passage above almost verbatim (*PL* 26, 616A).

[61] *Sat.* 13. 40.

[62] For another scurrilous and ironic use of *vertex*, see Letter 130. 7. 13. Cf. Juvenal 6. 501-507 and Paulinus of Nola, *Carmen* 25. 85–86 (*PL* 61, 635). This poem of Paulinus is itself a masterpiece of antifeminist satire.

ceaseless tears to wash away the white lead with which women's faces were polluted.[63]

These harsh words represent Jerome's final exposure of women's failings based on his own observation of their behavior. The great polemicist was in the end unable to sustain his battle against the sins of the world from the heart of Babylon itself. It is one of those striking incongruities of which Jerome's life is so full that his exile from Rome was the result both of his venomous attacks on women and of his close relationships with women. In his thirty-seventh letter Jerome caustically defends the violence of his moral critique and especially his remarks directed against women. As long as eight years after his departure from Rome, he was to be called upon to mitigate the harshness of his antifeminist strictures, and he was, superficially, at least, to do so in a long apology (Letter 49). And yet in his farewell epistle to Rome he pleads against the charges, brought by his enemies, of immorally close relationships with his female companions:

Before I became acquainted with the house of the holy Paula, the whole city was united in its enthusiasm for me. . . . Never did I enter the house of any wanton, did I? . . . No lady at Rome could subdue my mind unless she was grief-stricken and fasting, squalid with filth, almost blinded by tears, a woman whom the rising sun often surprised when she had prayed night after night for the mercy of the Lord. . . . No woman could afford me delight except one whom I never saw eating.[64]

In spite of this rather ridiculously exaggerated plea, Jerome was completely routed by the two-pronged attack of his enemies and fled, destined to take up the battle against the life of "the world" from the secure refuge of his Bethlehem monastery.

The earliest of the Bethlehem letters in which women and marriage are the focal points of an ascetic attack on society is

[63] Letter 38. 4.   [64] Letter 45. 3.

his *Apology to Pammachius*.[65] This document purports to be Jerome's defense against those who accused him of excessive hostility toward matrimony. The letter begins mildly enough as Jerome clearly states his position on marriage: "We accept marriage to the extent that we prefer virginity which is born of marriage."[66] But as he continues to write, Jerome is unable to conceal his true feelings. His deep bitterness toward marriage is revealed when, in a reference to Persius 2. 16, he compares those Christians who receive the eucharist *post coitum* to pagans who before they pray to their deities *noctem flumine purgant*.[67] There soon follows a list of marital inconveniences: *infantum vagitus, filiorum mortes, uxorum abortia, damna domus et cetera istiusmodi*.[68] Subsequently, Jerome makes one of his most strongly misogamistic comments when he refers to those who desire to marry as *subantibus semper ad coitum*.[69]

One of St. Jerome's most trenchant and angry polemics against marriage is found in his letter of exhortation addressed to the noble Roman widow Furia in which he urges her not to remarry (Letter 54). It is a highly artificial composition, full of gross flattery and farfetched classical allusions. Furia was personally unknown to Jerome, and Grützmacher believes that the ascetic party in Rome had called upon Jerome as their leading spokesman to try to prevent Furia's remarriage. Grützmacher sees in these efforts an attempt of the ascetic party to gain control of

---

[65] Letter 49 in Labourt's edition, 48 in Vallarsi's.

[66] Letter 49. 2.   [67] Letter 49. 15.

[68] Letter 49. 18.

[69] Letter 49. 21. For *subare* used in coarse reference to marriage, cf. *Adv. Iovin.* i. 38 (*PL* 23, 276A) and ii. 36 (*PL* 23, 349A). See also Jerome's ironic remark, Letter 123. 12. 1, *adhinniamus ad omnes feminas.* Cf. Letter 50. 5, *Volo omnes qui propter nocturos forsitan metus soli cubitare non possunt uxores ducere.* Even when Jerome tries to depict domestic life in a favorable light, a crude and mocking note creeps into his writing. Thus in Letter 47. 4, Jerome tries to portray the loving concern of a mother for her daughter: *Lavit pannorum sordes et immundo saepe foedata est stercore.*

Furia's immense wealth.[70] If this were true, and if Jerome were knowingly an accomplice in such a plot, a most unpleasant light would be thrown on his ascetic propaganda. It is difficult, however, to credit a theory which would make a complete mockery of Jerome's character and career. Grützmacher's opinion is the more difficult to believe because he has conveniently ignored the obvious fact to be derived from internal evidence within this letter that Furia herself had requested advice from Jerome.[71] More consistent with what we know of Jerome's life and character is the view that his deep and sincere emotional attachment to the cause of asceticism led him to make violent and extravagant remarks against marriage in an effort to induce Furia to abandon the world. Jerome begins by comparing marriage to the flesh of quails on which the children of Israel glutted themselves to nausea.[72] Marriage is most bitter bile, sour and unwholesome food. In a shocking display of poor taste, Jerome compares Furia's loss of her husband to the relieving of a heaving stomach. To remarry would be to return like a dog to its vomit or a pig to its mud. Then, in words of caustic irony, Jerome ridicules Furia's desire for children. *An vereris ne proles Furiana deficiat, et ex te parens tuus non habeat pusionem qui reptet in pectore et cervices eius stercore linat.*[73] This is coarse and humorless satire, completely wanting in any sympathy for human feelings. These remarks to Furia well illustrate how impossible it is to divorce Jerome's satiric critique of society from a certain callousness toward normal human hopes and aspirations inherent in his character. In the following passage Jerome tries to reinforce his point by exposing the voluptuousness of the married life. Servants are a corrupting influence. Nurses and maids seek to satisfy their own bellies at the expense of your flesh, Jerome

---

[70] Grützmacher, II, 180.

[71] See section 6: *Numquam enim exhortatorias litteras postulares si ambigeres de bono matrimoniae.*

[72] Letter 54. 4. Cf. Numbers 10:31–32.   [73] Letter 54. 4.

warns Furia: *Quidquid non tulerint, sibi ablatum putant, nec considerant de quanto, sed quantum accipiant. . . . Hi rumores turpissimos serunt, et quod ab ipsis egressum est ab aliis audisse simulant, idem auctores et exaggeratores.*[74] This "servant problem," which was to form an important theme in Jerome's attack on the married life, is also frequently found in pagan satire, for example Juvenal's ridicule of a rich man's servants in his fifth satire and his summary remark:

Maxima quaeque domus servis plena est superbis.[75]

From an attack on the servants of wealthy houses Jerome passes insensibly to a satiric tirade against the matrons who are their mistresses:

Videas plerasque rabido ore saevire et tincta facie, viperinis orbibus, dentibus pumicatis carpere Christianos. Hic aliqua,
"cui circa humeros hyacinthina laena est
rancidulum quiddam balba de nare locuta
perstrepit ac tenero supplantat verba palato."
Omnis consonat chorus et latrant universa subsellia.[76]

The quotation is adapted from Persius 1. 32–35. Jerome here uses against worldly women a satiric description originally intended for a completely different purpose, the ridiculing of effeminate poets.[77] Thus Jerome again shows his ability to draw from his memory and to remodel appropriate passages from pagan satire with which to flay the failings of his own Christian society.[78] Such insertions of pagan satire into his own polemic strongly suggest that Jerome was fully conscious of the similarity between his own censorious attacks on his society and the satire of the

[74] Letter 54. 5. In this passage Jerome views the "servant problem" as a true inconvenience of the secular life, but later in this letter (54. 16) he ridicules complaints about servants as a screen for female lewdness.

[75] Juvenal 5. 66. However, Heinrich brackets this line.

[76] Letter 54. 5.   [77] Letter 22. 29.

[78] Jerome's substitution of *perstrepit* for Persius' *eliquat* suggests that he was quoting from memory.

pagans and was striving to reproduce their spirit in his own age.

Of all aspects of women's behavior, their manner of dress excites the greatest indignation in Jerome. In his letters of advice to Furia against the ways of the world he finds an opportunity to lampoon women's *crispantes mitras, stridentes calceolos,* and *orbes stibio fuliginatos:*

Quid facit in facie Christianae purpurissus et cerussa? Quorum alterum ruborem genarum labiorumque mentitur, alterum candorem oris et colli: ignes iuvenum, fomenta libidinum, inpudicae mentis indicia. Quomodo flere potest pro peccatis suis quae lacrimis cutem nudat et sulcos ducit in facie? . . . Qua fiducia erigit ad caelum vultus quos conditor non agnoscat? frustra obtenditur adulescentia et aetas puellaris adseritur.[79]

This denunciation of women's dress and make-up presents a brilliantly witty transformation of a standard moralistic and rhetorical theme which was probably introduced into Christian literature by Tertullian in such works as De cultu feminarum and De virginibus velandis. Among Jerome's contemporaries, John Chrysostom wrote scathing passages of satire against women's

ἀσχημονοῦν πρόσωπον, ἠμαγμένα χείλη, στόμα ἄρκτου αἵματι πεφοινιγμένῳ προσεοικὸς ἠσβολωμένας ὀφρῦς, ὡς ἀπὸ χύτρας τινός, κεκονιαμένας παρειὰς κατὰ τοὺς τοίχους τῶν τάφων.[80]

Even the pagan Ammianus Marcellinus is revolted by the sight of *feminas affatim cirratas* wherever he turned his eyes.[81]

The literary effectiveness of a satiric artist lies largely in his ability to depict in the most lively detail the sins against which he preaches, and satirists often betray the keenest delight in elaborating such descriptions. St. Jerome is no exception to this general rule. In his exhortation to Furia against gluttony he

---

[79] Letter 54. 7. For another example of this satiric *sulcus,* see above, p. 129.

[80] *Hom. in Matt.* XXX, 5; PG 57, pt. i, 369.

[81] Amm. Marc. xiv. 6. 19.

expresses one of his standard ideas in repellently graphic terms: *Nihil sic inflammat corpora et titillat membra genitalia, nisi cibus ructusque convulsus.*[82] Then he enters upon a lengthy admonition against the sensual behavior which he implies was characteristic of wealthy women:

Iuvenum fuge consortia. Comatulos, comptos atque lascivos domus tuae tecta non videant. Cantor pellatur ut noxius; fidicinas et psaltrias, et istius modi chorum diaboli, quasi mortifera sirenarum carmina proturba ex aedibus tuis. Noli ad publicum subinde procedere, et spadonum exercitu praeeunte viduarum circumferri libertate. . . . Nec procurator calamistratus, nec formosus conlactaneus, nec candidulus et rubicundus adsecula adhaereant lateri tuo; interdum animus dominarum ex ancillarum habitu iudicatur.[83]

After these general remarks Jerome turns to a particular instance of immoral luxury. *Vidimus nuper ignominiosum per totum Orientem volitasse; et aetas et cultus et habitus et incessus, indiscreta societas, exquisitae epulae, regius apparatus Neronis et Sardanapalli nuptias loquebantur.*[84] In spite of the masculine (or neuter) adjective *ignominiosum*,[85] it has been conjectured that Jerome is here describing St. Silvia, the stepsister of Rufinus, the powerful Praetorian Prefect of the Orient. About the year 394 this lady made a lengthy pilgrimage to the Holy Land, an account of which from her own hand has been preserved.[86] Cer-

---

[82] Letter 54. 10.   [83] Letter 54. 13.
[84] *Ibid.*

[85] Vallarsi reads *ignominiosum quendam;* evidently the *quendam* has been struck out by later editors because it conflicts with the theory that a woman is meant.

[86] Published in *CSEL*, IX. The *Peregrinatio ad loca sancta* is now generally attributed to a Spanish abbess Aetheria (or Eucheria or Egeria; her name is much disputed) whose voyage can be dated about 395–400. Whether this person is in fact identical with Silvia appears to be a disputed question. See Dom G. Morin "Un passage énigmatique de S. Jérôme," *Rev. Bénédict.*, XXX (1913), 174–186, and H. Pétré, *Journal de Voyage* (Paris, 1948). Whoever this woman was, her manner of travel makes it certain that she was of high station.

tainly the context of the passage suggests that Jerome is portraying a woman, and Silvia's powerful connections would explain Jerome's care in concealing the true identity of the object of his satire.[87] Although the lady's identity remains obscure, Jerome clearly reveals his relish in portraying her indecent behavior.

Obviously, the cumulation of details in Jerome's polemic against women goes far beyond the needs of his case. As a trained rhetorician Jerome plainly enjoyed summoning all his literary powers for a tirade against moral failings. Certainly the desire to convince Furia of the corruption of secular life did not require him to list the types of lewd and effeminate attendants found in the houses of wealthy women. Nor did Jerome's purpose require the artful alliterations (*comatulos, comptos; tuae tecta; calamistratus, conlactaneus, candidulus; adsecula adhaereant*) or the emphatic polysyndeton (*et aetas et cultus et habitus et incessus*) with which he elaborates his description. Like many satirists, Jerome seems to revel in the evils he exposes and to be happy for an opportunity to describe them in detail.

Subsequently, in his letter to Furia, Jerome, in evident fear that he has not yet impressed the lady sufficiently with the horrors of the worldly life, caps his exhortation with a grimly satiric picture of second marriages:

Scribuntur tibi nunc sponsales tabulae ut post paululum testamentum facere conpellaris. Simulabitur mariti infirmitas, et quod te morituram facere volet ipse victurus faciet.[88] Aut si evenerit ut et de secundo marito habeas filios, domestica pugna, intestinum proelium. Non licebit tibi amare filios, nec aequis aspicere oculis quos genuisti. Clam porriges cibos, invidebit mortuo, et nisi oderis filios adhuc

---

[87] See Labourt's edition of the Letters, III, 237–238, for the latest discussion of this passage. Certainly *regius apparatus* suggests a person of very high position.

[88] Cf. Amm. Marc. xxviii. 4. 26, for a very similar tale of testamentary trickery.

eorum amare videberis patrem. Quodsi de priori uxore habens subolem te domum introduxerit, etiamsi clementissima fueris, omnes comoediae et mimographi et communes rhetorum loci in novercam saevissimam declamabunt.[89]

The last remark in this passage is perhaps a subtle indication that in drawing up his prognosis Jerome borrows at least as much from the *topoi* of rhetoric as from his own personal experience.

In his polemic against the luxury of mundane women Jerome implies that never before his own day had such depths of wantonness been reached. Yet Jerome had before his eyes the pious example of Paula and her daughters to prove that women could in fact abandon the debauchery of the secular life. As an edifying symbol, the conversion of these ladies had enormous propaganda value for Jerome the rhetorical preacher; their spiritual reformation might serve as a secure starting point for a vividly drawn contrast between the worldly and ascetic lives. Jerome makes good use of his opportunity. In an epistle addressed to the Roman senator Pammachius (Letter 66), which purports to be a eulogy of Pammachius' deceased wife but which is in reality another ascetic handbook, Jerome contrasts strikingly the lives of Paula and Eustochium before and after their conversion: when they were slaves to the world, they could not bear the dirt of the streets, they were carried by the hands of eunuchs, they thought it a burden to walk over the uneven ground, even silk was too heavy for them, and the sun's heat seemed to them like fire. *Nunc sordidatae et lugubres et sui comparatione forticulae, vel lucernas concinnant vel succendunt focum, pavimenta verrunt, mundant legumina.*[90] Jerome's ac-

[89] Letter 54. 15.
[90] Letter 66. 13. Luebeck has suggested (p. 198) that *pavimenta verrunt* here and *pavimenta verrerint* in *Adv. Helvid.* 20 (*PL* 23, 214B) may be derived from Juvenal 14. 60:
"verre pavimentum, nitidas ostende columnas."
It is unlikely, however, that Jerome is here thinking of Juvenal, for the phrase may well be a commonplace, and furthermore Jerome is at this point completely serious.

count of the ladies' preascetic mode of life is purely a product of his satiric imagination. His ironic remark on the excessive weight of silk has a parallel in Juvenal's description of pampered ladies:

> Hae sunt quae tenui sudant in cyclade, quarum
> delicias et panniculus bombycinus urit.[91]

For once Jerome has the honesty to imply that his satiric description does not represent the unvarnished truth. He prefaces his account of Paula's worldly behavior with the remark, *Ego quidem Romae non eram et tunc me tenebat heremus . . . sed tamen audio.*[92] In spite of the exaggerations and inconsistencies of Jerome's denunciations of the world in which he lived, this seems to be the only occasion on which he feels the need of justifying his censorious descriptions as a trustworthy representation of reality.

Jerome finds another opportunity for a graphic contrast of wantonness and piety in his epitaph for Fabiola, a devout noblewoman (Letter 77). Fabiola had committed the sin of marrying her second husband while her first was still alive. However, after the death of the second husband, remorse seized her, and she did public penance in the Lateran basilica. Jerome makes use of this incident to sketch the usual behavior of Roman widows:

> Quis hoc crederet, ut post mortem secundi viri in semet reversa, quo tempore solent viduae neglegentes, iugo servitutis excusso, agere se liberius, adire balneas, volitare per plateas, vultus circumferre meretricios, saccum indueret, errorem publice fateretur.[93]

We may note in this passage how Jerome achieves ironic emphasis by two characteristic techniques, the careful collocation

[91] Juvenal 6. 259–260.

[92] There is another brief contrast between Paula's two lives in her epitaphium: *Quae prius eunuchorum manibus portabatur, asello sedens profecta est* (Letter 108. 7).

[93] Letter 77. 4.

of sounds (*agere, adire; volitare, vultus*) and the extended asyndeton.

Among Jerome's letters of advice and exhortation, that addressed to the Princess Salvina (Letter 79) is at once the most surprising and most revealing. The recipient was the daughter of the powerful Count Gildo of Mauretania. She had been given in marriage by the Emperor Theodosius himself to his nephew Nebridius, the son of the Praetorian Prefect. Since Salvina was well known to be a supporter of the severe reforming policies of John Chrysostom and hence presumably a pious lady, Jerome saw fit upon the death of her husband to offer her some unsolicited advice on how to behave as a widow. Jerome was well aware that his taking the initiative in writing to a member of the imperial circle might easily be interpreted as a bold intrusion.[94] How was he to address an invective against worldliness and luxury to a lady who lived in the midst of imperial splendor? Jerome solved the problem by assuaging the bitterness of his satiric polemic with the saccharine sweetness of obsequious flattery. After Jerome's numerous tirades against the corrupting power of wealth, it is curious to find him claiming *nec diviti obsunt opes, si bene utatur* and insisting that a camel can after all pass through the eye of a needle.[95] Jerome devotes page after page to admiring remarks on Salvina's inherited and acquired virtues and only then does he venture to satirize the corruption of her surroundings. He begins by suggesting that Salvina was subject to the vice of gluttony: *Procul sint a conviviis tuis Phasides aves, crassae turtures, attagen Ionicus, et omnes aves, quibus amplissima patrimonia avolant.*[96] He then proceeds to make some wrathful comments on worldly women: "Let those women hear these words who are anxious about how they may please men. Let those women eat flesh who are slaves to the flesh, in whom fervor for intercourse boils up, who, bound to

[94] *Vereor ne officium putetur ambitio* (Letter 79. 1).
[95] Letter 79. 1 and 3.   [96] Letter 79. 7.

husbands, give their attention to procreation and children. Let those women whose wombs carry offspring fill their intestines with flesh."[97] Then Jerome grows bolder and dares to make reference to Salvina's meretricious make-up. *Tu vero . . . quae litam purpurisso et cerussa faciem super feretrum eius [mariti] lacrimis diluisti . . . nihil habes necesse aliud, nisi perseverare.*[98] But then, as if frightened by his own boldness, he retreats, assuring Salvina that he is speaking in general terms and means no personal insult.[99] However, his courage returns sufficiently for him to suggest that a perverted and debauched army of flunkies attends Salvina:

Non ambulet iuxta te calamistratus procurator, non historio fractus in feminam, non cantoris diaboli venenata dulcedo, non iuvenis vulsus et nitidus. Nihil artium scenicarum, nihil tibi in obsequiis molle iungatur.[100]

But Jerome then again tries to mitigate somewhat the virulence of this attack by quoting two passages of Horatian satire:

> "Nam vitiis nemo sine nascitur; optimus ille est
>   qui minimis urguetur,"
velut si
> "Egregio inspersos reprehendas corpore naevos."[101]

We can conjecture how well Princess Salvina received this arrogant missive from Jerome's failure ever to mention her again, except in one brief reference to this letter.[102]

A much more attractive work is the booklet *De institutione filiae* (Letter 107), which Jerome composed for Laeta, Paula's daughter-in-law. It is by far the best of the educational treatises. In it Jerome reveals a totally unexpected sensitivity of feeling for childhood. Written nearly two decades after the similar work for Eustochium (Letter 22), this letter shows some softening of Jerome's earlier severity. As Cavallera says, in this booklet "Jé-

[97] *Ibid.*   [98] *Ibid.*
[99] Letter 79. 8.   [100] Letter 79. 9.
[101] *Ibid.*; Horace *Sat.* i. 3. 68 and i. 6. 67.   [102] Letter 123. 17.

rôme s'y fait petit avec les petits."[103] Yet even when he is trying to be tender, Jerome cannot check completely the violence of his satiric temper. It bursts forth several times in the course of this letter. Thus in instructing Laeta how properly to dress her daughter, he delivers a blow at the current fashion in ladies' clothing: *Cave ne aures perfores, ne cerussa et purpurisso consecrata Christo ora depingas, ne collum margaritis et auro premas, ne caput gemmis onores, ne capillum inrufes, et ei aliquid de gehennae ignibus auspiceris.*[104] The key satiric words in this passage are *premas* and *onores,* for they are the brush strokes by which mere descriptive exhortation is distorted and transformed into parody.

Later in this letter Jerome's indignation at the corrupting influences to which worldly women are subject flares up once again, as he warns Laeta: *Nullus ei [Paulae] iuvenis, nullus cincinnatus adrideat. . . . Placeat ei comes non compta atque formonsa, quae liquido gutture carmen dulce moduletur. . . .*[105] Jerome then turns again to attack women's clothing: *Spernat bombycum telas, Serum vellera, et aurum in fila lentescens. Talia vestimenta paret, quibus pellatur frigus, non quibus corpora vestita nudentur.*[106] Subsequently Jerome warns Laeta to keep her daughter away from *maritae feminae,* who with *tumentibus uteris* present a hideous sight to the eye.[107]

In our modern collections of St. Jerome's correspondence, immediately after the treatise for Laeta there follows Jerome's finest and most moving letter, perhaps the greatest of his literary works, the funeral eulogy for the elder Paula (Letter 108). In

[103] Cavallera, II, 292.   [104] Letter 107. 5.
[105] Letter 107. 9.
[106] Letter 107. 10. The final phrase is one of Jerome's favorites. Cf. Letter 127. 3: *Nostra vidua talibus usa est vestibus, quibus obstaret frigus, non membra nudaret.* For an appreciation of this letter, see M. D. Diederich, "The Epitaphium S. Paulae," *Class. Journ.,* XLIX (1953–1954), 369–372.
[107] Letter 107. 11.

spite of the traditional rhetoric with which this letter is filled, Jerome's deep and sincere affection for Paula illuminates its every page. The description of Paula's funeral, with the train of monks carrying the coffin and intoning the psalms and the priests and bishops carrying lighted tapers, breathes a truly medieval spirit.[108] In keeping with the high seriousness of the work, Jerome tries to suppress his natural proclivity for malevolent and ridiculing remarks. Nonetheless, he cannot avoid using the opportunity offered by his praise of Paula's virtues to castigate the vices found in most women. Thus in eulogizing Paula's freedom from hypocrisy, he contrasts ordinary women: *Solent pleraeque matronarum bucinatoribus suis dona conferre, et in paucos largitate profusa, manum a ceteris retrahere.*[109] Later, Jerome praises Paula's extremely abstemious diet: she despised wine, gravy, milk, honey, and eggs, *in quibus sumendis quidam se abstinentissimos putant; et si his ventrem ingurgitaverint, tutam pudicitiam suspicantur.*[110] Thus in his last tribute to the beloved Paula, Jerome cannot restrain himself from seizing the opportunity to propagandize for the ascetic cause to which his life and Paula's had been devoted.

In his relationship with Paula alone does Jerome reveal any natural tenderness or affection. The tone of his relationship with other people was determined above all by the harsh and inexorable nature of a scholarly and doctrinaire ascetic. Even in his letters of advice and counsel, the severe preaching of moral improvement or the discussion of scholarly questions takes the place of the friendly concern which one human being might be expected to show for another. In fact, so little interest does Jerome reveal in his correspondents as human beings that he was

---

[108] Letter 108. 28–29.   [109] Letter 108. 16.

[110] Letter 108. 17. The word *pudicitiam* certainly suggests that Jerome is here thinking of women, according to the principle which he lays down in *Adv. Iovin.* i. 49 (*PL* 23, 294B–C): *Mulieris virtus proprie pudicitia est.* Perhaps he uses masculine forms (*quidam, abstinentissimos*) in order to give his remarks wider applicability.

able to compose for fictional addressees artificial letters of advice which are scarcely distinguishable from those letters written to actual persons. Such a work is Letter 117, supposedly addressed to an immoral matron and her daughter in Gaul.[111] In this rhetorical exercise Jerome, by pondering an imaginary case of female misbehavior, is able to stimulate his imagination sufficiently to indite as caustic a description of corrupt womanhood as any based on experience or autopsy. He addresses the daughter in a tone of piercing irony: *Absit quippe, ut quamvis proximi sint et cognati, virorum te suspicer captare consortia. Obsecro ergo te, virgo, ut mihi respondeas: sola vadis in comitatu propinquorum, an cum amasio tuo? . . . vos cunctorum digiti denotabunt.*[112] This is but the prelude to a satiric account of the dangers which lurk about a too worldly virgin:

Sin autem sola ieris (quod et magis aestimo) utique inter servos adulescentes, inter maritas feminas atque nupturas, inter lascivas puellas, et comatos linteatosque iuvenes, furvarum vestium puella gradieris. Dabit tibi barbatulus quilibet manum, sustentabit lassam; et pressis digitis aut temptabitur, aut temptabit. Erit tibi inter viros matronasque convivium: expectabis aliena oscula, praegustatos cibos. . . . Personabit interim aliquis cantator ad mensam, et inter psalmos dulci modulatione currentes, quoniam alienas non audebit uxores, te, quae custodem non habes, saepius respectabit.[113]

Then Jerome proceeds to reveal considerable knowledge of the arts of seductive women. In the following description he illustrates the principle that *vestis ipsa vilis et pulla* can conceal a lewd spirit, if

[vestis] rugam non habeat; si per terram, ut altior videaris, trahatur; si de industria dissuta sit tunica, ut aliquid intus appareat, operiatque

---

[111] See above, p. 84. Reich, *Der Mimus*, 760–763, discusses the influence of the rhetorical schools and through them of the mime on this letter.

[112] Letter 117. 6. Jerome may here be recalling Persius 1. 28:
   "At pulchrum est digito monstrari et dicier *hic est!*"
Cf. also Horace *Carmen* iv. 3. 22.

[113] Letter 117. 6.

quod foedum est, et aperiat quod formosum. Caliga quoque am-
bulantis nigella ac nitens stridore iuvenes ad se vocat. Papillae fasciolis
comprimuntur et crispanti cingulo angustius pectus artatur. Capilli,
vel in frontem, vel in aures defluunt. Palliolum interdum cadit, ut
candidos nudet umeros, et quasi videri noluerit, celat festina, quod
volens retexerat. Et quando in publico quasi per verecundiam operit
faciem, lupanarum arte id solum ostendit, quod ostensum magis
placere potest.[114]

Since the recipient of this letter was almost certainly fictional,
it is difficult to see why Jerome took the trouble to elaborate
this portrayal of a flirt in a nun's habit. The description is composed with great care. Note the word play *appareat, operiat,
aperiat* and the alliteration of *comprimuntur, crispanti, cingulo;
angustiis, artatur*. But this extreme care in effectively depicting
the details of female dress seems superfluous. We can only conclude that Jerome derived pleasure from simply elaborating at
length such satiric descriptions and in portraying in detail the
absurd minutiae of human behavior.

Although during the greater part of his life, the last forty-six
years, St. Jerome had no actual contact with worldly women,
the impressions of their behavior which he had received during
his sojourns in Antioch and Rome remained extraordinarily vivid
in his mind. Even in the letters of the last decade of his life he
can lampoon in great detail the absurdity of women's lives. The
heat of his indignation never seems to have cooled. One would
hardly think that for nearly twenty-five years St. Jerome had
seen few women except nuns when he described those ladies

quae vinosae et curiosae atque verbosae domus circumeunt matronarum, quarum deus venter est et gloria in confusione earum, quae
nihil aliud de scripturis nisi digamiae praecepta noverunt, quae in
alieno corpore sua desideria consolantur ut, quod ipsae fecerunt, alias
facere videant et malorum societate palpentur.[115]

[114] Letter 117. 7.   [115] Letter 123. 17.

Yet this is in fact a stereotyped portrayal of feminine foolishness and sensuality. Since it could not possibly have been based on recent autopsy, it must be more a routine and somewhat artificial piece of moralism than the expression of spontaneous indignation.

No less artificial are the strictures found in Jerome's last two educational manuals. The first of these (Letter 128) is addressed to a three-year-old girl who had already been dedicated by her parents to the ascetic life. Obviously under these circumstances the following warning had no immediate purpose but was simply a mordant statement of the standard ascetic view of women:

Pudet dicere et tamen dicendum est: nobiles feminae nobiliores habiturae procos vilissimae condicionis hominibus et servulis copulantur ac sub nomine religionis et umbra continentiae interdum deserunt viros, Helenae sequuntur Alexandros nec Menelaos pertimescunt.[116]

This passage again reveals the obvious pleasure Jerome takes in satirizing female behavior, whether such satire was appropriate to the occasion or not. Certainly he is trying to give the impression that his knowledge of such misdeeds is based on autopsy, although at the time the letter was written (413), Jerome had been living for nearly three decades in the retirement of his Bethlehem monastery.

Jerome's last educational treatise (Letter 130) is addressed to Demetrias, the daughter of wealthy and aristocratic Roman parents who had fled to Africa at the time of Alaric's sack of the city.[117] On the point of marriage with a noble Roman, Demetrias suddenly decided to dedicate herself to the Church. Her mother thereupon consulted four of the most important ecclesiastics of the day for advice on the proper conduct of Demetrias' life. In reply to her request, St. Jerome, St. Augustine, Pope Innocent, and the heresiarch Pelagius all wrote works for Demetrias'

[116] Letter 128. 4.
[117] On Demetrias' aristocratic connections, see Grützmacher, III, 252.

guidance.[118] Jerome's letter is generously spiced with those mocking pictures of the world by which he sought to promote zeal for asceticism. Early in the letter he congratulates Demetrias for maintaining the ascetic life: *inter eunuchorum et puellarum catervas et adulationem ac ministeria familiae perstrepentis et exquisitas epulas. . . .*[119] He praises her for laying aside *pretiosa monilia et graves censibus uniones ardentesque gemmae.*[120] He later launches into one of those parodies of women's dress at which he was so adept:

Quando eras in saeculo, ea, quae erant saeculi diligebas: polire faciem purpurisso et cerussa ora depingere, ornare crinem et alienis capillis turritum verticem struere, ut taceam de inaurium pretiis, candore margaritarum Rubri Maris profunda testantium, zmaragdorum virore, cerauniorum flammis, hyacinthorum pelago, ad quae ardent et insaniunt studia matronarum.[121]

But even this lengthy catalogue has not satisfied Jerome's obvious fondness for describing the details of corrupt elegance, for later in the letter he inserts a similar account of those lascivious girls,

quae ornant capita, crines a fronte demittunt, cutem poliunt, utuntur lomentis, adstrictas habent manicas, vestimenta sine ruga soccosque crispantes, ut sub nomine virginali vendibilius pereant.[122]

Jerome then exhorts Demetrias to choose her friends from girls who do not realize their own beauty, who, when they walk in

[118] Augustine's letter (CLXXXVIII) is found in Goldbacher's edition, *CSEL*, LVII, 119–130; Pelagius' in *PL* 23, 1099–1120 and *PL* 30, 15–45. An anonymous letter on the same subject will be found in *PL* 54, 161–180. A discussion of all these works by M. Gonsette is published in *Nouvelle Revue Théologique*, LX (1933), 783–801.

[119] Letter 130. 4.

[120] Letter 130. 5. Cf. Letter 125. 3: *uniones, quibus nobilium feminarum ardet ambitio.*

[121] Letter 130. 7. 13. Note the lofty and poetic word *vertex* satirically used. In Letter 148. 27, Jerome sets forth the scriptural precepts on proper dress for women.

[122] Letter 130. 18. 2.

public, do not expose their neck, back, and bosom to the crowd, but rather conceal their entire face, except for one eye, which Jerome permits them to leave uncovered, so that they can see where they are going. The extremism of this last directive seems utterly ridiculous to the modern reader and all the more so when it is remembered that at an earlier and perhaps less fanatic period of his life Jerome had ridiculed those hypocritical nuns who *operta facie vix unum oculum liberant ad videndum.*[123]

The exposure of the scandalous behavior of carnal women in this letter leads naturally to a vignette of those well-known objects of Jerome's hatred, the sybaritic fops who attend upon ladies:

Cincinnatulos pueros et calamistratos et peregrini muris olentis pelliculas de quibus illud Arbitri est, "non bene olet qui bene semper olet," quasi quasdam pestes et venena pudicitiae virgo devitet.[124]

Here again Jerome has made good use of this knowledge of the pagan satiric tradition, for he is quoting Martial II. 12. 4, to reinforce his denunciation of worldliness. His memory, however, has failed him, for he mistakenly attributes the line to Petronius.

It is not, however, the worldly women alone who come under attack in Jerome's letter to Demetrias. In a rare moment of candor, Jerome is forced to admit that the life of extreme asceticism has a debilitating effect on certain women: they become insane. After living in cold, damp cells they do not know where they are, where they are going, or what they are saying. But the sad plight of these women wins from Jerome not sympathy, but ridicule. He complains that such women begin to think they know something about Scripture; they cannot keep their mouths shut; they insist on lecturing about biblical passages of which they understand nothing; and finally they adopt the arrogant

---

[123] Letter 22. 27. See above, p. 125.

[124] Letter 130. 19. 1. On the moral danger presented by these youths, cf. Letter 128. 4. 5: *Solent lascivi et comptuli iuvenes blandimentis, affabilitate, munusculis aditum sibi per nutrices ad alumnos quaerere.*

airs of scholars. These are the women whom Paul describes as *semper discentes et numquam ad scientiam veritatis pervenientes.*[125] Jerome's attack on feminine pretensions to biblical learning is a Christian version of Juvenal's lampoon of the type of female:

> quae cum discumbere coepit
> laudat Vergilium, periturae ignoscit Elissae,
> committit vates et comparat, inde Maronem
> atque alia parte in trutina suspendit Homerum.[126]

As in so many of St. Jerome's letters, the elaboration of these caustic descriptions bears little relationship to the purpose at hand, in this case the spiritual guidance of a young girl who had willingly adopted the ascetic life. As Jerome grew older and more remote from the society which he describes, the pictures of corrupt and worldly women lose their appearance of reality and take on the aspect of stereotyped literary devices. We shall now see that this misogyny, which so often seems theoretical and forced, plays a large role not only in Jerome's letters but also in his other literary productions.

Polemical Works

As a treasure house of antifeminist sentiments Jerome's polemical works surpass even his letters, for the most important of these treatises were written specifically to combat that body of opinion which opposed the misogyny and misogamy fostered by the partisans of extreme asceticism. Jerome felt therefore called upon in these works to repeat and elaborate the charges brought by the monastic movement against women and marriage. The earliest of his controversial tracts, *Adversus Helvidium,* written while Jerome was still in Rome, is directed against a

---

[125] Eph. 4:14; II Tim. 3:7. See Jerome, Letter 130. 17.
[126] Juvenal 6. 434–456.

theologian who, in his zeal to defend marriage against the current glorification of chastity, had denied the perpetual virginity of Mary.[127] In championing such views Helvidius left himself defenseless before Jerome's satiric barbs. In order to ridicule Helvidius' theory that Mary had participated in normal conjugal relations, Jerome describes some of the delights which carnal marriage would have brought:

novem mensibus uterum insolescentem, fastidia, partum, sanguinem, pannos. Ipse tibi describatur infans, tegmine membranorum solito involutus. Ingerantur dura praesepia, vagitus parvuli, octavae diei circumcisio, tempus purgationis, ut probetur immundus. Non erubescimus, non silemus.[128]

As Vallarsi points out in his note on this passage, Jerome is here imitating Tertullian's arguments against the heretic Marcion: *Describe uterum de die insolescentem, gravem, anxium, nec somno tutum, incertum libidinibus fastidii et gulae.*[129] Vallarsi has failed to point out, however, that Tertullian in this passage is ridiculing the excessively ascetic views of Marcion but that Jerome imitates Tertullian's words in attacking the carnality of Helvidius' opinion. Tertullian is here parodying asceticism, but Jerome makes use of his parody as if seriously meant. It is not surprising that Jerome does not mention Tertullian by name in this passage, since in the immediately preceding paragraph, commenting on Helvidius' use of Tertullian's testimony in support of antiascetic views, Jerome scornfully says, *Et de Tertulliano quidem nihil amplius dico quam Ecclesiae hominem non fuisse.*[130] Such inconsistency is characteristic of Jerome. He was not an honest debater but seized his ammunition wherever he could

---

[127] Cavallera (II, 24) gives the date as 384. Jerome's work is also known as *De perpetua virginitate B. Mariae.*
[128] *Adv. Helvid.* 18 (PL 23, 212B).
[129] *De carne Christi* iv. 1; CC 2, 878.
[130] *Adv. Helvid.* 17 (PL 23, 211B).

find it, not hesitating to attack a writer openly in one passage and then surreptitiously use him in the next.[131]

Later in his polemic against Helvidius, Jerome draws up an elaborate satiric contrast between the married life and the life of chastity. He begins with a plea against the misunderstanding of his satire: *Et quia de comparatione virginitatis et nuptiarum sum aliqua dicturus, obsecro lecturos ne me putent nuptiis detraxisse in virginum laude.*[132] But the reader can quickly see how hollow are Jerome's protestations. He begins his comparison by asking,

Idem tu putas esse diebus et noctibus vacare orationi, vacare ieiuniis; et ad adventum mariti expolire faciem, gressum frangere, simulare blanditias? Illa hoc agit, ut turpior appareat, et naturae bonum infuscet iniuria. Haec ad speculum pingitur, et in contumeliam artificis conatur pulchrior esse quam nata est.[133]

This hardly looks like a fair presentation of marriage. But Jerome has not yet said his worst. He seems to lose sight of the life of chastity altogether as he becomes absorbed in painting a domestic scene:

Inde infantes garriunt, familia perstrepit, liberi ab osculis et ab ore dependent, computantur sumptus, impendia praeparantur. Hinc cocorum accincta manus carnes terit, hinc textricum turba commurmurat. . . .[134]

Into this fantastic scene of noise and confusion comes the lady's husband:

Nuntiatur interim vir venisse cum sociis. Illa ad hirundinis modum lustrat universa penetralia, si torus rigeat, si pavimenta verrerint, si ornata sint pocula, si prandium preparatum.

[131] The major example of this is the use of Porphyry in *Adv. Iovin.* See below, p. 153.

[132] *Adv. Helvid.* 20 (*PL* 23, 213B).

[133] *Ibid.* (*PL* 23, 214A).

[134] *Ibid.* Cf. the brief caricature of a matron's household in Letter 57. 13: *inter muliercularum radios et textrina.*

Now Jerome draws the moral from this detailed depiction of married life:

Responde, quaeso, inter ista ubi sit Dei cogitatio: Et hae felices domus? Caeterum ubi tympana sonant, tibia clamitat, lyra garrit, cymbalum concrepat, quis ibi Dei timor? Parasitus in contumeliis gloriatur: ingrediuntur expositae libidinum victimae, et tenuitate vestium nudae impudicis oculis ingeruntur. His infelix uxor aut laetatur et perit, aut offenditur, et maritus in iurgia concitatur. Hinc discordia, seminarium repudii. Aut si aliqua invenitur domus in qua ista non fiant, quae rara avis est; tamen ipsa dispensatio domus, liberorum educatio, necessitates mariti, correctio servulorum, quam a Dei cogitatione non avocent?[135]

Jerome closes his parody with one of his most powerful expressions of the ascetic ideal:

Quae non est in partus anxietatibus et dolore, quae deficientibus mentrui cruoris officiis, mulier esse desiit, a Dei maledictione fit libera.

Plainly, this extended satire of domestic life is not the spontaneous expression of moral indignation but a highly artificial caricature. In a moment of candor Jerome admits that this picture was not based on what he had seen of domesticity, for referring to his parody he says, *Rhetoricati sumus et in morem declamatorum, paululum lusimus.*[136] This admission is indicative of the complex intermingling in St. Jerome's satire of genuine moral fervor, traditional moralistic rhetoric, and delight in extravagant parody. As the leading champion of the monastic movement, Jerome sincerely believed in the superiority of the

---

[135] *Adv. Helvid.* 20. *Rara avis* is almost certainly a reference to Juvenal 6. 165, since it is women who are being satirized in both Juvenal and Jerome. Cf. *Adv. Iovin.* i. 47 (*PL* 23, 290B).

[136] *Adv. Helvid.* 22 (*PL* 23, 216A). Cf. *Adv. Iovin.* i. 13 (*PL* 23, 241A): *Non est huius loci nuptiarum angustias describere, et quasi in communibus locis rhetorico exultare sermone. Plenius super hac re contra Helvidium . . . arbitror absolutum.*

ascetic life over the worldly, yet he confesses that in drawing up one of his most extreme statements in support of this superiority he was indulging in a pleasant game by making free use of rhetorical material.

A much lengthier and more elaborate attack on marriage is contained in the tract *Adversus Iovinianum.* Jovinianus, though a monk, was a leading spokesman for antiascetic views, holding that virginity was not superior to marriage and that eating *cum actione gratiarum* was as holy as fasting.[137] Although this heretic had already been condemned by Pope Siricius, the ascetic leaders at Rome called upon Jerome to deal the viper the death blow.[138] In the first book of his tract Jerome approached his task of attacking *uteros tumescentes et infantum vagitus et fructus atque opera nuptiarum* with enthusiasm and relish.[139] He began by collecting from earlier antifeminist writers a large body of misogamistic material. He tells us in the course of his work: *Scripserunt Aristoteles et Plutarchus et noster Seneca de matrimonio libros ex quibus et superiora nonnulla sunt, et ista quae subicimus.*[140] He also inserts into this treatise a long and highly satiric burlesque of marriage drawn from Theophrastus' *aureolus liber de Nuptiis.*[141]

Little did Jerome know when he candidly admitted the derivative nature of much of his material how great a storm of controversy he would one day arouse. Modern *Quellenforscher* have seized upon this vague designation of his sources and have exercised their ingenuity in an effort to assign definite parts of Jerome's tract to each of the authors whom he names. The

---

[137] Jovinianus' own writings are lost. The *testimonia* are collected and studied by W. Haller in *Texte und Untersuchungen,* XVII, 2 (1897). For an impossibly biased view of the heretic, cf. Brochet, *St. Jérôme et ses Ennemis,* 64–79.

[138] Jerome does in fact compare Jovinianus and his followers to snakes, *PL* 23, 224B and C.

[139] *Adv. Iovin.* i. 12 (*PL* 23, 239C).   [140] *Ibid.* i. 49 (*PL* 23, 293A).

[141] *Ibid.* i. 47 (*PL* 23, 288C–293A).

fact that all the works mentioned, with the exception of Plutarch's *Praecepta coniugalia*, are lost stimulated the argument by opening the door to free conjecture. A complicating factor was the likelihood that Jerome had not actually derived his extract of Theophrastus' work from that writer himself but from an intermediary. Further puzzlement was caused by the resemblance between certain passages of the extract from Theophrastus and Juvenal's sixth satire, although Jerome does not name the satirist as a source.

E. Bickel has made the most complete and scholarly analysis of these problems in his *Diatribe in Senecae Philosophi fragmenta*.[142] Bickel succeeded in showing that a major portion of Jerome's denunciation of women is derived from a writer whom he did not even mention, the Neoplatonic philosopher Porphyry, who had attacked marriage in a work now lost. Naturally Jerome was reluctant to reveal the dependence of his arguments on the hated anti-Christian thinker.[143] Bickel has also tried to show that Jerome's knowledge of Aristotle's views and his extract from Theophrastus were derived from Porphyry. Jerome's other major source, says Bickel, was Seneca's lost work, *De matrimonio*. Bickel explained the resemblances between Juvenal and the extract from Theophrastus as follows: when Jerome was copying Theophrastus from Porphyry, memories of Juvenal's sixth satire entered his mind and he added these reminiscences to the extract, although Bickel admits *certa cognatio inter Iuvenalem et Theophrastea Hieronymi probari nequit*.[144] These views were seriously challenged by J. van Wageningen, who explained the apparent reminiscences of Juvenal by the theory that Jerome derived the *ecloga Theophrasti* from Seneca's *De matrimonio*,

---

[142] Bickel also prints as an appendix to this work his critical edition of the crucial passages of *Adversus Iovinianum*.

[143] Jerome expresses an unfavorable opinion of Porphyry's intelligence in *Comm. in Dan.* (PL 25, 520C).

[144] *Diat. in Sen. Phil. frag.*, 10–11. He excepts the phrase *rara avis*, which he sees as a borrowing from Juvenal 6. 165. See above, note 135.

which was also used by Juvenal in composing his sixth satire.[145] Van Wageningen's argument takes too little account of Bickel's cogent demonstration that the *ecloga Theophrasti* shows numerous traces of Jerome's own Latin style.[146] This would not, of course, have been so had the extract come from the pages of Seneca. On the other hand, Van Wageningen's case is strengthened by the almost complete absence of close *verbal* similarities between the extract and Juvenal, although similarities of *matter* are numerous. It is likely that if Jerome had been inserting into the *ecloga Theophrasti* his reminiscences of Juvenal, the verbal parallels would be more striking. In view of the loss of both Seneca's and Porphyry's works on marriage, it is impossible to solve this problem with any certainty. The argument is, nonetheless, of value because it casts light on the descent of Jerome's satire from pagan sources. Jerome's satiric attacks on women and marriage are revealed as a Christian continuation of the antifeminism of certain pagan thinkers. The argument, moreover, furthers our knowledge of Jerome by showing that in spite of his own considerable gifts as a satirist, his tendency to compose mosaics of extracts plagiarized from earlier writers extends even to those passages of his writings in which satire is used as the chief weapon in his campaign for the dearly cherished cause of asceticism. In praise of Jerome, however, it may be said that if he had not admitted that Theophrastus' attack on women was not his own original work, the reader would hardly have guessed

---

[145] J. van Wageningen, "Seneca et Iuvenalis," *Mnemosyne*, n.s. XLV (1917), 417–429. In emphasizing Seneca, Van Wageningen is following F. Haase, *L. Annaei Senecae opera quae supersunt*, III (Leipzig, 1853), 248ff. Felix Bock tried to show that the excerpt from Theophrastus was derived from a lost work of Tertullian. See Bock's *Aristoteles Theophrastus Seneca de matrimonio, Leipziger Studien*, XIX (1899), 1ff. He was refuted by G. Grossgerge, *De Senecae et Theophrasti libris de matrimonio* (Königsberg, 1911). For a summary of the whole problem, see Hagendahl, *Latin Fathers*, 147–157.

[146] Bickel, *Diatribe*, 1–6.

it, so markedly is his adaptation of the passage stamped with his own satiric style. A few citations may reveal this:

Fertur aureolus Theophrasti liber de nuptiis, in quo quaerit, an vir sapiens ducat uxorem, et cum definisset, si pulcra esset, si bene morata, si honestis parentibus, si ipse sanus ac dives, sic sapientem inire aliquando matrimonium, statim intulit: "haec autem raro in nuptiis universa concordant. Non est igitur uxor ducenda sapienti. . . . Multa esse quae matronarum usibus necessaria sint, pretiosae vestes, aurum, gemmae; sumptus, ancillae, suppellex varia, lecticae et esseda deaurata."[147]

Most of the items in this list are standard fixtures of Jerome's satire of women. We may compare Letter 54. 11, where Jerome attacks women's *amorem monilium atque gemmarum sericarumque vestium;* also in Letter 66. 5, *ardentes gemmas, quibus ante collum et facies ornabatur* and in Letter 130. 19, the *ancilla virgo dominis ornatior.* But the following description has no parallel in Jerome's original satire:

Dein per totas noctes garrulae conquestiones: "illa ornatior procedit in publicum," "haec honoratur ab omnibus, ego in conventu feminarum misella despicior." "Cur aspiciebas vicinam?" "Quid cum ancillula loquebaris?" "De foro veniens quid adtulisti?"[148]

Van Wageningen compares Juvenal 6. 149–152:

> Poscitque maritum
> pastores et ovem Canusinam ulmosque Falernas—
> quantulum in hoc! —pueros omnes, ergastula tota,
> quodque domi non est, sed habet vicinus, ematur.

Although the general significance of the two passages is the same—that women are envious and complaining—there is no verbal similarity which might indicate that Jerome was thinking of Juvenal when copying Theophrastus. The excerpt from Theophrastus then continues:

[147] *PL* 23, 289A; Bickel, 388.   [148] *PL* 23, 289B; Bickel, 388.

Attendenda semper eius est facies et pulcritudo laudanda, ne si alteram aspexeris, se aestimet displicere. Vocanda domina, celebrandus natalis eius, iurandum per salutem illius, ut sit superstes optandum. Honoranda nutrix eius et gerula, servus paternus et alumnus et formosus adsecula et procurator calamistratus et in longam securamque libidinem exectus spado; sub quibus nominibus adulteri delitescunt.[149]

With these sentiments we may compare Jerome's own warnings against the corrupt servants who surround women: in Letter 54. 5, he inveighs against the *nutrix et gerula*, in Letter 54. 13, against the *procurator calamistratus, rubicundus adsecula* and *eunuchorum exercitus*, and again in Letter 79. 9, against *procurator et calamistratus*. Since St. Jerome wrote *Adversus Iovinianum* in 393, Letter 54 in 395, and Letter 79 about 400, how is it that the expressions *procurator calamistratus* and *nutrix et gerula* occur both in his translation of Theophrastus and his own original writings? It is possible to claim that these phrases are quite literal translations of the actual words of Theophrastus and that Jerome found the expressions so striking that he stored them in his mind for later use elsewhere. If this is true, it follows that Jerome's satiric references to corrupt servants are based as much on his reading of Theophrastus as upon his personal observation of servants' behavior. Another explanation is that the phrases are part of Jerome's stock of original satiric expressions, that he himself was the translator of the excerpt from Theophrastus, as Bickel conjectured, and that he inserted the phrases into his translation. The implications of these alternatives are important: if the former view is correct, it suggests that Jerome's satire is highly contrived and artificial, consisting of borrowed phrases inserted into his writings according to the demands of his propaganda. The second view leaves more room for sincere *indignatio* and for original satiric invention. Since the original

[149] *PL* 23, 289C; Bickel, 388–389.

of Theophrastus' work is lost, it is impossible to resolve this problem with any certainty.

The extract from Theophrastus goes on:

Porro liberorum causa uxorem ducere, ut vel nomen nostrum non intereat vel habeamus senectutis praesidia et certis utamur heredibus, stolidissimum est. Quid enim ad nos pertinet recedentes e mundo, si nomine nostro alius vocatur, cum et filius non statim patris vocabulum referat et innumerabiles sint qui eodem appellentur nomine? Aut quae senectutis auxilia sunt enutrire domi, qui aut prior te forte moriatur, aut perversissimis moribus sit, aut certe, cum ad maturam aetatem venerit, tarde ei videaris mori?[150]

Van Wageningen compares Juvenal 6. 38–40:

> Sed placet Ursidio lex Iulia: tollere dulcem
> cogitat heredem, cariturus turture magno
> mullorumque iubis et captatore macello.

However, Juvenal is here stating his case less than wholeheartedly, for the arguments he adduces against child-bearing are intentionally nugatory. The sense of the passage from *Adversus Iovinianum* is better paralleled in Jerome's words to the widow Furia, urging her not to remarry:

An vereris ne proles Furiana deficiat, et ex te parens tuus non habeat pusionem qui reptet in pectore et cervices eius stercore linat? quippini? Omnes habent filios quae habuere matrimonia, et quibus nati sunt liberi suo generi responderunt? Exhibuit Ciceronis filius patrem in eloquentia? Cornelia vestra. . . . Graccos suos se genuisse laetata est? Ridiculum sperare pro certo, quod multos et non habere videas, et cum habuerint perdidisse.[151]

It is plain that in this attack on marriage Jerome is often making use of an inherited corpus of moralistic material, reworking it from a Christian point of view, and expressing it in his satiric language. In fact, so anxious is Jerome to combat marriage and

---

[150] *PL* 23, 290C; Bickel, 390.   [151] Letter 54. 4.

so filled is his mind with rhetorical arguments derived from the misogamistic tradition that he has ignored an important consideration—that the satiric excerpt from Theophrastus is not entirely suitable to his case. He wants to show that for *women* virginity is superior to marriage. But then why take the trouble to ridicule women as a terrible burden to men? Obviously Jerome was so fond of vivid, satiric exposures of women that he could not resist inserting Theophrastus' description, even though it was not completely applicable to his argument.[152]

We turn now from Jerome's adaptation of Theophrastus to his own satiric remarks against marriage in *Adversus Iovinianum*. He begins by interpreting antifeminist passages of the Bible: *"Mulier insipiens et audax, inops panis efficitur."* Cuius panis? *Nempe illius qui de caelo descendit. . . . Et rursum in alio loco: "Sicut in ligno vermis, ita perdit virum suum uxor malefica."*[153] But some will object, says Jerome, that these statements apply only to bad women. He has his answer ready:

Quam rarum sit uxorem sine vitiis inveniri, novit ille qui duxit uxorem. . . . Si domus communis mariti et uxoris erigit uxorem in superbiam, et contumeliam viro facit: quanto magis si ditior uxor fuerit, et in domo eius vir manserit! Incipit enim non uxor esse sed domina; et viro si offenderit migrandum est. Stillicidia eiciunt hominem in die hiemali de domo sua, similiter et mulier maledica de propria domo. (Prov. 27:15.) Assiduis quippe iurgiis et quotidiana garrulitate facit perfluere domum eius, et eicit eum de aedibus suis. . . .[154] Non hic de meretrice, non de adultera dicitur, sed amor mulieris generaliter accusatur, qui semper insatiabilis est, qui extinctus accenditur, et post copiam rursum inops est, animumque virilem effeminat, et excepta passione quam sustinet, aliud non sinit cogitare. . . . Qui enim ducit uxorem, in ambiguo est, utrum

---

[152] This is the view of Reich, *Der Mimus*, 756.

[153] *Adv. Iovin.* i. 28 (*PL* 23, 260D–261A). Biblical quotation from Prov. 9:13 and 25:30.

[154] Cf. *Anecdot. Mared.*, III, 2, 327 (*CC* 78, 459), where Jerome describes domestic life as *turbae et frequentia et dissensiones et rixae.*

odiosam, an amabilem ducat. Si odiosam duxerit, ferri non potest. Si amabilem, amor illius inferno, et arenti terrae, et incendio comparatur.[155]

The depth of Jerome's fear and hatred of marriage is bared by the grotesque argument that the love of woman renders the virile mind effeminate! Those who desire to marry, exclaims Jerome, *pecudum more lasciviunt.*[156] Men commonly marry women better endowed with money than with chastity, which proves the truth of the saying that *multos non oculis sed digitis uxores ducere.*[157] Later in his tract against Jovinianus, Jerome delivers the following denunciation:

Certe qui dicunt se causa reipublicae, et generis humani, uxoribus iungi, et liberos tollere, imitentur saltem pecudes, et postquam uxorum venter intumuerit, non perdant filios; nec amatores uxoribus se exhibeant, sed maritos. Quorundam matrimonia adulteriis cohaeserunt; et, o rem improbam! iidem illis pudicitiam praeceperunt, qui abstulerant. Itaque cito eiusmodi nuptias satietas solvit. Cum primum lenocinium libidinis abscessit, quod libebat, eviluit. Nam quid, ait Seneca, de viris pauperibus dicam, quorum in nomen mariti, ad eludendas leges quae contra caelibes latae sunt, pars magna conducitur.[158]

Such coarse and extravagant satire is praised by J. Brochet as "le plaidoyer le plus savant, le plus vaste, le plus curieux, sinon le plus profonde qu'on ait jamais écrit en faveur de la doctrine ascetique."[159] A less prejudiced view would see in Jerome's harsh comments on marriage the attempt of an immoderate polemicist to strengthen the case for Christian asceticism by

---

[155] *Adv. Iovin.* i. 28 (*PL* 23, 261A–262A).

[156] *Ibid.* i. 38 (*PL* 23, 276A). Cf. *Adv. Vigilantium* 2. Vigilantius urges marriage, *ut nihil sit quo distemus a procis, quo differamus a brutis animantibus, quo ab equis* (*PL* 23, 356A).

[157] *Adv. Iovin.* i. 46 (*PL* 23, 288B).

[158] *Ibid.* i. 49 (*PL* 23, 294A). Bickel (pp. 360 and 393) attributes *quorundam—eviluit* to Seneca's *De matrimonio*.

[159] Brochet, *St. Jérôme et ses Ennemis*, 76.

adducing some of the most extreme arguments of the pagan antifeminist tradition.[160]

Exegetical Works

The major vehicles of Jerome's propaganda were his letters and polemical works. When composing his biblical commentaries, however, he naturally found it difficult to suppress entirely thoughts of those causes for which he was simultaneously campaigning in his other works. Satiric comments, therefore, intended to promote such causes frequently obtrude themselves incongruously into his exegesis. Thus Jerome is roused to an antifeminist attack by Paul's exhortations on the proper behavior of aged women: "Bid the older women likewise to be reverent in behavior, not to be slanderers or slaves to drink; they are to teach what is good" (Titus 2:3). Jerome satirically contrasts such virtuous old women with those whom he has himself observed:

Quia ipsae adulescentiam iam transgressae sunt, de adulescentularum aetatibus disputent, et dicant: Illa sic ornatur, illa sic comitur, sic illa procedit; amat illum, amatur ab illo. . . . Solent hae aetates, quia corporis frixere luxuria (licet sint plurimae, quae nec canos suos erubescant, et ante gregem nepotum trementes virgunculae componantur), vino se dedere pro libidine; et cum inter pocula sibi prudentes visae fuerint et facundae, morum quasi austeritatem assumere, loquentes hoc quod sibi videntur esse, et non recordantes illud quod fuerunt.[161]

---

[160] *Adversus Iovinianum* exercised great influence on the Middle Ages. Through Jerome, pagan antifeminism became part of medieval tradition. See the study of P. Delhaye, "Le Dossier Anti-matrimoniale de l'*Adv. Jov.* et son Influence sur Quelques Écrits Latins du XIIième Siècle," *Medieval Studies*, XIII (1951), 65–86. Also, August Wulff, *Die Frauenfeindlichen Dichtungen in den Romanischen Literaturen des Mittelalters* (Halle, 1914).

[161] *PL* 26, 615C–616A. For a severe attack on marriage, see Jerome's remarks on Mic. 7:5–7 (*PL* 25, 1279C).

This description again indicates how little Jerome's satiric diction changed with the passage of time. We may compare a picture of elderly women which Jerome had drawn in a letter written to Marcella three to five years before this commentary:

Illae Christianos oculos potius scandalizent . . . quas nec numerus annorum potest docere quod vetulae sunt, quae capillis alienis verticem instruunt . . . *quae denique ante nepotum gregem trementes virgunculae conponuntur.*[162]

Jerome appears to have memorized a notebook of misogynous phrases upon which he can easily draw whenever aroused by the satiric spirit.

Profound antifeminism is found also in Jerome's commentary on Isaiah. The prophet's words, *Populum meum exactores sui spoliaverunt, et mulieres dominatae sunt eis* (3:12), allow a doubly antifeminist interpretation. First, Jerome claims that the oppressors are called women, *quia propter libidinem omnia faciant, et sint dediti voluptatibus.* Secondly, the prophetic words are interpreted as an attack on the excessive influence of women on Church affairs:

Caveamus ergo et nos, ne exactores simus in populo; ne iuxta impium Porphyrium matronae et mulieres sint noster senatus, quae dominantur in Ecclesia et de sacerdotali gradu favor iudicat feminarum.[163]

The problem of the pernicious influence of women on religion seems to have been at the top of Jerome's mind at the time he was expounding Isaiah (A.D. 408–410), for he mentions it once again in this commentary. To entrust the selection of Church officials to *muliercularum precibus* is to throw pearls before swine, he declares.[164] The same protest against female influence is found in another work of this period, the *Dialogus contra*

---

[162] Letter 38. 3. The letter was written in 383; the *Comm. in Titum* belongs to the period 387–389 (Cavallera, II, 156).

[163] PL 24, 67C. On the reference to Porphyry, see above, Chapter II, note 38.

[164] *PL* 24, 591A–B.

Pelagianos (dated 415). The orthodox interlocutor challenges the heretical view that women can have *legis scientiam,* alleging Paul's teaching (I Corinthians 14:34) that women should keep silent in church and if they have any questions should consult their husbands. The orthodox speaker adds: *Quis enim ignorat psallendum esse feminis in cubiculis suis absque virorum frequentia et congregatione turbarum?*[165] It is difficult to reconcile such statements with Jerome's encouragement of the scholarly labors of the aristocratic ladies of Rome. But that had been many years before, and Jerome was never known, even among his contemporaries, for the consistency of his views. He may have been angered by the unwholesome influence of some particular woman on the Church, but if so her identity can no longer be determined.

It is possible, however, that Jerome's harsh words on the proper role of women in religion were elicited by an aspect of female behavior which particularly irritated him, provoking a seemingly endless stream of caustic remarks, namely, women's peculiar fondness for heretical sects. Jerome frequently describes such women with the words of Paul: *mulierculas oneratas peccatis, quae ducuntur variis desideriis* [or, *quae circumferuntur omni vento doctrinae*], *semper discentes et numquam ad scientiam veritatis pervenientes* (II Timothy 3:6–7). This scornful description is used twice in the commentary on Isaiah, as well as in many other works.[166] According to Jerome, the most foul and foolish heresies were invented and spread with the help of women.[167] He complains that flighty and empty-headed females cannot even begin to comprehend the orthodox doctrine of the

---

[165] *Dial. contra Pelag.* 25 (PL 23, 542B). Cf. Ambrose, *De Helia et leiunio* 18, 66: *Apostolus mulieres tacere etiam in ecclesia iubet, domi viros suos praecipit interrogare.*

[166] PL 24, 571D and 646D. Cf. Letters 75. 3 and 133. 4. 1.; *Adv. Vig.* 3 (PL 23, 356C); *Comm. in Jer.,* PL 24, 859B; *Comm. in Ezech.,* PL 25, 418A.

[167] Jerome gives a catalogue of these heresies in Letter 133. 4.

resurrection of the flesh. Such women are portrayed with scornful fury:

Non mihi dives Ciceronis lingua sufficiat, non fervens Demosthenis oratio animi mei possit inplere fervorem, si velim hereticorum fraudulentias prodere. . . . Solent enim mulierculae eorum mammas tenere, ventri adplaudere, lumbos et femina et puras adtrectare maxillas et dicere: "Quid nobis prode est, si fragile corpus resurget? Futurae angelorum similes angelorum habebimus et naturam."[168]

The scurrility of this ridicule appears to have shocked Jerome's contemporaries. Rufinus decries the immoderation and bad taste of this very passage in his *Apology*.[169] But Jerome was not moved by popular disapproval to temper his statement of the cherished antifeminist principle. According to Jerome, the odious Gnosticism of Basilides had a special attraction for witless women.[170] It is such frivolous creatures who are angrily mocked in the commentary on Isaiah as "receivers of the portents of Basilides, Balsamus, Thesaurus, Barbelon, and Levisbora," all monstrous names connected with Gnosticism.[171] These attacks on the female partiality for outlandish and eccentric forms of religion recall Juvenal's lampooning of women's fondness for foreign superstitions:[172]

Si candida iusserit Io,
ibit ad Aegypti finem calidaque petitas
a Meroe portabit aquas, ut spargat in aede
Isidis, antiquo quae proxima surgit ovili.
credit enim ipsius dominae se voce moneri.[173]

Jerome's ridicule of credulous women is, however, more controlled than Juvenal's. It is in fact relatively free of that rhetori-

---

[168] Letter 84. 6.   [169] Ruf., *Apol.* i. 7 (*PL* 22, 546A).

[170] Letter 75. 3. Cf. John Chrysostom, Hom. VIII in *Epist. ad Col.*, 5 (*PG* 68, 358). He inveighs against women's superstitions and pagan passion for amulets and incantations.

[171] *PL* 24, 646C. The Hebrew origin of those *portentosa nomina* is explained by Vallarsi, *PL* 22, 687, note b.

[172] *Sat.* 6. 511–591.   [173] *Ibid.*, 526–530.

cal extravagance and exaggeration which characterizes his satiric attacks on other aspects of female behavior. This may imply that in exposing the feminine penchant for heresy Jerome was expressing his concern over a truly serious spiritual problem and not merely voicing commonplace thoughts on a traditional topic.

Conclusion

In studying St. Jerome's relationships with women, we are faced with a striking incongruity: Jerome's closest companions and staunchest supporters were women, yet some of his most vitriolic and revealing satire was directed against the female character and female behavior. Indeed, at times Jerome seems to condemn the sex as a whole. The source of this incongruity is not far to seek. Although he does not seem to have been by nature a misogynist, Jerome's attachment to the cause of extreme asceticism compelled him to reject the feminine influence on society as corrupting and immoral. To be sure, one might object that there was no compelling reason why Jerome, in his voluminous writings in support of the ascetic ideal, should constantly emphasize *feminine* uselessness and *feminine* corruption. Indeed, it may appear most strange that in exhorting women against marrying, Jerome emphasizes *feminine* failings. Surely in describing marriage in black colors in letters addressed to women, it would have been more natural for Jerome to lampoon male faults. However, trained as he was in the schools of rhetoric and thoroughly acquainted with pagan literature, perhaps it was easy and natural for him to draw upon the pagan tradition of hostility to women in voicing his disapproval of marriage and to borrow the vivid and highly colored phrases of the rhetorical schools. The traditional and derivative nature of the material which Jerome used in support of his asceticism resulted in such incongruities as the insertion of Theophrastus' attack on women and marriage into a work aimed at persuading women not to marry; it also may account for the lack of variety in Jerome's satiric pictures. For if his descriptions were based on continuing autopsy, we would hardly find the same caustic portrayals in works separated by many decades. Tradition and school rhetoric, as well as the recollection of early experience, supplied Jerome with ridiculing pictures of worldly ladies many years after he had retired to his Bethlehem cloister.

But the uncovering of the derivative character of Jerome's satire of women proves nothing as to the genuineness of his moral indignation. Jerome's championship of asceticism was surely sincere; hence it was inevitable that he should be shocked by the lives of the worldly and wealthy ladies of Rome and by the behavior of the corrupt nuns who were proving an embarrassment to the monastic movement. But John Chrysostom was also rhetorically trained, yet his acid denunciations of the women of Antioch and Constantinople have not therefore been attacked as fabrications.[174] However, since exaggeration is the essence of satire, it would be wrong to accept Jerome's satiric pictures as accurate descriptions of the society of his day. Moreover, through sheer love of language Jerome was inclined to elaborate his descriptions far beyond the requirements of his propaganda.[175] In fact it is possible on rare occasions to discover a softening of the bitter tone he had adopted toward women. We have no reason to question the sincerity of a sentence in which Jerome joins to his ascetic enthusiasm a suggestion that his harsh satire of women and marriage resulted from idealism rather than malice. *Laudo nuptias, laudo coniugium, sed quia mihi virgines generant, lego de spinis rosas, de terra aurum, de conce margaritum.*[176]

[174] Probably because John continued to live amid the luxury and corruption of Antioch and Constantinople and hence, unlike Jerome, had firsthand knowledge of what he was describing.

[175] Samuel Dill well warns against literal acceptance of Jerome's heated descriptions (*Roman Society in the Last Century of the Western Empire* [2d ed.; London, 1899], 130–131).

[176] Letter 22. 20.

CHAPTER V

Heretics, Jews, and Pagans

AMMIANUS MARCELLINUS recounts how the Emperor Julian, wishing to assure the disunity of the Christian world, called together the numerous quarreling Christian factions and urged them all fearlessly to follow their own beliefs, "knowing by experience that no beasts are as hostile to men as many Christians are bestial to each other."[1] Julian was probably thinking in particular of the physical violence that frequently broke out between adherents of rival Christian sects, but his observation was scarcely less applicable to the scurrilous abuse and scorn that Christian writers poured out upon the holders of opinions they considered erroneous or heterodox. Among the masters of malignant vilification aimed at intellectual opponents, St. Jerome stands supreme. Unorthodox views were utterly abhorrent to him, and no one who dared hold them could escape his vitriolic invective. As Jerome justly says in defending the intellectual honesty of his polemical writings, "I shall briefly reply that I have never spared the heretics and have striven with all zeal that the enemies of the Church might become my enemies too."[2]

[1] Amm. Marc. xxii. 5. 4. Julian refers to Christian violence toward pagans and heretics in *Against the Galilaeans* 206A.

[2] *Dial. contra Pelag., Praefat.* 2, PL 23, 519B. Cf. the horrifying

Heretics

The violent scurrility with which Jerome attacked heresy should be viewed both as a sign of his deep personal attachment to the cause of orthodoxy and as an inheritance from the apologetic tradition. The harsh and mordant tone which the apologists had adopted toward paganism had naturally been transferred to heresy, when the latter began to be looked upon as a greater danger to right religion.[3] Thus Polycarp had reviled the heresiarch Marcion as the first-born of the devil.[4] For Justin too heretics were followers of Satan. Tertullian had turned the harshness of his invective not only against pagan religion but also against such monstrous aberrations from Christianity as Valentinian Gnosticism and Monarchianism.[5] St. Jerome quotes a highly satiric passage from a certain Apollonius, who had castigated the Montanist leaders as lewd and avaricious gamblers and usurers.[6] The gradual emergence of a system of dogma, the acceptance of which became the inescapable test of orthodoxy, naturally hardened forever the lines between sound and reprehensible opinion and exposed those who stubbornly maintained their own views to the tongue-lashings of the orthodox. This was especially true after the Council of Nicaea had condemned Arianism. Forever afterward this dread heresy evoked the vehement denunciations of right-thinking theologians. Thus, Hilary of Poitiers and Apollinarius of Laodicea, one of Jerome's teachers, directed polemics against the Arians. We find Gregory

---

remark on heresy, *Ego si patrem, si matrem, si germanum adversum Christum meum audivissem ista dicentes, quasi rabidi canis blashphemantia ora lacerassem, et fuisset in primis manus mea super eos (Contra Joannem 8, PL 23, 378A).*

[3] Cf. above, Chapter I.

[4] The remark of Polycarp is quoted by Irenaeus *Adversus haereses* 3. 3. 4.

[5] In *Adversus Valentinianos* and *Adversus Praxean.*

[6] See *De vir. ill.* XL (PL 23, 690).

of Nyssa hurling words of scornful malevolence against the Arian Eunomius.[7]

These "torrents of abuse which one saint poured on another" have been viewed by one scholar as the continuation of the mutual vilification and invective of rival philosophical schools.[8] This violent behavior of philosophers toward their opponents is illustrated brilliantly, though of course with exaggeration, in the dialogues of Lucian. In the *Icaromenippus* Zeus complains of the scurrility of philosophers: "Whoever of them is the most noisy and impudent and reckless in calling names is held to be the champion."[9] In the *Hermotimus* we read of a philosophical quarrel which broke out at a banquet between a Stoic and a Peripatetic. The dispute ended only when the Stoic wounded his rival on the head "with a cup as big as Nestor's."[10]

It is doubtless true that the abuse indulged in by representatives of quarreling Christian sects is in part the descendant of this traditional philosophical vilification. But one may see another force stimulating Christian invective, the influence of the legal rhetoric. The history of ancient invective is as old as Archilochus and Alcaeus, but with the development of rhetoric, vilification became a specialized art whose natural home was the law court. Gorgias was the first writer to justify on theoretical grounds the orator's adoption of a humorously abusive tone.[11] The vital role that ridicule played in the subsequent development of forensic eloquence is clearly shown by Cicero's lengthy analysis

---

[7] *Against Eunomius* i. 30–36 and 72–80, in W. Jaeger's 2d ed. (Leiden, 1960), I, 31–34 and 41–50.

[8] Hatch, *The Influence of Greek Ideas,* 329.

[9] *Icaromenippus* 31, in A. M. Harmon's Loeb ed., II (London and New York, 1915).

[10] *Hermotimus* 12, in K. Kilburn's Loeb ed., VI (Cambridge, Mass., 1959).

[11] Cicero *Brutus* 47 on invective in early Roman oratory. For an excellent brief essay on ancient invective, see R. G. M. Nisbet's edition of Cicero's *In Pisonem* (Oxford, 1961), App. VI.

in *De oratore* of the nature and proper use of humor in oratory.[12] In his own speeches Cicero followed the earlier Roman orators in outrageously vilifying his opponents.[13] Quintilian too, although he states his preference for gentle wit, says: "And yet it is, of course, permissible to address one's adversaries insultingly and bitterly, just as it is allowable to accuse them openly of crimes and to ask for their lives."[14] This tradition of forensic wit and abuse was the natural heritage of the Christian apologists, for many of them, both Greek and Latin, had received the old rhetorical education. Indeed, Tertullian not only had been trained in the law but had actually practiced as a lawyer in Rome. One of his most bitterly satiric works, the *Apologeticum*, is written in the form of an argument delivered before a tribunal. Arnobius and his pupil Lactantius were by profession teachers of rhetoric and were consequently well equipped to employ in their defense of Christianity the polemic of the law courts.[15] Of Greek writers, Gregory Nazianzen and Basil studied rhetoric in Athens under Prohaeresius and Himerius, and John Chrysostom was a pupil of the famous Libanius.[16] Their writings reveal them as well versed in the techniques of abuse. We have conclusive evidence from St. Jerome himself that scurrilous wit and invective were still vigorously employed in the legal debates of the fourth century. Writing of his own rhetorical education, Jerome says, "When as a very young man I was declaiming *controversiae*

---

[12] *De oratore* ii. 54–71. Cf. *De off.* i. 103–104 and *Orator* 88. On this subject see M. A. Grant, *The Ancient Rhetorical Theories of the Laughable* (*University of Wisconsin Studies in Language and Literature*, XXI; Madison, 1924). On Cicero's humor in general see A. Haury, *L'Ironie et l'Humeur chez Cicéron* (Paris, 1955).

[13] For invective in the earlier orators see Nisbet's *In Pisonem*, 193.

[14] Quintilian vi. 3. 28.

[15] Jerome complains (Letter 58. 10) that Lactantius was better at destroying opponents' arguments than in constructing his own.

[16] Gregory was of course one of Jerome's mentors. E. Hatch, *The Influence of Greek Ideas*, devotes his fourth chapter to tracing the influence of rhetoric on Christianity.

at Rome and through fictitious cases practicing for real struggles, I would sometimes run to the judges' tribunals and see the most eloquent of the orators battle each other with such bitterness that they would often abandon their business and turn to insulting and biting one another with jocular tooth."[17] Thus Jerome was able both in his reading to observe earlier Christian writers burying their intellectual opponents beneath a torrent of invective and also to acquire through his rhetorical education the techniques of doing so himself. Certainly nothing was more natural than that the irascible *Ciceronianus* should learn from his favorite author the modes of piercing opponents with barbed epithets.

Yet another force, the Cynic diatribe, can be seen influencing, somewhat indirectly, St. Jerome's adoption of a scurrilous tone toward the enemies of his ascetic propaganda. The Cynic preachers, in their efforts to spread their moralistic doctrines among the mass of men, made abundant use of coarse and vivid wit. This abusive humor was, of course, later appropriated by Roman satire for similar purposes.[18] But the Cynic diatribe was also the prototype of the Christian sermon. The wandering Christian missionaries, who spread the moral teachings of the new faith, easily borrowed the rough style of exhortation characteristic of those pagan preachers with whose ethical doctrines Christianity had so much in common.[19] The polemical methods of the diatribe thus became naturalized in Christian writing. The Cynic diatribe may be said, then, to have exercised a twofold

---

[17] *Comm. in Gal.* i. 2 (*PL* 26, 363A–B).

[18] See Horace *Epist.* ii. 2. 60 and Fiske, *Lucilius and Horace*, 180–201.

[19] P. Wendland, *Die Hellenistisch-Römische Kultur* (Tübingen, 1907), 39–53, and N. Terzaghi, *Per la storia della satira* (Turin, 1933), 7–57. See also A. Dirking, *S. Basilii Magni de divitiis et paupertate sententiae quam habeant rationem cum veterum philosophorum doctrina* (Münster, 1911), and "Diatribe" by W. Capelle and H. I. Marrou, in ed. T. Klauser, *Reallexikon für Antike und Christentum*, III (Stuttgart, 1957), cols. 990–1009.

influence on St. Jerome's adoption of a vituperative tone toward his enemies, both indirectly through Roman satire and again through its effect on the Christian style of preaching.

But abusive invective is not satire, it may be objected. Yet the relationship between satire and invective is so close that it would be wrong to omit the less subtle and harsher form of ridicule from a study of St. Jerome's satire. The earliest Roman satire, that of Lucilius, is characterized as much by fierce and censorious invective as by the subtlety of the author's wit. In several fragments of his thirtieth book, we find Lucilius defending the unrestrained venom of his critique.[20] Horace in his criticism of Lucilius reveals that excessive harshness was a major element in the earlier satirist's denunciations of men and morals. When Horace writes,

Ridiculum acri
fortius et melius magnas plerumque secat res,

he is showing that bitterness, rather than true humor, was the chief quality of earlier satire.[21] Again, in the fourth satire of his first book, Horace represents an opponent of his sharpness thus complaining:

"Laedere gaudes,"
inquit, "et hoc studio pravus facis." . . .[22]

The poet implies in these words that satire was looked upon as an instrument of malicious abuse. The harsher type of satiric invective may, then, be said to fall under that category of humor

---

[20] Fragments 970, 971, 1014, 1015, 1016, 1022, in Marx's edition. See Fiske, *Lucilius and Horace*, 90. On Cicero's view of Lucilius' vitriol, see Grant, *Ancient Rhetorical Theories*, 100.

[21] *Sat.* i. 10. 14. Cf. Juvenal 1. 165–67:
"ense velut stricto quotiens Lucilius ardens
infremuit, rubet auditor cui frigida mens est
criminibus, tacita sudant praecordia culpa."
Cf. Persius 1. 114–115.

[22] *Sat.* i. 4. 78.

which Cicero describes as *illiberale, petulans, flagitiosum, obscenum*, in contrast to wit, which is *elegans, urbanum, ingeniosum*.[23] If then we should find that Jerome in denouncing his adversaries inherits both from Cicero and from earlier defenders of orthodoxy a complete lack of restraint, a boldness of diction, and a certain absence of subtle wit, we should not on this account exclude such invective from a study of his satire. In the words of Quintilian, *a derisu non procul abest risus*.[24]

We can further demonstrate that according to ancient rhetorical theory Jerome's coarse and bitter invective is closely linked to classical satire. W. S. Anderson has shown that many of Juvenal's satires belong rhetorically to the *genus demonstrativum* and to that particular aspect of the *genus* known as *vituperatio*.[25] The chief surviving prose example of *vituperatio* is Cicero's scurrilous speech *In Pisonem*. Anderson reveals a great similarity in the abusive techniques employed by Cicero and Juvenal. He states that "the stylistic techniques adopted by Cicero to convey his hatred of all that Piso represents . . . constitute prose analogues to what Juvenal employs in his satires."[26] But we will see that Jerome's violent attacks on his opponents do not merely show a general resemblance to *In Pisonem* but in fact borrow directly from that speech. Jerome's polemics should be regarded then as part of that tradition of rhetorical *vituperatio* to which both Cicero's scurrility and Juvenal's satire belong.

---

[23] *De off.* i. 104. This distinction between the liberal and illiberal jest, emphasized in all ancient theoretical discussions of humor, was formulated by Aristotle in *Ethics* iv. 8 (1128A) ff. and discussed also in a portion of the *Poetics* now lost. Cf. Aristotle's *Rhetoric* iii. 18. 7 (1419b). See Grant, *Ancient Rhetorical Theories*, 27ff.

[24] Quintilian vi. 3. 7.

[25] See *Rhetorica ad Herennium* iii. 6. 10 in H. Caplan's Loeb ed. (Cambridge, Mass., and London, 1954); and W. S. Anderson, "Juvenal and Quintilian," *Yale Classical Studies*, XVII (1961), 3–93.

[26] Anderson, 92.

It is important, however, to note while studying Jerome's malevolence toward his opponents that such contentious vituperation is directly contrary to the theory which he himself sets forth of the apologist's proper role: *prava non acriter confutare, disputantem contra se magis docere quam vincere.*[27] Furthermore in one of the earliest of his exegetical works, the commentary on the Epistle to the Ephesians, St. Jerome makes the important distinction between the intellectual and moral sins of the heretics:

Inter peccatum autem carnis et mentium hoc esse puto: quod carnis peccatum est impudicitia atque luxuria, et ea quae ministerium eius in libidinibus explentur. Mentium vero delictum ad dogmata pertinet contraria veritati et haereticam pravitatem, ita ut possimus dicere plerosque haereticorum (quamquam hoc rarum sit) voluntates mentium facere˜ et non voluntates carnis, et multos contra ecclesiasticos carnis et non mentium facere voluntates.[28]

We shall see Jerome completely ignoring exactly this distinction in his satiric attacks on heretics. He rarely seeks to refute their intellectual errors, except in his expressly polemical works, but instead hurls accusations of every conceivable moral crime against them. This tendency is already foreshadowed in the passage above, for Jerome here suggests that it is rare to find a heretic who is not also befouled by sensual faults.

Letters

By far the most dangerous heresy to agitate the Christian world in St. Jerome's day was Arianism. In an early letter to Pope Damasus from the desert of Chalcis, Jerome complains that his departure from Rome to seek peace in the desert proves the dictum of Horace:

Caelum, non animum mutant, qui trans mare currunt,

[27] Letter 60. 10. He there praises Nepotianus' ability to achieve this ideal.
[28] *PL* 26, 497B–C.

for even in those distant wastes *Ariana rabies fremit.*[29] In a later letter he refers to an Arian interpretation of a biblical passage with the words *Arius caput levat.*[30] Jerome, it would seem, is by implication describing the heresiarch as a snake, an animal to which he was inordinately fond of comparing his enemies. Jerome confirms our suspicion when he uses against another heresy the same expression in a fuller form: *Olim emortua vipera contritum caput levat.*[31]

A heresy that played a far greater role in St. Jerome's own personal life than Arianism was Origenism. No incident of Jerome's career has been more carefully studied and more thoroughly documented than the complex Origenist controversy, and there seems little purpose in repeating what has so often been well set forth.[32] Suffice it to say here that Jerome had been a fervent admirer of the great Origen and had done much to spread his fame in the West until in 393 an obscure priest named Atarbius called upon Jerome to reject Origen's heretical views.[33] With surprising alacrity Jerome did a complete *volte-face* and from that time on spoke only with the greatest bitterness and scorn of the supporters of Origen's heterodox views.[34] Thus in his ninety-seventh letter, referring to his own supposed connection with Origenism, he speaks of the heresy as *coluber tortuosus, venenatissima viper* and *heresis quae sibilabat in mundo, et . . . latratu impudentissimorum canum ad inducendos simplices, nostrum mentiebatur adsensum.*[35] This rapid passage from snake to dog imagery is characteristic of Jerome's most unrestrained style

---

[29] Letter 16. 2; Horace *Epist.* i. 11. 27.   [30] Letter 65. 13.

[31] Letter 69. 1.

[32] The clearest and most complete account is by F. X. Murphy, *Rufinus of Aquileia* (Washington, D.C., 1945), 59–157. The unreasonable partiality of J. Brochet largely invalidates his *St. Jérôme et ses Ennemis.*

[33] On Jerome's attitude toward Origen see esp. Cavallera, II, 115–127.

[34] On the causes of Jerome's abrupt change of opinion, see Murphy, *Rufinus,* 69–70.

[35] Letter 97. 1. Apollinarianism is included in this condemnation.

of abuse. His comparison of Origen's followers to dogs betrays his facility in maligning former friends and in adapting his scurrility to the needs of his argument; many years before he had abused Origen's enemies as *rabidi canes* who hated the great scholar, not because of his supposed heresy but on account of their own jealousy.[36]

In other attacks on Origenism, Jerome hounds the snake image to death. In his educational letter to Demetrias, he warns her against Origenism, which indeed has lost its hissing hydra-heads yet still lies hidden in viper's holes and with its scorpion sting threatens to wound the innocent.[37] It is curious that Bishop Theophilus of Alexandria, Jerome's ally in the struggle against Origenism, also uses serpent imagery to refer to the heresy. In his pastoral letter translated into Latin by Jerome, Theophilus calls Origen *hydram omnium haereseon* and declares his followers to be snakes who creep along the ground.[38] This similarity of abusive terminology implies either that ecclesiastical writers had a common vocabulary of scurrilous epithets or that Jerome has impressed his own polemical style on Theophilus' work.[39] The first conjecture is more probable, since it was entirely natural for a Christian writer to employ serpent imagery: we read in Luke that Jesus gave his disciples *potestatem calcandi supra serpentes et scorpiones,* and these words were easily applied by the orthodox to their adversaries.[40] Tertullian's use of

---

[36] Letter 33. 5.   [37] Letter 130. 16. 2; 130. 16. 3; and 130. 16. 5.

[38] Letter 98. 9 and 98. 19.

[39] In letter 99. 2 Jerome praises Theophilus for having attacked Origenism *absque invidia personarum.* This does not mean that all scurrilous abuse was absent from Theophilus' work before translation, for Jerome would not have considered the epithet *hydra* hurled at the long dead Origen as a piece of *personal* malice. For another possible example of Jerome's tampering with the text of Theophilus, see above, Chapter II, n. 93.

[40] Luke 10: 19. We find Jerome using this very passage against the Origenists when he writes *inter scorpiones et colubros incedendum est* (Letter 124. 2). Cf. Letter 124. 15.

the title *Scorpiace* (*Antidote for the Scorpion's Sting*) for one of his polemical works implies this traditional comparison of his enemies, the heretics, to scorpions.

We must not, however, suppose that in his attacks on his intellectual adversaries Jerome relied simply on hurling abusive epithets. He sometimes concentrates his feelings of contempt and disgust into brief caricatures of his enemies, as when refuting certain heterodox opinions of the Origenists he says, *sicut quidam stertentes sopore gravissimo somniant.*[41] This picture may have been inspired by Cicero, who frequently portrays his opponents as excessively sleepy.[42] In another caricature Jerome describes the Origenists "mumbling in corners" (*per angulos mussitare*) and asking each other foolish questions, which Jerome quotes at length in an effort to ridicule through mimicry: *"Cur illa anima in illa est nata provincia? Quid causae extitit, ut alii de Christianis nascantur parentibus, alii inter feras et saevissimas nationes, ubi nulla dei notitia est?"*[43] Jerome combats erroneous opinions on the marriage of bishops by recounting verbatim a dialogue that took place between Jerome himself and a representative of these mistaken views. He prefaces this with a physical description of his opponent: *Primum spinosulus noster obmutuit; postea vero, Pisoniano vitio, cum loqui nesciret tacere non potuit. Sudare tamen frons, pallere genae, tremere labia, haerere lingua, saliva siccari, et plus timore quam aetate contrahi.*[44] This grotesque cartoon is a product of Jerome's imagination and reveals his delight in finding occasion for satire, for there can be little doubt that the argument described in the letter never actually took place. Jerome's comparison of his adversary to Piso suggests that in his abusive treatment of heretics he thought of

---

[41] Letter 121. 1.

[42] *In Pisonem* x. 22 and *Phil.* ii. 13. 30; Süss, *Giess. Beitr.*, LX, 235.

[43] Letter 130. 16. 3.

[44] Letter 69. 2. Cf. Cicero *In Pisonem* i. 1 and Martial vi. 41:
"Qui recitat lana fauces et colla revinctus
hic se posse loqui, posse tacere negat."

himself as heir to Cicero's forensic scurrility. Later in this letter, at the conclusion of the dialogue, Jerome ridicules the condition of mental dizziness into which his own brilliant argumentation had thrown his adversary: "I was tossing darts and hurling quivering spears at my drowsy opponent. He merely yawned and as if in a state of intellectual inebriation, sea sick and belching, vomited forth the following reply: 'That's what the Apostle said, so taught Paul.' "[45] Jerome's obvious pleasure in his triumph over a nonexistent adversary is curious but also characteristic.

In the course of his correspondence Jerome found opportunity to fling at least one abusive remark at most of the current heresies. In describing the Gnosticism of Basilides he speaks of "a most foul and filthy heresy raging through Spain like a pestilence and a disease."[46] He frequently makes reference to the crazy female prophets of Montanism and once called Montanus himself a castrated halfman (*abscisum et semivirum*).[47]

But Gnosticism and Montanism were no longer vital movements in the late fourth century. A novel heresy, much more dangerous because so persuasive, was Pelagianism, which Jerome combated in the last years of his life, in concert with St. Augustine. Jerome devoted two works to a refutation of this movement, his Letter 133 to Ctesiphon and the *Dialogus contra Pelagianos*. These two documents present a striking contrast: while the latter work is full of the extreme bitterness which we expect to find in Jerome's attacks on heresy, the former work is remarkably calm. At one point in the letter Jerome exclaims, "My mind is aboil, I cannot check my words."[48] Yet he does in fact control himself, although he goes so far as to describe the followers of the heresy as

[45] Letter 69. 2. It is curious to note that in this letter Jerome is not in fact satirizing a heretical view but is unwittingly defending one. See Labourt's note on this passage, *Letters*, III, 235.

[46] Letter 75. 3.   [47] Letters 41. 4; 21. 3; 120. 9; 133. 4. 3.

[48] Letter 133. 11. 3. On Pelagius, see G. de Plinval, *Pelage* (Lausanne, 1943), and J. N. L. Myers, *Journ. of Rom. Stud.*, L (1960), 21–36.

mulierculae oneratae peccatis, quae circumferuntur omni vento doctrinae semper discentes et numquam ad scientiam veritatis pervenientes et ceteri muliercularum socii prurientes auribus et ignorantes quid audiant, quid loquantur.[49]

But his indignation never reaches a higher pitch. The relative mildness of this attack is almost surely due to the circumstance, which Jerome repeatedly emphasizes in the course of the letter, that the Pelagians had not yet openly declared themselves.[50] Jerome was still unsure of his ground.[51] But with greater knowledge came more impassioned indignation, and the following year Jerome was ready to loose a storm of satiric abuse on the Pelagians.[52]

Polemical Works

Cicero had taxed his enemy Piso with avarice, sensuality, and ignorance, and Jerome frequently hurls these same charges against the heretics in general and especially against the Pelagians. In the *Dialogus contra Pelagianos* the orthodox interlocutor ridicules the heretics' passion for riches. "You claim to take no thought for the morrow," he exclaims, "and to be like birds, content with what you already have. Then whose papyrus letters keep flying across the rivers of Ethiopia, so that from the midst of she-apes and peacocks more gifts might be sent to you, a new Solomon?"[53] Pelagius, swollen with the shoulders of a

---

[49] Letter 133. 4. See above, p. 162.   [50] See Letter 133. 12.

[51] Letter 133 belongs to the year 414 (Cavallera, II, 54–55) and hence was written one year before the *Dialogus* and two years before the Pelagian attack on Jerome's monastery.

[52] The *Dialogus* is already adumbrated as a *promissum opus* in Letter 133. 13. 1.

[53] *Dial.* ii. 12 (*PL* 23, 572B). Vallarsi's interpretation of this passage as applying to the avarice of Pelagius is reasonable. Vallarsi notes that the diction is borrowed from the LXX version of Isa. 18:2. Cf. *Comm. in Jer.* iii. *Praefat.*, on Pelagius: *Mittit in universum orbem epistolas biblinas prius auriferas, nunc maledicas.*

Milo and the arrogance of a Cato, vomits forth his doctrines.[54]
The orthodox speaker in Jerome's work has a penchant for
applying lines from Roman comedy to his opponent. Ridiculing
the literary style of Pelagius, he declares that his heretical
language is so eloquent that it moves with the speed and grace of
a tortoise. He here recalls Plautus, *Aulularia*, 49:

> Testudineum istum tibi ego grandibo gradum.[55]

Twice the orthodox speaker says, "You heretics keep rolling
around in the same old mud." Furthermore, "your arguments
are trifling. You accomplish nothing more than if you should
wash a brick, ignorant of the saying, 'Settled for once, settled
forever.' You seek to deceive the innocent, knowing that
obsequiousness produces friends, truth enemies." Jerome here
tries to ridicule his opponents by drawing together scattered
lines from Terence's *Phormio* and *Andria*.[56] The remark about
being stuck in the mud comes from *Phormio*, 780:

> in eodem luto haesitas.

"Settled for once, settled forever" (*Actum ne agas*) is quoted
verbatim from *Phormio*, 419. The comparison of foolish argumentation to washing a brick is found in *Phormio*, 186. The
saying *Obsequium amicos, veritas odium parit*, is borrowed from
Andria, 68.

Homilies

St. Jerome thought it wise on occasion to warn the monks
gathered in the Bethlehem church against the subtle heresies that
lay in ambush, ready to lead the unwary astray. His method of
attack was to use a biblical text as the starting point of his invec-

[54] *Dial.* i. 28 (*PL* 23, 546A); i. 32 (*PL* 23, 549C). Hagendahl, *Latin
Fathers*, 265, thinks that the reference to Milo's shoulders recalls *Cato
Maior*, 33.
[55] *Dial.* iii. 16 (*PL* 23, 614). Cf. the same line applied to Rufinus, *Contra
Ruf.* i. 17.
[56] *Dial.* i. 23 (*PL* 23, 541B) and *Dial.* i. 26 (*PL* 543B).

tive. Thus when the psalmist prays for the destruction of his enemies, "For there is no faithfulness in their mouth; their inward part is very wickedness," Jerome seizes the opportunity to caricature heretics:

Arius, Eunomius, and all the other heretics have tongues like arrows; their jaws are a tomb. "Their throat is an open sepulchre." . . . For whenever anyone, being deceived wishes to walk into their jaws, the heretic is ready and swallows him down. Never do the heretics close their mouths but are always gaping wide.[57]

The heretics are wild beasts that seize and murder souls. They are clever *Platonici et Aristotelici,* lovers of the meretricious gold of worldly eloquence.[58] The talk of heretics is crafty and artificial: *Si illos tenueris in uno testimonio, ad aliud transeunt. Si in scripturis tenueris, ad Aristotelem fugiunt. Si Aristotelem tenueris, in Platonem transeunt.*[59] A hard thing it is to escape a heretic, once he has caught you in the snares of dialectic, syllogism, and worldly knowledge. Heretics are furthermore greedy lovers of riches. *Videas enim magistros haereticorum nihil aliud facere, nisi studere divitiis. Divitiis student, et pauperem Christum contemnunt. Boves eorum crassi.* The heretics are, in fact, the fat Egyptian cattle which Pharaoh saw in his dream.[60]

Exegetical Works

In reading Jerome's biblical commentaries, one feels that the author's whole being was ceaselessly gripped with profound horror at the evil of heresy. There is scarcely a page in any one

[57] Psalms 5:9; *Anecdot. Mared.,* III. 2. 14.

[58] *Anecdot. Mared.,* II. 2. 42 and 63, on Psalm 67 (A.V. 68): 30 and Psalm 77 (A.V. 78): 9.

[59] *Anecdot. Mared.,* III. 2. 284.

[60] *Anecdot. Mared.,* III. 2. 283–285, on Psalm 143 (A.V. 144). Jerome's Vulgate version and the Authorized Version of this Psalm are strikingly different. The latter could never have been interpreted as applying to heretics. The differences can be explained as follows: the Vulgate Psalter is Jerome's revised Latin version of the LXX and is not based on the Hebrew text.

of his exegetical works which is not filled with ridicule and abuse of the heterodox. Such violent attacks are particularly frequent in the commentaries on the Old Testament prophets, for the fiery denunciations so numerous in these books could easily be applied to the heretics. Yet even in the books of the New Testament, Jerome found ammunition for his campaign against heresy. As he says in one of his biblical commentaries, *Iuxta spiritalem intelligentiam laborandum est, quomodo omnia haereticis coaptemus.*[61] It would obviously be impossible to examine here every such passage, but we can try to form a general picture of the means adopted by Jerome to expose and ridicule the evils of heresy.

We find in Jerome's biblical commentaries innumerable descriptions of the heretics as avaricious. In one of his earliest Old Testament commentaries, that on Micah, the gross venality of the unorthodox is heavily emphasized. In seducing the souls of the innocent they seek only their own profit, declaring, *Non necesse est ut vivas continenter et sancte.*[62] These are the siren songs which deceive the unwary.[63] The seductive actions of the heretics are guided by motives of pride and love of lucre— *haeretici, qui omnia gloriae et lucri causa faciunt, et orant in angulis platearum, rectam semitam relinquentes.*[64] This theme is continued in many of Jerome's other exegetical works. In the commentary on Amos, we find him flinging this charge repeatedly: on the one hand, heretics attack the poor, thinking to find them easy prey. On the other hand, they flatter the rich: *Cum divitibus prospera quaeque promittant, tantum apud pauperes truculenti sunt et severi.*[65] In the commentary on Hosea, the heretics are accused of devouring houses for the sake of base

---

[61] *Comm. in Osee,* PL 25, 906B. Although Jerome is referring here to one passage in particular, the sentiment is applicable to all the biblical commentaries.

[62] *PL* 25, 1180C, 1221C.   [63] *PL* 25, 1158C.

[64] *Comm. in Zach.,* PL 25, 1531A.

[65] *PL* 25, 1646B and 1447A. Cf. 1006D and 1007A.

lucre.⁶⁶ In Jerome's work on Ezekiel, we read that when the destruction of the earthly Tyre comes, the heretics will bewail their *male divitias congregatas*.⁶⁷ In the commentary on Isaiah, Jerome declares that the heretics are engaged in a foul struggle to seize booty from the deceived:

Propter luxuriam, et voluptatem, et lucra de populis inter se habent discordiam, ut de una haeresi duae fiant, et rursum ipsae dividantur in partes, ut proprios abducant greges et devorent domos viduarum et mulierum peccatricum.⁶⁸

Gluttony is another failing repeatedly ascribed to heretics in Jerome's biblical commentaries. The unorthodox preach against the flesh while living a life of carnality and nourishing their obese paunch (*pinguissimum ventrem*).⁶⁹ In an outburst of hatred, Jerome paints the following choleric portrait of the life of heretics:

Contemplemus haereticos, quomodo semel desperantes salutem, gulae se tradant et deliciis, vescantur carnibus, frequenter adeant ad balneas; musco fragrent; unguentis variis delibuti quaerant corporum pulchritudinem.⁷⁰

The chiliastic *Semiiudaei*, who foresee a life of sensual luxury after death, "making ready exquisite foods for a thousand years," are particularly subject to the charge of gluttony.⁷¹ Jerome draws up a satiric list of their hopes in the next world: "abundance of wealth and luxurious foods, and bodily fatness and pheasants and stuffed turtledoves, honeyed wine, the beauty of

---

⁶⁶ PL 25, 876C. Also 856B: *et lucra quaerunt de populis*.

⁶⁷ PL 25, 264C. Cf. 308A: *haereticorum . . . propter voluptatem et terrenam opem cuncta facientium*.

⁶⁸ PL 24, 136A. Cf. 326C: *omnia mercedis causa faciunt*. Same sentiment in 365B.

⁶⁹ *Comm. in Jonam*, PL 25, 1136B. Cf. Cicero on Gabinius, *In Pisonem* xvi. 41: *nam ille gurges atque helluo, natus abdomini suo*.

⁷⁰ *Comm. in Jer.*, PL 24, 857A.   ⁷¹ *Ibid.*, PL 24, 541C.

wives, troops of children."[72] God cures heretics by abandoning them to their pleasures, "so that by eating and being fattened on flesh they might become nauseated and vomit forth through their nostrils and begin to hate those whom they followed with such great zeal."[73] As slaves of their bellies, heretics are rightly called *vaccae pinguissimae*.[74] In brief, *nulla . . . haeresis nisi propter gulam ventremque construitur.*[75]

A charge closely related to that of gluttony is lewdness. The church of the heretics is called a house of prostitution (*conciliabulum*).[76] When we join the heretics, we are helping to build a brothel.[77] Heretics are spawned in drunkenness and incest, and during their entire lives *deliciis vacant*.[78] They are thoroughly debauched voluptuaries: "*Volutantur in sordibus libidinum, vacant stupris, et quidquid loquuntur et putaverint se in laudem Dei dicere, ululatus luporum et baccharum insanientium sonitus est.*[79] Horrendous crimes can daily be seen in the house of heretics, for their masters are fornicators who pollute the people.[80]

The imagery of Jerome's exposure of the heretics' crimes is sometimes borrowed directly from the biblical passage he is

[72] *Comm. in Isa., PL* 24, 550D. Those charges are repeated in 609D, 610B, and 665D.

[73] *Comm. in Osee, PL* 25, 936B.

[74] *Comm. in Amos, PL* 25, 1024D. Cf. 1022C.

[75] *Comm. in Jer., PL* 24, 729C.

[76] *Comm. in Mic., PL* 25, 1155D and 1157C. Also *Comm. in Ezech., PL* 25, 293B. *Conciliabulum* is used in Roman comedy as a synonym for *lupanar*: Plautus, *Bacchides* 1. 1. 17; *Trinummus* 2. 2. 38.

[77] *Comm. in Ezech., PL* 25, 147A.

[78] *Ibid., PL* 25, 234A–B and 293B. Cf. *Comm in Amos, PL* 25, 1063D: *principes haereticorum, qui propter delicias meum populum devorant.*

[79] *PL* 25, 880B. Cf. 897A.

[80] *Comm. in Osee, PL* 25, 872B. For other references on sensuality of heretics, see *In Isaiam, PL* 24, 570D, 573D, and 290B. In the last of these passages heresy is elaborately compared to a prostitute. Cf. Cicero on Piso, *In Pisonem* xxvii. 66–67: *Nihil scitote esse luxuriosius, nihil libidinosius, nihil posterius, nihil nequius.*

expounding. Thus in interpreting the words of Jeremiah, "Hast thou seen that which backsliding Israel has done: she is gone up upon every high mountain and under every green tree, and there hath played the harlot," Jerome declares: *Secundum anagogen autem de haereticis prophetia est: qui . . . carnis huius voluptatibus deliniti sub omni ligno frondoso et amoeno exponunt fornicationem suam.*[81]

The pride and arrogance of the heretics are frequently described in satiric vignettes.

Quis enim haereticorum non superbus est? qui ecclesiasticam despiciens simplicitatem, ita habet Ecclesiae homines quasi bruta animalia, et intantum superbiae iniuriaeque tumore erigitur ut contra ipsum creatorem armet os suum.[82]

By constantly using the words *tumor* and *inflare* to refer to heretics, Jerome seeks to place before the reader an almost visible picture of their swollen pomposity: *Inflati enim tument, et sacratiora se invenisse gloriantur.*[83] The heretics are empty windbags: *Inflati sunt et nihil sciunt, et languent circa quaestiones.*[84] Another descriptive phrase frequently employed to caricature heretics is *os positum in excelsum.* Ignorant arrogance is briefly but vividly portrayed as Jerome describes the heretics: *Quorum os in caelum ponitur . . . et sensu quem a Deo in bonam partem acceperunt, abutuntur in contrarium atque perversum.*[85] So great is the pride of heretics, *ut . . . gaudeant in sceleribus suis, et erecta cervice gradiantur.*[86]

A heretic's haughtiness is derived from his claims to wisdom, for, *sibi sciolus videtur.*[87] The truth is, however, that heretics

[81] Jer. 3:6; *Comm. in Jer.*, PL 24, 728C.

[82] *Comm. in Jer.*, PL 24, 243C–D.

[83] *Ibid.*, PL 24, 276B. Cf. *Comm. in Osee*, PL 25, 923A.

[84] *Comm. in Mic.*, PL 25, 1222B and 1224A–B. Also *Comm. in Amos*, PL 25, 1031A: *Et quia semper haeretici tumentes superbia.*

[85] *Comm. in Isa.*, PL 24, 141A. Cf. 215A, 547C, and 572A–B. Also *In Ezech.*, PL 25, 140A.

[86] *Comm. in Osee*, PL 25, 849C.   [87] *Comm. in Ezech.*, PL 25, 61B.

creek and rattle with meaningless verbal noises (*vano sermonum strepitu concrepantes*).[88] They have fallen into a deep sleep and can only emit the raucous sound of snoring from their noisy nose.[89]

In seeming contradiction to this ridicule of heretical ignorance, but in complete accord with the usual practice of opponents of heresy, Jerome constantly mocks the unorthodox for their addiction to worldly knowledge.[90] Learned in the philosophy and dialectic of the pagans, they are able with their slick and artificial talk to deceive the innocent believers. *Vide haereticos in dialectica sibi et rhetorica et omnium sophismatum dogmatibus applaudentes, contemnere Ecclesiae rusticitatem.*[91] In one passage Jerome mimics the cunning but empty verbosity of the heretics:

Opprimitur pauper ecclesiasticus verbositate et argutiis haereticorum, qui postquam aliquos deceperint, solent dicere: Divites facti sumus, habemus plurimam multitudinem, discipulorum turba nos sequitur; invenimus idolum vel refrigerium nobis.[92]

These are the *verba pompatica* of the unorthodox.[93] Yet when their doctrines try to fly aloft, though full of cleverness, they fall miserably to the ground and find their place *inter Aristotelis et Chrysippi spineta.*[94] With the verbal cunning of the heretics

[88] *Comm. in Osee, PL* 25, 907C.

[89] *Comm. in Jonam, PL* 26, 1125C. Jonah asleep within the whale is interpreted as the torpid heretics. For the sleep and snore imagery, cf. *Comm. in Isa., PL* 24, 19B, 151B, and 657B–C; *Comm. in Jer., PL* 24, 860A.

[90] This is a commonplace of the antiheretical polemic. Cf. Hippolytus, *Refutatio omnium haeresium, passim.*

[91] *Comm. in Soph., PL* 25, 1365C. Cf. 1361C; also *Comm. in Isa., PL* 24, 380D.

[92] *Comm. in Osee, PL* 25, 927A–B.

[93] *Comm. in Ezech., PL* 25, 61D.

[94] *Comm. in Naum, PL* 25, 1269C. For other passages denouncing heretics' clever language and use of pagan learning, see the commentaries: *In Ezech., PL* 25, 249B; *In Osee, PL* 25, 863D, 893B, 912B; *In Dan., PL* 25, 506B; *In Amos, PL* 25, 994A, 996C, 1044B; *In Isa., PL* 24, 82C, 119B, 244D, 458C, 656B; *In Jer., PL* 24, 776A and C, 778B.

Jerome frequently contrasts the artless language of the orthodox, meaning himself in particular. Addressing the Roman senator and Christian ascetic Pammachius in his commentary on Hosea, Jerome claims: *Neque enim Hebraeum prophetam edisserens, oratoriis debeo declamatiunculis ludere, et in narrationibus atque epilogis Asiatico more cantare.*[95] Although throughout his life Jerome took passionate pride in his literary training and in the refinement of his style, for the sake of his polemic he did not hesitate to dismiss linguistic elegance as *haereticorum supellectilem.*[96]

It is common for polemicists to attempt to ridicule their opponents by comparing them to various animals. Cicero in his speeches calls his antagonists dogs, donkeys, and unnatural monsters.[97] We have already seen examples of Jerome's use of animal imagery in his letters.[98] In deriding heretics in his exegetical works Jerome avails himself of a larger menagerie of abuse. Interpreting Isaiah 9:14, "Therefore the Lord will cut off from Israel head and tail," Jerome applies the words to the heretics: by using the word tail, he claims, the prophet, *non homines, sed iumenta, haereticos esse demonstrat, quae hoc membro utuntur ad stercora protegenda, et ad arcenda parva animalia.*[99] Elsewhere Jerome exposes the animal lust and the bestial stupidity of the heretics in one phrase, by calling them tortoises and oxen.[100] If in their stolidity and filth the heretics are cattle, yet

---

[95] *PL* 25, 839A.

[96] *PL* 25, 585A and 1025A. It need hardly be pointed out that this ambiguous attitude toward pagan rhetoric exists throughout early Christian literature. Many Christian writers denounce rhetoric while making good use of it. The classic account is E. Norden, *Die antike Kunstprosa* (5th ed.; Stuttgart, 1958), II, 529ff.

[97] *Verr.* II. 1. 133; II. 3. 28; II. 1. 126; *In Pisonem* xxx. 73; *Phil.* xiii. xxi. 49. See S. Seliga, "De contumeliis Hieronymianis," *Eos.*, XXXIV (1932–1933), 395–412.

[98] See above, p. 174.   [99] *Comm. in Isa.*, PL 24, 135C.

[100] *Comm. in Osee, PL* 25, 929C.

propter fraudulentiam ac nequitiam, they are like foxes.[101] Some, indeed, may argue that heavy stupidity and clever fraudulence are mutually exclusive characteristics, but Jerome was not likely to be bothered by such incongruities. The unorthodox, further-more, *instar porcorum volutantur in coeno.*[102] They are scrofu-lous animals and dogs who bark at Scripture.[103] In other passages Jerome tosses at the heretics the epithets *Hydra* and *Scylla.*[104] In his adoption of this monstrous terminology Jerome was probably recalling that Cicero had denounced Verres as more savage than Scylla and Charybdis.[105]

In the light of Jerome's efforts to cast scorn and ridicule upon heretics as the most debauched and foolish of creatures, we may test how well he achieved the goal that he himself set for an apologist: to avoid bitterness by teaching rather than conquering one's opponents.[106] Jerome's perfervid temper and the traditions of philosophic and forensic invective combined to destroy this ideal. Indeed so furiously angry is Jerome's treatment of heresy that satire tends to give way to unadorned vilification. We have seen that bitter invective was one of the original elements of Roman satire and that Horace criticizes Lucilius for its overuse. However, true satire has its origin in reality itself. The aim of satire is to seize upon reality and to distort it by emphasizing absurd or unpleasant details. Beneath the exaggeration of carica-ture and parody, real life is always visible. But when the evil and ridiculous elements of the actual are so monstrously exaggerated that reality itself is unrecognizable, satire degenerates into choleric malevolence. This process has, to some extent, taken place in Jerome's invective against heresy, and the reason is not

---

[101] *Comm. in Ezech.,* PL 25, 110B–C.

[102] *Comm. in Osee,* PL 25, 855B.

[103] *Comm. in Gal.,* PL 26, 430B and 433C. On Cicero's dog imagery, see Seliga, "De contumeliis," 397–398.

[104] *Comm. in Ezech.,* PL 25, 165.

[105] *Verr.* II. 5. 146. Seliga, "De contumeliis," p. 140.

[106] See above, p. 173.

far to seek. In denouncing the clergy or women, Jerome was able to base his attacks on behavior he had actually witnessed. Hence his descriptions, though heavily influenced by tradition and rhetoric, are firmly rooted in actuality. In attacking heresy, on the other hand, Jerome was dealing with abstract concepts which were not open to the same extremely detailed realistic caricature that he applies to female and clerical behavior. Hence in an effort to place heresy squarely within a context which would lend itself to satiric treatment, he is reduced to casting the most absurd charges of immorality against the heretics themselves. Jerome then attempts to describe this immoral behavior in the lively terms of satiric caricature. But since such portrayals are not based on autopsy, there is but little life in them. The satiric kernel often dries up, leaving only the husk of vilification.

Jews

In view of the angry terms of abuse and mockery which St. Jerome employed against those of his fellow Christians whose opinions he considered erroneous, it is hardly likely that he would have adopted a gentle tone toward those archenemies of Christianity—the Jews.[107] In the traditions of Christian apologetics he could find no source for any mildness. By the fourth century the body of Christian anti-Jewish literature was already large.[108] Tertullian had subjected the Jews to harsh invective in

[107] On the depressed social and economic position of the Jews in the fourth century, especially in Palestine, see H. Graetz, *History of the Jews* (Philadelphia, 1893), II, 531–603; J. Juster, *Les Juifs dans l'Empire Romain* (Paris, 1914), II, 323–326; S. W. Baron, *A Social and Religious History of the Jews* (New York, 1952), II, 241–251. See also J. E. Seaver, *Persecution of the Jews in the Roman Empire* (*University of Kansas Humanistic Studies*, XXX, 1952), J. Parkes, *Journal of Rom. Stud.*, XLIII (1953), 235, and Parkes's own *Conflict of Church and Synagogue.*

[108] See Juster, *Les Juifs*, I, 43–76; A. Harnack, *Texte und Untersuchungen* (Leipzig, 1883), I, Heft 3, 56–134; A. Lukyns Williams, *Ad-*

a work with which Jerome was familiar.[109] Cyprian had written his *Testimonium* in part as a polemic against the Jews. Eusebius specifically directed his *Demonstratio evangelica* against Judaism, and Origen in his *Contra Celsum* assaulted Jews as well as pagans. Ephraem Syrus had denounced the Jews in the most violently abusive terms. Jerome claims to have read this work in translation and praises Ephraem's "sublime genius."[110] Among Jerome's contemporaries, John Chrysostom directed eight homilies against the Jews, and Prudentius had hard words for them also.[111] Pagans too, until the very end of the old religion, continued to express bitter hatred for the Jews: Rutilius Namatianus hurls a most foul and heated tirade against the *obscaena gens* and their customs.[112]

It is worth remarking before Jerome's satire of the Jews is studied that he owed them an enormous intellectual debt. His earliest Hebrew training was provided by a converted Jew in the desert of Chalcis. He read Hebrew Scripture with the Jew Bar Anina, who surreptitiously removed books from the synagogue in order to instruct Jerome.[113] Throughout his life he had recourse to learned Jews for explanations of difficult biblical passages. His exegetical works are replete with Jewish interpreta-

---

versus Judaeos (Cambridge, 1953), 3–113; and esp. M. Simon, *Verus Israel* (Paris, 1948), 165–213. Also R. Wilde, *The Treatment of the Jews in the Greek Christian Writers of the First Three Centuries* (*Cath. U. of Am. Patristic Studies*, LXXXI; Washington, D.C., 1949). Of course the pagan satirists had little good to say of the Jews, e.g., Juvenal 14. 96-106.

[109] Jerome quotes from Tertullian's *Adversus Iudaeos* in *Comm. in Dan.*, PL 25, 549A.

[110] *De vir. ill.* CXV. Ephraem Syrus is now available in the *Corpus Scriptorum Orientalium* (Louvain, 1957), LXXVII–LXXIX.

[111] PG 48, pt. i, 839ff. Also Prudentius, *Apotheosis*, 348–354.

[112] *De reditu suo* i. 380–398.

[113] Letter 84. 3. Bar Anina was attacked under the insulting name Barabbas by Rufinus (*Apol.* ii. 12–13; PL 21, 595C).

tions.[114] Yet in spite of the learning Jerome had derived from the Jews, he is able in one of his letters to make the cruel remark, *Iudaeorum luctus Christianorum gaudium est*.[115] The conflict between Jerome's intellectual debt to the Jews and his hatred of them is clearly expressed in a passage in which, speaking with great pride of his Hebrew learning, Jerome suddenly adds: *Si expedit odisse homines et gentem aliquam destestari, miro odio aversor circumcisos*.[116]

Jerome's sincere animosity toward the Jews is eminently plain in the satiric pictures and abusive phrases he brings to bear against them. In one of his letters he implies that the Jews are lascivious. If we should follow their habits, *semper aestuemus ad coitum*.[117] This *gens inimica* has all sorts of foul and foolish customs, among which is the observance of the Sabbath:

Praeterea, quia iussum est, ut diebus sabbatorum sedeat unusquisque in domo sua et non egrediatur nec ambulet de loco, in quo habitat, si quando eos iuxta litteram coeperimus artare, ut non iaceant, non ambulent, non stent, sed tantum sedeant, si velint praecepta servare, solent respondere et dicere: "Barachibas et Symeon et Helles, magistri nostri, tradiderunt nobis, ut duo milia pedes ambulemus in sabbato."[118]

[114] Grützmacher, II, 114: "Aus zwei Quellen hat Hier. vor allem seine Kommentare geschöpft. . . . Es sind wieder Origines und die Hebräer." This subject has been studied by M. Palmer, *Die hebräischen Traditionen in den Werken des Hieron.* (Breslau, 1861) and by S. Krauss, "The Jews in the Works of the Church Fathers—VI, Jerome," *Jewish Quart. Rev.*, VI (1894), 225–261. See also Penna, *Esegesi*, 5–10, and Simon, *Verus Israel*, esp. ch. v.

[115] Letter 60. 6. Cf. Tertullian *De spectaculis*, 29: *Lugeamus ergo dum ethnici gaudent, ut dum lugere coeperint, gaudeamus.*

[116] Letter 84. 3. Cf. Letter 45. 4: *Haberem solacium non placendi eis quibus displicet Christus.*

[117] Letter 49. 8. Pagans and heretics are included in this remark.

[118] Letter 121. 10. 20. The filthy slander which immediately precedes this passage is too disgusting for repetition. Cf. also Letter 39. 4, where Jerome mocks the Jewish custom of mourning.

In another letter Jerome, describing the narrow limits of Palestine, comments, "Jew, you go through the different provinces boasting to the ignorant of the size and greatness of your homeland." He ridicules this Jewish mendacity by quoting Persius, 3. 30:

> Ad populum phaleras! Ego te intus et in cute novi.[119]

In another letter he remarks, if the Jews do not believe in the miracles of the Christians, "Let them go on swelling up and threatening us."[120]

Among Jerome's writings the greatest repository of mocking remarks on the Jews is the corpus of biblical commentaries.[121] Biblical texts rouse Jerome to cast the most foul aspersions on the Jews. When Isaiah attacks those that "sanctify themselves and purify themselves in the garden behind one tree in the midst, eating the swine's flesh and the abomination," Jerome applies the words to the "carnal Jews, who think that with water alone they can wash away their adulterous behavior and the filth of their lusts." To the Jews that saying of Persius is well fitted: *Noctem flumine purgant.*[122] So lecherous are they that they produce sons and grandsons like little worms (*instar vermiculorum*).[123] The Jews are not only lewd but also gluttonous. On the Sabbath they sit around panting after feasts (*epulis in-*

---

[119] Letter 129. 4. Cf. Letter 129. 7, where Jerome addresses to the Jews a curious speech on the reasons for their troubles. For John Chrysostom's polemic against the "arrogant, bold, shameless, and boundlessly conceited" Jews, see the passages quoted by C. Baur, *John Chrysostom and his Times* (2d ed.; Westminster, Md., 1959), I. 332.

[120] Letter 38. 2.

[121] This subject is handled, very briefly, by Sister M. J. Kelly in her *Life and Times as revealed in the Writings of St. Jerome Exclusive of his Letters* (Washington, D.C., 1944), 129–130.

[122] *PL* 24, 691C; Persius 2. 16. Cf. Letter 49. 15. Vallarsi strangely attributes this line to Horace.

[123] *Comm. in Isa., PL* 24, 479B.

hiant).[124] The Jews celebrate their festivities with wine and banquets.[125] As they look forward to the next world they think only of filling their maw, *et pro huius vitae continentia brevique ieiunio, bulbos sibi, et vulvas, et aves Phasidis et attagenem, nequaquam Ionicum, sed Iudaeum reprommittunt.*[126] When the end of this world comes, the Jews hope *se . . . in morem pecorum corporalibus donis Iudae opibusque complendos et pascendos herbis viridibus, et deletis cunctis gentibus, sibique subiectis, nullum posse residere qui eos exterreat.*[127] Thus they foresee for themselves, *beatitudinem ventri, et gutturi Iudaico servientem.*[128] Such vilification is of course entirely characteristic of the Christian anti-Jewish polemic. John Chrysostom speaks of the Jews who "live for their bellies, seek greedily after earthly riches and are no better than swine or goats in their dissipation and their excessive longing for pleasure."[129]

Avarice is a characteristic which Jerome too ascribes to the Jews. To them he applies the words of Horace, *semper avarus eget.*[130] Apart from the Romans, the Jews are the greediest people on earth.[131] Their god is money.[132]

As for the inflated arrogance of the Jews, it is totally unbearable: "They are wont to laugh at us, to raise their brows and, blowing out their cheeks, to belch forth their knowledge of Scripture."[133] Almost fanatic hatred breathes through Jerome's portrayal of *supercilium Iudaeorum, solutis labiis, et obtorta*

---

[124] *Ibid., PL* 24, 559A.   [125] *Comm. in Naum, PL* 25, 1243B.

[126] *Comm. in Zach., PL* 25, 1529C.

[127] *Comm. in Soph., PL* 25, 1380D–1381A.

[128] *Comm. in Ezech., PL* 25, 339A. Evidently the Jewish dietary laws were interpreted by some as a form of ascetic abstinence. Jerome combats this view, *In Zach., PL* 25, 1470D.

[129] Baur, *John Chrysostom*, I, 333. Baur curiously accepts every word of Chrysostom's vilification as literally correct.

[130] *Comm. in Isa., PL* 24, 49A–B. Horace *Epist.* i. 2. 56. This line is frequently used by Jerome.

[131] *PL* 24, 49A–B.   [132] *Comm. in Isa., PL* 24, 52B.

[133] *Comm. in Ezech., PL* 25, 346D.

lingua, et stridente saliva, et rauca fauce gaudentium.[134] Jerome
has chosen his blackest colors in which to paint this brief, odious
caricature.[135]

Jewish stupidity is also censured by Jerome. The Jews are
always quarreling over trivial points of Scripture, he says:

> Rixae quoque legales penitus respuendae sunt, et Iudaeorum stul-
> titiae relinquendae. Sunt enim inutiles et vanae, quae tantum speciem
> scientiae habent: ceterum nec dicentibus, nec audientibus prosunt.
> Quid enim mihi prodest scire quot annos vixerit Mathusalem, quoto
> aetatis suae anno Salomon sortitus sit coniugem, ne forsitan Roboam
> undecimo aetatis illius anno natus esse credatur?[136]

We possess amusing proof of Jerome's highly ambiguous attitude
toward Jewish learning: several years after he thus ridiculed the
Jews for quibbling over so minute a question as King Solomon's
age at the time of his marriage, he was to devote a letter of
exegesis to this very topic![137] Jerome can deride the learning of
the Jews as "belching and nausea,"[138] speak of Jewish scriptural
interpretations as foolish tales, inept inventions, and anile fables[139]
and then make proud claims to have derived his knowledge of
the Scripture from the Hebrews themselves, claims which he
often puts forth even when he is not in fact using Jewish
exegesis.[140]

The Jews, says Jerome, keep running to their synagogues as
if they are seeking God; "to the Jews this saying is well-fitted:
'The evil shall seek Me and shall not find Me.' "[141] The prayers
and chanting of the Jews are pure noise, the grunting of pigs,

---

[134] *Comm. in Titum, PL* 26, 631A.

[135] On Jewish pride, cf. *Comm. in Ezech., PL* 25, 296D and 480D;
Comm. in Amos, PL 25, 1087A; *Comm. in Jonam, PL* 25, 1116B.

[136] *Comm. in Titum, PL* 26, 631D–632A.   [137] Letter 72.

[138] *Praefat. in librum de nom. Heb., PL* 23, 816A.

[139] *PL* 25, 356C and 1411B.

[140] On this subject, see G. Bardy, "Saint Jérôme et ses Maîtres
Hébreux," *Revue Bénédict.*, XLVI (1934), 145–164, esp. 145–149.

[141] *Comm. in Isa., PL* 24, 582C–D.

the braying of asses.[142] The Jews are camels, forever chewing on the Law, ruminating and rolling it around in their mouths, but never coming to wisdom.[143] Their learning is dead, for they can no longer speak, but only mutter.[144] Their glory is departed, and to them can be applied the words of Terence: *Visa est vere quod dici solet, aquillae senectus.*[145]

Thus the Jews, along with heretics and pagans, are the most foul dregs (*spurcissimae faeces*).[146] If they have suffered terrible oppression, they have deserved it: *Propter peccata sua offendere Iudaei: ideo eos oppressimus, et ex pretio eorum divites facti sumus.*[147] And yet on one occasion Jerome does, very briefly, feel a somewhat gentler sentiment toward the Jews: "Believe me, as often as I see synagogues, I keep in mind the saying of the apostle, that we ought not exult over the olive tree whose branches are broken, but rather be fearful."[148]

Pagans

Scholars have frequently remarked with some surprise that St. Jerome spends very little time and effort in attacking paganism.[149] This is, in fact, quite untrue. Indeed, Jerome himself declares, *Tota opuscula mea, et maxime Commentarii, iuxta opportunitatem locorum gentilem sectam lacerant.*[150] It is true, however, that Jerome denounces paganism much more rarely than heresy. This was natural: in his day paganism was definitely on the wane, in spite of brief and transient revivals, while the

---

[142] *Comm. in Amos*, PL 25, 1054B–C.   [143] *PL* 25, 1535B.

[144] *Comm. in Amos*, PL 25, 1080A. Cf. on heretics Letter 130. 16.

[145] *Comm. in Mic.*, PL 25, 1164D; Terence, *Heauton*. III. 520. For other passages on Jewish ignorance, cf. commentaries: *In Mic.*, PL 25, 1204D; *In Aggaeum*, PL 25, 1412B; *In Soph.*, PL 25, 1364B; *In Isa.*, PL 24, 1442C.

[146] *Comm. in Joel.*, PL 25, 956C.   [147] *Comm. in Zach.*, PL 25, 1501A.

[148] *Anecdot. Mared.*, III. 2. 66.

[149] Grützmacher, I, 275; Weston, 92; C. Favez, "La Satire dans les Lettres de Saint Jérôme," *Rev. des Et. Latines*, XXIV (1946), 212; Hagendahl, *Latin Fathers*, 210.

[150] Letter 84. 3.

heresies were young and powerful enemies.[151] In fact, Jerome himself states that he was much less worried about pagans than about heretics: *facilius enim ab ethnicis captum liberes, quam haereticorum praestigiis inretitum.*[152] Nonetheless in many of his writings Jerome does ridicule, parody, and caricature pagans. Thus in two of his letters he cruelly mocks Fabia Aconia Paulina, widow of the recently dead pagan leader Vettius Agorius Praetextatus, for, *illa infidelem maritum translatum fingit in caelum.*[153] A malicious *double-entendre* may lie hidden in this sentence, for in the word *infidelem* Jerome probably wants to suggest both that Praetextatus did not believe in the Christian faith and that he was an unfaithful husband. There is perhaps special significance in Jerome's allusion to Praetextatus as *infidelis,* for fidelity both to the ancient deities and to his wife Paulina was one of the pagan leader's outstanding qualities.[154] On the famous inscription which preserves Praetextatus' epitaph, husband and wife exchange final greetings. The long list of Praetextatus' priesthoods is given, and Paulina celebrates the learned piety with which her husband worshipped the *numen multiplex.* Later in the inscription Paulina mourns her husband's death but declares that she is happy to have been and to be his, and looks forward to being his in death once again. Jerome, who surely understood the nature of Rome's outstanding citizen, perhaps chose the adjective *infidelis* expressly in order to imply malevolently that the loyalty on which Praetextatus prided himself was in fact vain and empty. Jerome may, in fact, have had direct knowledge of Praetextatus' epitaph and may have noticed

[151] *Cambridge Medieval History,* I, 97; E. Stein, *Histoire du Bas-Empire* (Paris-Bruges, 1959), I, 211–214; Fliche and Martin, *Histoire,* III, 506–519.

[152] *In Abdiam, PL* 25, 1110A. What did worry Jerome was an alliance between heresy and paganism, *PL* 25, 1109C.

[153] Letter 39. 3.

[154] On Praetextatus and his wife see H. Bloch, "Pagan Revival," *Harvard Theol. Rev.,* XXXVIII (1945), 199–244, esp. 216. Also P. de Labriolle, *La Réaction Païenne* (Paris, 1934), 349–351.

that Paulina's expectation of meeting her husband once again implied that he was in heaven, for in a letter written in 384[155] Jerome paints an inhumanly cruel and mocking picture of Praetextatus' true abode: "Now he is abandoned, naked, not in the milky palace of heaven, as his unhappy wife pretends, but imprisoned in the filthy darkness."[156]

In another epistolary attack on paganism Jerome ridicules the Emperor Julian, who, the mad dog, vomited forth seven books against Christ, and then, in imitation of the poets' accounts of heroes, tore himself apart with his own sword.[157] The followers of Isis and Cybele are also derided, *qui gulosa abstinentia Fasides aves et fumantes turtures vorant, ne scilicet Cerealia dona contaminent.*[158]

However, as Jerome himself states, his exegetical works are the richest treasury of attacks on the pagans. As might be expected, the heathen are in these works called voluptuaries: *Plurimi quippe gentilium in suis ignominiis gloriantur, et putant si expleverint voluptatem, quamdam se turpitudinum victoriam consecutos.*[159] The pagans' misuse of *sapientia saecularis* is often derided: "Their fine eloquence is in truth a drooping weed which soon withers and dies, while the simple seed of Gospel preaching grows into a glorious tree."[160] The Stoics even attempt to make profit of the souls of men by writing treatises *de officiis, de continentia,* and *de opibus contemnendis.* But they are deceiving their readers, foisting brazen vessels upon those who expect golden bowls.[161] Such are the gentile dogs who bark

---

[155] Jerome was of course in Rome at this time.   [156] Letter 23. 3.

[157] Letter 70. 3. Cf. *De vir. ill., Prologus* (PL 23, 634B), where Jerome calls Julian, Celsus, and Porphyry *rabidi canes.* In *Anecdot. Mared.,* III. 2. 320, Porphyry is said to vomit forth his madness. See De Labriolle, *La Réaction Païenne,* 111–169, 225–296, 369–436.

[158] Letter 107. 10.   [159] *Comm. in Gal.,* PL 26, 443A.

[160] *Comm. in Matt.,* PL 26, 93B; *Comm. in Ezech.,* PL 25, 253C–D. Cf. PL 25, 258D and 291D.

[161] *Comm. in Abdiam,* PL 25, 1114B.

against the Christians.[162] During the persecutions of Maximinus and Diocletian, the pagans thumbed their noses at the Church (*subsannaverunt Ecclesiam*).[163] But Jerome can now glory that pagan thought and learning are dying: "How few men nowadays read Aristotle? How many know Plato's name, to say nothing of his works? Even old men sitting in corners with nothing to do hardly recall them."[164]

Conclusion

Students of St. Jerome's character and writing will find nothing surprising in the fierceness of his attitude toward pagans, Jews, and heretics. This attitude follows naturally from his inherently irascible and intolerant personality, from his high conception of his own role as an upholder of strict orthodoxy, and from the traditions that allowed controversialists to employ the most violent scurrility against their opponents. This tradition of vilification had flourished in the law courts, and the early apologists had adopted it in their battle against the pagan world. Invective thus became an integral part of Christian propaganda and naturally continued to be employed freely when the internal conflicts within Christianity began to assume greater importance than the struggle against the non-Christian world. Jerome is concerned above all with the moral threat posed, as he claimed, by heresy. He rarely attacks heresy on intellectual grounds except in his avowedly polemical works, such as the *Dialogus contra Pelagianos*. He much prefers to render heterodoxy vulnerable by claiming that it fosters and promotes immoral behavior. He can then attempt to portray this behavior with the exaggeration and vivid detail of satire. This attempt is not wholly successful, for the charges were false, and Jerome could not use his own observations as the basis for lifelike caricatures of heretics. He is therefore frequently reduced to hurling abusive

[162] *Comm. in Matt.*, PL 25, 159C.
[163] *Comm. in Ezech.*, PL 25, 339D.   [164] *Comm. in Gal.*, PL 26, 428C.

charges, most of which have parallels in Cicero's oratory but whose ultimate origin is probably to be sought elsewhere. Phillip De Lacy has convincingly maintained that when Cicero attacks the Epicurean Piso as an impious and gluttonous voluptuary and calls him a monster, a beast, a horse, and a pig, he is drawing from the anti-Epicurean propaganda of popular philosophy.[165] Since St. Jerome inherits just these arguments from *In Pisonem,* his polemic against the heretics appears as a Christian remodeling of pagan anti-Epicureanism. Christian satire has in common with that of the pagans an essentially Stoic orientation, even though Jerome often vilifies the Stoics themselves.

Jerome's assault against the Jews does not differ essentially from his attack on heretics. Naturally he pays much less attention to the Jews, for in his day they no longer constituted a threat to Christianity. However, Jerome evidently considered their religious views to be influential, for he spent no little effort in trying to destroy their intellectual credit by attacking their moral character. Yet it is significant that most of Jerome's outbursts against the Jews are found in his biblical commentaries; these attacks take their origin directly from biblical passages which brought the Jews to mind. If Jerome had had an overwhelming dislike or fear of the Jews, he would more frequently have attacked them spontaneously in his letters and in other works where they were not presented to his mind by the material he was discussing.

The general opinion that Jerome pays little attention to paganism cannot be wholly substantiated. On numerous occasions, especially in his exegetical works, he ridicules the intellectual and moral emptiness of paganism. He was well aware, however, that paganism was moribund, and he does not waste too many words in trying to injure it further. So caught up was Jerome in the *internal* conflicts of contemporary Christianity

---

[165] "Cicero's Invective against Piso," *TAPA*, LXXII (1941), 49–58.

that he did not have much time to devote to its relatively minor *external* enemies.

We may summarize Jerome's attitude toward heretics, Jews, and pagans and also epitomize his method of denouncing them by quoting a passage in which he bewails what he considers their unjust prosperity:

Quantos enim cernimus ethnicos, Iudaeos, hereticos et diversorum dogmatum homines volutari in coeno libidinum, madere sanguine, feritate lupos, rapinis milvos vincere, et nihilominus flagellum non adpropinquare tabernacula eorum.[166]

[166] Letter 68. 1.

CHAPTER VI

Personal Enemies

IN his impassioned fight against the enemies of orthodoxy Jerome did not limit himself to denouncing and lampooning heretics in general. On the contrary, one large class of his personal enemies was made up of heretics, and these individuals too felt the sting of Jerome's satiric invective. The second major group of personal foes consisted of individuals who had the audacity, or courage, to suggest that Jerome's scholarship was not beyond criticism. The virtue of considering these two groups together is that this procedure will illustrate the inextricable mingling of personal ill will and religious zeal that underlay much of Jerome's satire.

Anonymous Enemies

We begin with Jerome's lampoons of those foes whose names he did not choose to mention. So numerous were his antagonists that he was unable, much as he may have wished it, to denounce each one by name. In one of his letters he exclaimed, "I thank God that I am worthy of the world's hatred," and hated he was—by those who were deeply disturbed by his rejection of the Septuagint and older Latin versions of the Bible in favor of his own new translation, by those who took offense at the extremism of his ascetic propaganda, and by those who found his arrogant and harsh personality intolerable.[1] His life was an unending struggle with such antagonists. As early as 375 he complained in a letter written from the desert of Chalcis, *Et licet me sinistro Hibera excetra rumore dilaniet, non timebo hominum iudicium habiturus iudicem meum.*[2] The identity of this "Spanish snake" is unknown.[3] The word Jerome used to describe him, *excetra,* is so rare, especially in its figurative sense, that Jerome must be borrowing it from an earlier writer. In fact *excetra* is twice used as an abusive term by Plautus to describe crafty, scheming women.[4] Hence Jerome may here be adopting the language of Roman comedy to vilify his anonymous foe. Even at this early stage of his career we find a foreshadowing of the personal animosity which was to dominate so much of his later life.

A much more complex document of Jerome's struggle with his enemies is Letter 27. Certain clerics had attacked Jerome for his insufferable pride and for his revolutionary tampering with the text of the Bible. In answering them Jerome deployed all the satiric ammunition at his command. Of course such trivial little men (*homunculi*) could not understand his scholarly work on the Bible—*Asino quippe lyra superflue canit,* says Jerome, here adapting the Greek proverb ὄνος λύρας ἀκούων to suggest the bestial stupidity of his enemies.[5] These men claim to be disciples of the Fishermen (the Apostles), but they resemble them only in their extreme simplicity, which is a sign not of holiness but of gross vulgarity. Referring to his efforts to purify the text of

[1] Letter 45. 6.   [2] Letter 6. 2.
[3] Cavallera, II, 75.
[4] *Casina,* III. 5. 19; *Pseudolus,* I. 2. 82. Jerome also uses *excetra* in Letter 147. 8; *Praefat. in Ezram, PL* 28, 1474; *Praefat. in Comm. Abacuc, PL* 25, 1307A. Cavallera suggests that the word may be applied only to women. However, Jerome often uses the word of Rufinus.
[5] Letter 27. 1. Cf. Letter 61. 4, where Jerome uses the Greek original of the proverb against Vigilantius. See Otto, *Sprich. der Röm.,* p. 41.

the Bible, Jerome writes: *Si displicet fontis unda purissimi, caenosos rivulos bibant, et diligentiam qua avium salivas et concharum gurgites norunt, in scripturis legendis abiciant.*[6] Here again Persius has come to the aid of biblical scholarship. The satiric phrase *avium salivas norunt*, one of Jerome's favorite descriptions of gluttony, is adapted from Persius' *turdarum nosse salivas.*[7] *Concharum gurgites nosse* is another of Jerome's standard expressions characterizing excessive interest in food.[8]

Subsequently Jerome addresses his foes with the insulting words: *Revertimur ad nostros bipedes asellos, et in eorum aurem bucina magis quam cithara concrepamus.*[9] Jerome here takes a phrase from Juvenal 9. 92:

Neglegit atque alium bipedem sibi quaerit asellum.

At the very end of the letter Jerome writes:

Ad extremum illi gaudeant Gallicis canteriis, nos solutus vinculis et in salvatoris mysterium praeparatus Zachariae asellus ille delectet qui postquam Domino terga praebuit coepit Esaiae consonare praeconio: "beatus qui seminat secus omnem aquam, ubi bos et asinus calcant."[10]

What are these *Gallici canterii* in which Jerome's adversaries are told to rejoice while he takes his delight in the donkey ridden by Christ? Vallarsi in his note on the passage points out that Jerome has taken the phrase *Gallicis canteriis* from Plautus' *Aulularia*, 495.[11] The word *canterius* means literally a castrated horse, a gelding. The adjective *Gallicus*, however, presents a problem, since we have no indication that Jerome's foes had anything to do with Gaul. *Gallicus* is probably not a geographic

---

[6] Letter 27. 1.

[7] Persius 6. 24. This phrase is frequently used by Jerome. Cf. Letter 33. 3.

[8] Cf. Letter 33. 3 and 52. 6.   [9] Letter 27. 3.

[10] Letter 27. 3. Cf. Zech. 9:9, and Matt. 21:9.   [11] PL 22, 432.

term here but is calculated to suggest the *Galli*, the castrated priests of the Great Mother.[12] Thus the adjective reinforces the pejorative meaning of *canterii*, and also adds a suggestion that the *homunculi* in question were tainted with paganism. The whole phrase carries through the donkey-horse imagery with which the letter began. Jerome is saying to his attackers, "You asses, the Bible in which *you* seem to take such delight is only a wrecked and tainted nag, while *I* rejoice in Scripture pure and undamaged, which may be compared to the beast on which Christ rode in triumph."

Evidently Jerome did not succeed in crushing his critics with this bitter missive, for in a later letter (40) he singles out one of this group for even harsher treatment. The object of this extremely clever attack had taken exception to Jerome's denunciation of the immorality of the age, feeling that his satiric barbs were directed particularly against himself. Jerome replies:

Placet mihi de larvis, de noctua, de bubone, de Niliacis ridere portentis: quicquid dictum fuerit in te dictum putas. In quodcumque vitium styli mei mucro contorquetur te clamitas designari, conserta manu in ius vocas, et satiricum scriptorem in prosa stulte arguis.[13]

The addressee of this letter is called Onasus Segestanus by Jerome, but one sentence reveals that this was not his real name: *An ideo tibi bellus videris quia fausto vocaris nomine?*[14] Since the name Onasus is not particularly *faustus*, Jerome is probably concealing the man's true identity. But why has Jerome undertaken to attack him under this name in particular? This question has been carefully studied by J.-G. Préaux, who has discovered the origin of the name in a passage of the Verrines, where Cicero speaks of *Onasum Segestanum, hominem nobilem . . . vir pri-*

---

[12] So used, for example, by Ovid *Amores* ii. 13. 18. Cf. Cicero, *In Pisonem* ix. 18, where the orator refers to his enemy as a *maialis*, a gelded hog.

[13] Letter 40. 2 with reference to Letter 22. 28.   [14] Letter 40. 2.

marius, homo nobilissimus.[15] Préaux has conjectured from this passage that Jerome's adversary was a well-known and highly-placed personage, and hence Jerome has chosen this ironic pseudonym. But other motives entered into the choice of name. Onasus suggests both the Greek word ὄνος, donkey, and the Latin *asinus.* Thus Jerome is here continuing the insult which, as we have seen, played such an important role in Letter 27. The name furthermore suggests *nasus,* and throughout the letter Jerome mocks his adversary's malformed and foul nose. *Disposui nasum secare fetentem,* declares Jerome, *timeat qui strumosus est.*[16] The other fault for which Jerome ridicules Onasus is his swollen eloquence: *Volo corniculae detrahere garrienti: randiculam se intellegat cornix.*[17] These two themes are closely connected in Jerome's attack:

Numquid unus in orbe Romano est, qui habeat "truncas inhonesto vulnere nares?"[18] numquid solus Onasus Segestanus cava verba et in vesicarum modum tumentia buccis trutinatur inflatis?[19] dico quosdam scelere, periurio, falsitate ad dignitatem nescio quam pervenisse: quid ad te qui te intellegis innocentem? rideo advocatum qui patrono egeat; quadrante dignam eloquentiam nare subsanno: quid ad te, qui disertus es?[20]

Préaux believes that when composing the last two clauses Jerome was thinking of Persius 5. 91:

Disce, sed ira cadat naso rugosaque sanna.[21]

It is also clear from Jerome's mockery of Onasus that this man considered himself somewhat of a beau, in spite of his disgusting nose:

[15] *De suppliciis* v. 45. 120. See J.-G. Préaux, "Procédés d'invention d'un sobriquet par S. Jérôme," *Latomus,* XVIII, 4 (1958), 659–664.

[16] Letter 40. 2.   [17] For *cornicula,* see Horace *Epist.* i. 3. 19.

[18] Cf. *Aeneid* vi. 497.   [19] Cf. Persius 3. 82.

[20] Letter 40. 2.

[21] Cf. Horace *Epist.* i. 5. 23. As Préaux points out, Persius frequently makes fun of noses: 1. 33; 1. 109 (imitated from Lucilius).

An ideo tibi bellus videris quia fausto vocaris nomine? quasi non et lucus ideo dicatur quod minime luceat, et Parcae ab eo quod nequaquam parcant, et Eumenides Furiae et vulgo Aethiopes vocentur argentei. Quodsi in descriptione foedorum semper irasceris, iam te cum Persio cantabo formosum:

> Te optent generum rex et regina, puellae
> te rapiant: quicquid calcaveris tu, rosa fiat.[22]

Jerome's satiric use of the argument *lucus a non lucendo* has a close parallel in Juvenal 8. 30–38, where the poet warns an aristocrat against believing that nobility consists in high birth alone:

> Quis enim generosum dixerit hunc qui
> indignus genere et praeclaro nomine tantum
> insignis? Nanum cuiusdam Atlanta vocamus,
> Aethiopem Cycnum, pravam extortamque puellam
> Europen; canibus pigris scabieque vetusta
> levibus et siccae lambentibus ora lucernae
> nomen erit pardus, tigris, leo, si quid adhuc est
> quod fremat in terris violentius; ergo cavebis
> et metues ne tu sic Creticus aut Camerinus.

This whole letter is, indeed, as Préaux says, "un chef-d'oeuvre d'humeur satirique." It is disconcerting, however, to find Jerome completely unable or unwilling to defend himself by reasoned argumentation. We may conclude this discussion of Letter 40 by mentioning Labourt's conjecture, probably correct, that Onasus' real name was Onesimus (i.e. ὀνήσιμος, beneficial), which would indeed be a *faustum nomen*.[23]

The bitterly sarcastic tone, arising from offended pride, is

---

[22] Letter 40. 2. The lines of Persius are adapted from *Satire* 2. 37–38. Préaux (p. 660) thinks that Onasus felt personally insulted by Jerome's lampoon of priests who sought access to women through their profession (Letter 22. 28).

[23] Labourt's ed. of the *Letters*, II, 196.

typical of Jerome's reaction toward his critics and is perhaps best exemplified by one of the most acid and ironic of his letters, *Ad Domnionem* (Letter 50). Domnio, one of Jerome's partisans at Rome, had written that a certain monk was in the habit of ridiculing and reviling him in aristocratic circles, attacking in particular Jerome's tract against Jovinianus and claiming that he himself could have done better. Jerome replies to his critic in a letter addressed to Domnio. He begins by describing his foe as an ignorant and verbose fop:

Scribis eos, immo nescio quem de trivio, de compitis, de plateis circumforanum monachum rumigerulum, rabulam, vafrum tantum ad detrahendum, qui per trabem oculi sui festucam alterius nititur eruere, contionari adversum me, et libros quos contra Iovinianum scripsi canino dente rodere, lacerare, convellere; hunc, dialecticum urbis vestrae et Plautinae familiae columen, non legisse quidem κατηγορίας Aristotelis, non περὶ ἑρμηνείας, non ἀναλυτικά, non saltim Ciceronis τόπους, sed per imperitorum circulos muliercularumque συμπόσια syllogismos ἀ'συλλογίστους texere, et quasi σοφίσματα nostra callida argumentatione dissolvere. Stultus ego qui me putaverim haec absque philosophis scire non posse; qui meliorem stili partem eam legerim quae deleret, quam quae scriberet. Frustra ergo Alexandri verti commentarios; nequiquam me doctus magister per ἐ'ισαγωγὴν Porphyrii introduxit ad logicam.[24]

Jerome attempts to emphasize the monk's profound want of literary culture in comparison with his own by mingling Greek amidst his Latin. By hurling at him the epithet *Plautinae familiae columen* he probably is insinuating a comparison between his enemy and the disreputable characters of Roman comedy. And yet the phrase may perhaps have a further significance. The adjective *plautus* was frequently applied to dogs. We read in Festus: *Plauti appellantur canes, quorum aures languidae sunt*

[24] Letter 50. 1.

ac flaccidae et latius videntur patere.[25] Jerome has succeeded in including two insults in the one phrase *Plautinae familiae columen.* He continues the comparison of his critic to a dog by alluding to *canina eloquentia,* which probably signifies senseless growling.[26] Jerome's irony becomes even more penetrating as he continues to scoff at his opponent's supposed learning:

Inventus est homo absque praeceptore perfectus, πνευματοφόρος καὶ θεοδίδακτος, qui eloquentia Tullium, argumentis Aristotelen, prudentia Platonem, eruditione Aristarchum, multitudine librorum χαλκέντερον Didymum, scientia scripturarum omnes sui temporis vincat tractatores. Denique dicitur materiam poscere, et Carneadeum aliquid referens in utramque partem, hoc est et pro iustitia et contra iustitiam, disputare. Liberatus est mundus de periculo, et hereditariae vel centumvirales causae de barathro erutae, quod hic forum neglegens se ad ecclesiam transtulit. Quis hoc nolente fuisset innoxius? quem criminosum non huius servasset oratio, cum coepisset in digitos partiri causam et syllogismorum suorum retia tendere? nam si adplosisset pedem, intendisset oculos, rugasset frontem, iactasset manum, verba tornasset, tenebras ilico ante oculos iudicibus offudisset.[27]

Later Jerome turns upon his enemy's verbosity:

Non est grande, mi Domnion, garrire per angulos et medicorum tabernas ac de mundo ferre sententias: "hic bene dixit, ille male; iste scripturas novit, ille delirat; iste loquax, ille infantissimus est." Ut de omnibus iudicet cuius hoc iudicio meruit? contra quemlibet passim in triviis strepere et congerere maledicta, non crimina, scurrarum est et paratorum semper ad lites. . . . Det nobis occasionem respondendi disertitudini suae. Possum remordere, si velim, possum genuinum laesus infigere; et nos didicimus litterulas, "et nos saepe

---

[25] Paul. ex Fest., 231; Lindsay's ed. (Leipzig, 1913), 259. In *Casina,* 34, Plautus alludes to his canine name: *Plautus cum latranti nomine.*

[26] This is a common phrase in Jerome's invective. Süss, "Hieron. u. die Formen," 221, justly says, "Durch allzu häufige Wiederholung geschädigt hat Hier, die *canina eloquentia* aus den Historien des Sallust."

[27] Letter 50. 2.

manum ferulae subtraximus," de nobis quoque dici potest: "faenum habet in cornu, longe fuge."[28]

Jerome's penchant for replying to his enemies' objections by charging them with the grossest moral crimes is illustrated in this letter. A man who could be shameless enough to criticize Jerome must necessarily be a seducer of women:

> Audio praeterea eum libenter virginum et viduarum cellulas cir- cumire, et adducto supercilio de sacris inter eas litteris philosophari. Quid in secreto, quid in cubiculo mulierculas docet? ut hoc sciant esse virgines quod maritas, ut florem aetatis non neglegant, ut come- dant et bibant, ut balneas adeant, munditias adpetant, unguenta non spernant? an magis pudicitiam et ieiunia et inluviem corporis? utique illa praecipit quae plena virtutis sunt: fateatur ergo publice quod domi loquitur, aut si et domi eadem docet quae publice, a puellarum consortio separandus est. Non erubescere iuvenem et monachum et, ut sibi videtur, disertum . . . lustrare nobilium domos, haerere salutationibus matronarum, religionem nostram pugnam facere et fidem Christi contentione torquere verborum, atque inter haec fratri suo detrahere![29]

We would learn much about St. Jerome's methods of satire if we could discover whether he had indeed heard these allegations of immorality brought against his critic. In a letter addressed to Domnio, Jerome would probably not have used the word *audio* if Domnio himself in his previous letter had actually described the immorality of Jerome's critic. *Audio* implies another source of such information, aside from Domnio. But there is no indica- tion anywhere in this letter that Jerome even knew of the

---

[28] Letter 50. 5. The last sentence contains references to Persius 1. 115, Juvenal 1. 15, and Horace *Sat.* i. 4. 34. For a fuller discussion of this passage, see below, p. 253. For other references to the empty loquacity of this critic of Jerome, see Letter 50. 4: *Est quippe proverbium balbum melius balbi verba cognoscere* (cf. Otto, *Sprich. der Röm.*, 50) and Letter 50. 4, the imaginary and ironic words of protest put by Jerome into the mouth of Jovinianus: *In tantam opinionem venit eloquentiae, ut soleant dicta eius cirratorum esse dictata* (reference to Persius 1. 29).

[29] Letter 50. 3. For *adducto supercilio*, see Persius 3. 82.

existence of his anonymous critic from any source except Domnio's earlier letter. If other acquaintances of the critic had in fact described to Jerome the man's immoral behavior, Jerome would surely have said so openly and clearly. But he avoids doing so. Thus we may well conjecture that the whole account of his antagonist's dissipation was invented by Jerome himself. In spite of the probably fictitious nature of the charge of wanton behavior, Jerome repeats it toward the end of the letter, calling his antagonist an impious Epicurus, a sybaritic Aristippus, a grunting, pregnant sow.[30]

Thus far we have seen St. Jerome replying to particular detractors who remain unnamed. More often he scatters his anonymous shafts at his critics in general. In replying to adversaries who opposed his scholarly labors as destructive of tradition, he compares himself to Terence, for the comic poet was forced in the prologues of his plays to defend the products of his pen: *Urguebat enim eum Luscius Lanuinus, nostro Luscio similis, et quasi publici aerarii poetam furem criminabatur.*[31] Jerome goes on to say, in a tone of self-pity, that Vergil too and Cicero had been attacked by enemies: "It is not surprising that filthy sows grunt against me, an insignificant little man, and crush pearls beneath their feet, since malice has blazed forth against the most learned of men whose glory ought to have been proof against envy."[32] Evidently Jerome liked to think of him-

[30] Letter 50. 5. On Epicurus and Aristippus cf. Letter 33. 6.

[31] *Praefat. in Librum Hebraicarum quaestionum in Genesim,* PL 23, 983. Cf. the prologue to Terence's *Andria.* Vallarsi reads *Lanuinus* instead of the more usual *Lanuvinus.* Jerome is probably here attacking his enemies in general, not an individual. In the preface to the twelfth book of the commentary on Isaiah, Jerome again refers to Luscius Lanuinus. Cavallera (II, 113) conjectures that Rufinus is there meant. However, the earlier reference cannot be to Rufinus because at the time of the *Lib. Heb. quaest.* (389–392) the controversy with Rufinus had not yet broken out.

[32] PL 23, 983A–B. Cf. Letter 119. 11; *Cur me lacerant inimici mei, et adversum silentem crassae sues grunniunt?*

self as a latter-day Terence, for he makes the comparison frequently. On one occasion he does so indirectly; W. Süss has pointed out that, in the preface to the second book of the commentary on Micah, Jerome refers no less than six times, without any acknowledgment, to the prologues of Terence's plays:

Semper invidis respondemus, quia non cessat invidia, et librorum nostrorum exordia aemulorum maledicta confutant. . . . Moneo autem tauros pingues, qui circumdederunt me, ut quiescant et desinant maledicere, malefacta ne noscant sua, quae proferentur post, si pergent laedere. Nam quod dicunt, Origenis me volumina compilare, et contaminari non decere veterum scripta: quod illi maledictum vehemens esse existimant, eamdem laudem ego maximam duco, cum illum imitari volo, quem cunctis prudentibus et vobis placere non dubito. Si enim criminis est Graecorum benedicta transferre, accusetur Ennius et Maro, Plautus, Caecilius et Terentius, Tullius quoque. . . . Quorum omnium aemulari exopto neglegentiam, potius quam istorum obscuram diligentiam.[33]

Malefacta ne noscant is borrowed from *Andria*, 23; *quae proferentur post si pergent laedere*, from *Eunuchus*, 18; *contaminari non decere*, from *Andria*, 16; *quod illi . . . placere non dubito*, from *Adelphi*, 17–19; and *obscura diligentia*, from *Andria*, 21.[34]

St. Jerome's vitriolic ridicule of his personal enemies represents a perfect fulfillment of the rhetorical rule laid down by the *auctor ad Herennium:*

From the discussion of the person of our adversaries we shall secure goodwill by bringing them into hatred, unpopularity, or contempt. We shall force hatred upon them by adducing some base, high-handed, treacherous, cruel, impudent, malicious, or shameful act of theirs. . . . We shall bring our adversaries into contempt by

[33] *PL* 25, 1189C–1190C.

[34] Süss, "Hieron. u. die Formen," 232. In two passages Jerome employs against his enemies an accusation brought against Terence by his foes, *de Graecis bonis Latina facere non bona*, *Praefat, in Lib. Didymi de Spir. Sanct.*, *PL* 23, 108A (against Ambrose); and *Comm. in Osee*, *PL* 25, 860A.

presenting their idleness, cowardice, sloth, and luxurious habits.[35]

Jerome's critics are of course lazy and avaricious. "Since Holy Scripture contains the sum of all knowledge," says Jerome,

miror quosdam exstitisse, qui aut ipsi se inertiae et somno dantes, nolint quae praeclara sunt discere, aut caeteros, qui id studii habent, reprehendendos putent. Quibus cum possim districtius respondere, et breviter eos vel offensos dimittere, vel placatos, multo esse melius Scripturas legere, quam augendis et cumulandis opibus inhiare. . . .[36]

The opponents of Jerome's scholarly work on the text of the Bible are furthermore, not unexpectedly, gluttons: "Most perverse of men! While they are constantly seeking out new lusts, and the treasures of neighboring seas do not suffice their gullet, in the study of Scripture alone are they satisfied with old flavor."[37] But Jerome has no hatred for his enemies: *Quibus non invideo, si tantum amant terram ut in regno Christi terrena desiderent: et post ciborum abundantiam gulaeque ac ventris ingluviem, ea quae sub ventre sunt quaerant.*[38] Why indeed should he hate *umbras larvarum, quarum natura esse dicitur, terrere parvulos, et in angulis garrire tenebrosis?*[39] Jerome can scorn the so-called learning of his carping critics whose talk is nothing but garrulous mumbling (*mussitationem garrulam*), who think they have tongues for only one purpose, *ut proximos lacerent, et duritiam frontis attritae verborum rabie consolantur.*[40] Against his personal enemies Jerome hurls many of the same terms of opprobrium drawn from the animal kingdom which he had cast at the heretics. His opponents are serpents

---

[35] *Ad Herennium* i. v. 8. The translation is H. Caplan's in the Loeb ed.

[36] *Praefat. in Comm. in Epist. ad Eph.*, PL 26, 468C–469A. Cf. *Praefat. in Lib. Heb. quaest.*, PL 23, 984A–B: *Sic et illi [aemuli] noverint, non posse se notitiam Scripturarum, id est, divitias Christi, cum mundi pariter habere divitiis.* The text reads *notitia* but *notitiam* seems required.

[37] *Contra Ruf.* ii. 31, PL 23, 475A.   [38] *Comm. in Isa.*, PL 24, 651C.

[39] *Praefat. in Lib. Heb. quaest.*, PL 23, 986B.

[40] *Comm. in Isa.*, PL 24, 325A.

and scorpions beside whom he must walk.[41] One of them, who is unidentified, keeps hissing that Jerome is a plagiarist.[42] Such foes are also dogs who cannot cease barking.[43]

There is plainly very little originality or satiric freshness in this ridicule and abuse. Once Jerome has seized upon an image he is extremely loath to let it go. His enemies are lampooned time and time again for their *adducta supercilia* and *concrepantes digitos,* for their interest in *ventrem et quae sub ventre sunt,* and for their insatiable passion for gold. Jerome draws upon vividly sensuous and physical imagery to portray his enemies, but he has a tendency to apply the same abusive terms to all.

The question arises here why Jerome so often ill-uses his enemies without stating their names. We may feel certain that on many such occasions the enemy in question was a person of power and influence who might easily strike back against open satire. The important position of "Onasus" has been conjectured from his relationship to Cicero's Onasus Segestanus. St. Silvia and, as we shall see, St. Ambrose, both of whom would have been dangerous enemies, are also lampooned anonymously. H. Hagendahl goes so far as to say, "the insidious way of attacking a person without mentioning his name is characteristic of Jerome's polemic."[44] We shall see, however, in the following section that this statement is an exaggeration, for Jerome did not hesitate to abuse openly and by name many of his less influential antagonists.

---

[41] *Ibid., PL* 24, 652C–653A. Cf. Ezek. 2:6: "And thou . . . be not afraid . . . though . . . thou dwell among scorpions." Cf. also *PL* 24, 362D–363A: *Audio praeterea scorpionem, mutum animal et venenatum, nuper . . . nescio quid mussitare.* Cf. also *Comm. in Zach., PL* 25, 1498C.

[42] *Comm. in Osee, PL* 25, 820A; *Comm. in Mic., PL* 25, 1154A: *Lernaea bestia saeviente.*

[43] *Contra Ruf.* ii. 30 (*PL* 23, 474C); *Praefat. in Lib. Samuelis, PL* 29, 604A.

[44] Hagendahl, *Latin Fathers,* 115.

Jovinianus

St. Jerome did not know Jovinianus personally, but the heretic's views on the equal worth of marriage and virginity and his depreciation of extreme fasting were so serious a threat to his own cherished principles that he may well have felt a personal hatred for him.[45] As soon as he had begun to read Jovinianus' antiascetic writings, "il sentit s'éveiller sa verve satirique" (Cavallera, I, 157). Jovinianus' opposition to monastic practices exposed him to attack as *Epicurum nostrum subantem in hortulis suis inter adulescentulos et mulierculas.*[46] Jerome's elaborate description of Jovinianus' debauchery deserves to be quoted in its entirety. He begins with a quotation from the New Testament (II Peter 3: 3): *Venient enim in novissimis diebus illusores seducentes, iuxta propria desideria ambulantes.* Jerome then continues:

Descripsit sermo apostolicus Iovinianum loquentem buccis tumentibus et inflata verba trutinantem, repromittentem in coelis libertatem, cum ipse servus sit vitiorum atque luxuriae, canis revertens ad vomitum suum. Nam cum monachum esse se iactitet: et post sordidam tunicam, et nudos pedes, et cibarium panem, et aquae potum, ad candidas vestes, et nitidam cutem, ad mulsum et elaboratas carnes, ad iura Apitii et Paxami, ad balneas quoque ac fricticulas,

[45] Jovinianus' other heretical views are corollaries of the first two: (*a*) that the baptized cannot be tempted by the devil and (*b*) that all good Christians receive equal recompense in heaven. St. Augustine attacked Jovinianus in *De bono coniugali;* St. Ambrose's Letter XLII (*PL* 17, 1123–1129) is also devoted to denouncing him. The authoritative modern work is W. Haller's *Iovinianus, die Fragmente seiner Schriften . . . sein Leben u. seine Lehre*, in Gebhardt and Harnack, *Texte und Untersuchungen*, XVII, no. 2 (Leipzig, 1897). J. Forget in *Dictionnaire de Théologie Catholique*, s.v. *Jovinien*, takes Jerome's lampoon as a literal and accurate picture of Jovinianus. Grützmacher gives a balanced account in Schaff-Herzog, *Encyclopedia of Religious Knowledge*, s.v. Jovinianus.

[46] *Adv. Iovin.* ii. 30 (*PL* 23, 340A). Cf. i. 1 (*PL* 23, 221A): *Epicurum Christianorum.* Cf. also *Comm. in Ezech., PL* 25, 115A: Jovinianus and others like him are *libidinis doctores.*

et popinas se conferat, manifestum est, quod terram coelo, vitia virtutibus, ventrem praeferat Christo, et purpuram coloris eius putet regna coelorum. Et tamen iste formosus monachus, crassus, nitidus, dealbatus, et quasi sponsus semper incedens, aut uxorem ducat, ut aequalem virginitatem nuptiis probet: aut si non duxerit, frustra contra nos verbis agit, cum opere nobiscum sit.[47]

This portrayal is made up of a typical mélange of pagan and Christian elements. Jerome again borrows his favorite line of Persius, the centurion's portrayal of philosophers:

> Atque exporrecto trutinantur verba labello [3. 82].

The picture of the dog returning to its vomit is taken from Proverbs 26: 11:

> Sicut canis qui revertitur ad vomitum suum
> sic imprudens qui iterat stultitiam suam.

In describing Jovinianus' *nitidam cutem*, Jerome was thinking of Horace, *Epistle* i. 4. 15–16:

> Me pinguem et nitidum bene curata cute vises
> cum ridere voles, Epicuri de grege porcum.[48]

The adjective *dealbatus* recalls Jesus' description of the Pharisees as *similes dealbatis sepulcris* (Matthew 23: 27). This list of references will help again to illustrate how in his satiric descriptions Jerome assists his own imagination by plucking brief but vividly colored phrases from both pagan and biblical sources.

We should not, however, imagine that Jerome confines his ridicule of Jovinianus' voluptuousness to one descriptive passage alone. Later in the work, after he has adduced an example of pagan austerity and abstemiousness, he contrasts the sybaritic heretic and his followers:

---

[47] *Adv. Iovin.* i. 40 (*PL* 23, 280A–B).
[48] This very line of Horace is employed against the followers of Jovinianus in *Adv. Iovin.* ii. 12 (*PL* 23, 315B).

Unius tantum philosophi exemplum posui, ut formosuli nostri et torosuli, et vix summis pedibus abumbrantes vestigia, quorum verba in pugnis sunt et syllogismi in calcibus, qui paupertatem Apostolorum et crucis duritiam aut nesciunt aut contemnunt, imitentur saltem gentilium parcitatem.[49]

Here we have a capsule description of little men at once effeminate and quarrelsome, sensualists walking mincingly on their toes, yet ready for a fight. It is possible however that Vallarsi's reading *torosulus* (little and muscular) should be changed to *trossulus*, which is indeed the reading of the manuscripts. *Trossulus* is a word used by Persius (1. 82) to describe effeminate dandies, and Jerome employs this adjective in another passage to lampoon a young and foppish clergyman—*iuvenem non quidem comatum, non vestium sericarum, sed trossulum et in sordibus delicatum.*[50]

Although Jerome had never set eyes upon Jovinianus, he is able to describe his physical appearance in detail. "When you were a true monk," he says to Jovinianus,

Ante nudo eras pede: modo non solum calceato, sed et ornato. Tum pexa tunica et nigra subucula vestiebaris, sordidatus, et pallidus, et callosam opere gestitans manum: nunc lineis et sericis vestibus, et Atrebatum ac Laodiceae indumentis ornatus incedis. Rubent buccae, nitet cutis, comae in occipitium et frontem tornantur: protensus est aqualiculus, insurgunt humeri, turget guttur et de obesis faucibus vix suffocata verba promuntur.[51]

The phrase *pexa tunica* is derived from Horace, *Epistle* i. 1. 95–6:

> si forte subucula pexae
> trita subest tunicae.

---

[49] *Adv. Iovin.* ii. 14 (*PL* 23, 319A). Cf. also ii. 37: *Habes praeterea in exercitu plures succenturiatos, habes scurras et velites in praesidiis, crassos, comptos, nitidos, clamatores, qui te pugnis calcibusque defendant.*

[50] Letter 117. 8. Cf. Seneca *Epist.* 76. 2 and 87. 9.

[51] *Adv. Iovin.* ii. 21 (*PL* 23, 329B).

But either Jerome's memory has failed him or he has adapted Horace's words to his own purposes, for Horace uses the word *pexa* to mean elegant and unsoiled, but in Jerome's burlesque of Jovinianus the word means the opposite, soiled.[52] *Protensus aqualiculus* in this passage is of course taken from Persius 1. 57. The whole portrayal serves again to highlight the artificiality which pervades Jerome's satire. It is impossible to say that such a description reveals Jerome's power of observation, first because he has not in fact observed Jovinianus, and secondly because so many of the striking phrases are either borrowed from other writers (Horace and Persius) or are found elsewhere in Jerome's writings.[53] An important point must, however, be made in defense of Jerome's satiric originality: obviously he could not lampoon Jovinianus on the basis of personal experience. Hence he was reduced to repeating those phrases of his own which he had used elsewhere and to borrowing from pagan satirists.

It can be shown that on some occasions when Jerome does actually come into contact with his personal enemies he is able to satirize them with greater originality and inventiveness. To illustrate this we may quote from his vignette of the immoral deacon Sabinianus, who had lived for a time at Jerome's monastery:

Amiciris linteis, digitos anulis oneras, dentes pulvere teris; raros in rubenti calvaria digeris capillos, taurina cervix toris adipeis intumescens nec, quia fracta est, inclinatur. Super haec unguentis flagras, mutas balneas et contra renascentes pilos pugnas; per forum ac plateas nitidus et politus amator incedis.[54]

There are of course trite elements even in this passage: the ac-

[52] Cf. the reference to Jovinianus' *sordida tunica* (*Adv. Iovin.* i. 40). To the mind of the ascetic, of course, dirt is praiseworthy, and that is Jerome's meaning here.

[53] For *rubent buccae*, cf. *Comm. in Mic.*, PL 25, 1172A–C (*rubentes buccas*). For *nitet cutis*, cf. *Adv. Iovin.* i. 40 (*nitidam cutem*).

[54] Letter 147. 8. On the identity of Sabinianus, see Grützmacher, III, 151–153.

cusations that Sabinianus wears linen and walks *nitidus* through the street. Yet most of the brilliant details of the parody are found only here: the description of Sabinianus scrubbing his teeth, arranging his sparse hairs over his ruddy scalp, and constantly using depilatories. When Jerome was able to use his own observations as the basis of his description, the worn-out phrases disappear and his satire comes alive.

In describing Jovinianus, Jerome uses pagan sources to expose his adversary's ignorance:

Verum scriptorum tanta barbaries est, et tantis vitiis spurcissimus sermo confusus, ut nec quid loquatur, nec quibus argumentis velit probare quod loquitur, potuerim intelligere. Totus enim tumet, totus iacet: attollit se per singula, et quasi debilitatus coluber, in ipso conatu frangitur. Non est contentus nostro, id est, humano more loqui, altius quiddam agreditur.

> Parturiunt montes, nascetur ridiculus mus.
>
> Quod ipse,
>
> Non sani esse hominis, non sanus iuret Orestes.

Praeterea sic involvit omnia et quibusdam inextricabilibus nodis universa perturbat, ut illud Plautinarum litterarum ei possit aptari:

> Has quidem praeter Sibyllam leget nemo.[55]

Thus Jerome supports his ridicule of the heretic's ignorance by citing in rapid succession Horace (*Ars P.* 139), Persius (3. 118), and Plautus (*Pseudolus* I. 1. 25). Soon thereafter, Jerome prefaces an excerpt from Jovinianus' writings with the words, *exordium, quod hesternam crapulam ructans ita evomuit*—abusive terminology derived from Cicero.[56] After considering the out-

---

[55] *Adv. Iovin.* i. 1 (*PL* 23, 221A). For a further development of the snake image here adumbrated, cf. *Adv. Iovin.* i. 3: *Proponam breviter adversarii sententias, et de tenebrosis libris eius quasi de foveis serpentes protraham. . . .* Also *ibid.*, 1. 4: *Haec sunt sibila serpentis antiqui;* ii. 21: *Simulque miror, quomodo serpens lubricus et Proteus noster, in variarum se mutet portenta formarum.*

[56] *Phil.* v. 7. 20. Cf. also *Adv. Iovin.* i. 4: *Nec molestum lectori sit, si nauseam eius et vomitum legere compellatur.*

worn phrases of invective and the evil-tongued scurrility with
which Jerome seeks to overcome the arguments of Jovinianus,
the reader may find it difficult to agree with Cavallera's judgment of this polemic as "l'oeuvre la plus brilliante et l'une des
plus soigneés de Saint Jérôme."[57]

Vigilantius

The late fourth century was an age of vigorous intellectual
controversy, a time in which the greatest importance was given
to the ability effectively to defend one's own theological opinions
and cogently to refute conflicting views. It was inevitable, then,
that intellectual disagreement should frequently lead to personal
quarrels and, conversely, that personal dislike should stimulate
intellectual debate. Nothing better illustrates this close connection between intellectual disagreement and personal conflict
than the numerous disputes in which St. Jerome became embroiled. In his angry clash with the monk Vigilantius it is impossible to ascertain whether personal or doctrinal disagreement
first set the two churchmen against each other. Vigilantius was
a Gallic monk who, on the recommendation of Paulinus of Nola,
had been hospitably received at Jerome's Bethlehem monastery.[58]
During his stay there unpleasantness developed between him
and Jerome, which may have been in part the result of an amusing scandal of which Jerome had refused to speak for many
years—*ne laedere quempiam videar*, as he claims—but which he
dragged up at the time of his open battle against Vigilantius'

---

[57] Cavallera, I, 157.

[58] The year was 395. On Vigilantius, see Gennadius, *De vir. ill.*, ed.
E. C. Richardson, in Gebhardt and Harnack, *Texte und Untersuchungen*,
XIV, no. 1 (Leipzig, 1896), 74: *Scripsit et ipse zelo quidem aliquo, sed
fictus humana laude et praesumens supra vires suas.* See also A. Réville,
Vigilance de Calagurris (Paris, 1902); G. Bardy, in *Dictionnaire de
Théologie Catholique*, XV, cols. 2992–2994; Fliche and Martin, *Histoire
de l'Eglise*, III, 362. There has been some dispute as to whether Vigilan-
tius' home was the Gallic or the Spanish Calagurris.

theological theories. In the middle of the night a sudden earthquake shook the monastery, and Vigilantius, seized by fear, ran from his cell in a state of indecent undress which Jerome compares to that of Adam and Eve:

Tu et tunica et fide nudus . . . et aliquid habens nocturnae crapulae sanctorum oculis obscenam partem corporis ingerebas, ut tuam indicares prudentiam.[59]

Jerome may have strongly rebuked Vigilantius for such immodesty, for when the monk departed from Bethlehem the enmity between them was open.

Not long afterward Jerome heard that Vigilantius was accusing him in Rome of being a follower of the Origenist heresy. Jerome's reply (Letter 61) is a typical document of satiric exposure. He begins by ridiculing his adversary's intellectual failings: "To you alone, wisest of skulls, is it permitted to bear judgement on all Greek and Latin writers and like a censor's rod to drive out some from the library and accept others." *Non parum est scire quod nescias; prudentis hominis est nosse mensuram suam, nec zelo diaboli concitatum imperitiae suae cunctum orbem testem facere.*[60] But to Jerome's mind intellectual faults are inevitably accompanied by moral weaknesses:

Aliud a parva aetate didicisti, aliis adsuetus es disciplinis. Non est eiusdem hominis et aureos nummos et scripturas probare, degustare vina, et prophetos vel apostolos intellegere. . . . Postquam navigare coepisti, et ad intimum cerebrum tuum sentinae putredo pervenit, tunc nos haereticos recordatus es.[61]

The references above to wine and money have been explained as a slur on the profession of Vigilantius' father, who was an innkeeper. This is a likely interpretation, for the disparagement of an opponent's trade or that of his relatives is a traditional form

---

[59] *Contra Vig.* 11 (*PL* 23, 364B). Cf. Jerome's careful reticence in Letter 58. 11.

[60] Letter 61. 2 and 3.   [61] Letter 61. 3.

of abuse. Aristophanes had mocked Euripides for having a mother who was, he claimed, a vegetable seller. Tertullian used the profession of the heretic Hermogenes, who was a painter, and that of Marcion, a ship's captain, as a basis for ridicule.[62] The rhetorician Aphthonius recognizes the lampoon of an adversary's origins as an essential element of the correctly composed *vituperatio*.[63] Jerome employs another traditional form of attack when he writes to Vigilantius: *Ego reor et nomen tibi* κατὰ ἀντίφρασιν *inpositum. Nam tota mente dormitas, et profundissimo non tam somno stertis quam lethargo*.[64] Jerome is here punning on the name of Vigilantius by calling him sleepy. Cicero recognizes puns on personal names as an acceptable form of humor, and he himself uses the porcine associations of the name Verres to abuse his opponent.[65] Such wordplay is one of Jerome's favorite forms of ridicule; he uses the names Jovinianus, Macarius, and Melania as the basis for insulting remarks.[66] Jerome's play on the name Vigilantius, however, loses much of its force through ceaseless repetition. Time and time again he refers to Vigilantius as Dormitantius, eventually exhausting the joke of whatever humor it originally contained.[67]

Jerome concludes his letter with a shockingly severe remark. After taking Vigilantius harshly to task for an allegedly blasphemous misinterpretation of a biblical passage, Jerome suggests that the blasphemer's tongue should be cut out and chopped into little bits and pieces. Jerome continues: *Meam iniuriam*

---

[62] Süss, "Hieron. u. die Formen," 227–228.

[63] *Progymnasmata*, IX, 275, in R. Nadeau's trans.   [64] Letter 61. 4.

[65] Cicero defends the use of this type of pun in *De oratore* ii. 249.

[66] See above, p. 205, on Onasus. The name Jovinianus is ridiculed by Jerome for its pagan associations: *Cave Ioviniani nomen, quod de idolo derivatium est* (*Adv. Iovin.* ii. 38; PL 23, 352B). Cf. also Letter 127. 9, where he reveals that Rufinus' friend *Macarius*, "the happy one," is a source of *unhappiness*, and Letter 133. 3. 5, where Melania is mocked for the black sound of her name.

[67] Letter 109. 1 and 3; *Contra Vig.* 1 (PL 23, 355A) and 6 (PL 23, 360A).

patienter tuli: inpietatem contra Deum ferre non potui, unde et visus sum mordacius in extrema epistula scribere quam promiseram.[68] In this passage Jerome passes suddenly from attacking Vigilantius as a personal enemy to denouncing him as a foe of God. Jerome was eager to enlist God on his own side in his private quarrels. Although at the time of this letter Vigilantius had not yet propounded those heretical views for which he later became well known, Jerome wished to stigmatize Vigilantius as not only obnoxious to himself but also as offensive to God.

The dispute between Jerome and Vigilantius which had begun as a quarrel of personalities was now well on its way to becoming an intellectual debate between representatives of two religious points of view. The next document of the struggle reveals its intellectual aspect as more fully developed. Nine years had passed since the previous epistolary attack on Vigilantius, when St. Jerome received the news from his friend Riparius that his old opponent had now adopted antiascetic views and was rejecting the cult of martyrs, the veneration of relics, the custom of night-long vigils, and prayers to the saints.[69] To personal dislike of Vigilantius, Jerome could now add anger at his heterodox opinions. This combination was almost too much for Jerome to bear: the gates of abusive satire stood wide open. "You say," writes Jerome to Riparius, "that Dormitantius has again opened his stinking mouth and emitted some foul putrescence against relics of the martyrs. The pitiful Samaritan and Jew! His brain is crazed! His views are nothing but stupid dreams, or rather the belching forth of his repulsive drunkenness.[70] He is a monster (*portentum*) whose tongue should be cut out."[71] After drawing this caricature Jerome has at least the grace to suspect that such

[68] Letter 61. 4.
[69] Protestants have exalted Vigilantius as the precursor of their own views (Cavallera, I, 307, n. 3).
[70] Letter 109. 1.
[71] Letter 109. 2. Jerome makes the same grim suggestion in Letter 61. 4.

repulsive vilification might be thought in bad taste, for he says to Riparius, "You might perhaps chide me in the silence of your thoughts for inveighing against someone behind his back."[72] Yet objections of this nature had in fact no influence on him at all. In this letter Jerome declares himself ready to forge a shaft which will pierce the beast to the quick.[73]

Upon receiving a full account of Vigilantius' errors, Jerome approached the task of refuting him with such alacrity that in a single night he composed the poisonous libel known as *Contra Vigilantium*.[74] The briefness of the time in which Jerome wrote it necessitated drawing upon standard material already used in other contexts. There is scarcely a satiric portrait or cutting expression in this work which cannot be found elsewhere in Jerome's writings. But he does begin his invective with one of the most grotesquely exaggerated of his monster images:

Cerberum et Stymphalidas, aprumque Erymanthium, et leonem Nemaeum, chimaeram atque hydram multorum capitum narrant fabulae poetarum. Cacum describit Vergilius. Triformem Geryonem Hispaniae prodiderunt. Sola Gallia monstra non habuit, sed viris semper fortibus et eloquentissimis abundavit. Exortus est subito Vigilantius, seu verius Dormitantius, qui immundo spiritu pugnat contra Christi spiritum.[75]

Immediately after this vituperation Jerome turns in his usual manner to his enemy's moral delinquency:

Hic Romanae Ecclesiae auctoritate damnatus, inter Phasides aves et carnes suillas non tam emisit spiritum, quam eructavit. Iste caupo Calagurritanus, et in perversum propter nomen viculi mutus

[72] Letter 109. 3.   [73] Letter 109. 4.
[74] See *Contra Vig.* 17 (*PL* 23, 368A–B): *Haec . . . unius noctis lucubratione dictavi.*
[75] *Contra Vig.* 1 (*PL* 23, 355A). These monsters frequently appear in Jerome's abusive passages, but never so many in one piece of invective. The tone of this passage is quite Ciceronian.

Quintilianus miscet aquam vino . . . dum inter phialas philosophatur, et ad placentas liguriens, psalmorum modulatione mulcetur.[76]

Jerome is here re-using material from Letter 109. We had learned there that Vigilantius, if not himself an innkeeper (*caupo*), at least had relatives who were. We are also told there that Vigilantius' writings were emitted in unseemly fashion from his mouth. Moreover the *Phasides aves* here mentioned are Jerome's standard symbol of gluttony.[77] The phrase *miscet aquam vino* comes from *Isaiah* 1:22 and has a double significance: the expression is frequently used by Christian writers to describe the dilution of the wine of true religion with the water of heresy, but Jerome also intends it as a slur on the profession of Vigilantius' father.[78] In addition, Vigilantius is a "dumb Quintilian" because he has pretensions to eloquence and because his native town, the Aquitanian Calagurris, has the same name as Quintilian's Spanish birthplace.

Later in the work Jerome inserts another standard piece of satire. Vigilantius had used a spurious passage from the Bible to support his doctrines. Commenting on this, Jerome says:

Si tibi placuerit, legito fictas revelationes omnium patriarcharum et prophetarum; et cum illas didiceris, inter mulierum textrinas cantato, imo legendas propone in tabernis tuis, ut facilius per has naenias vulgus indoctum provoces ad bibendum.[79]

Like many of Jerome's other enemies Vigilantius is a dandy who can be found among the looms of matrons. We may compare an expression Jerome had used in a letter written about ten

[76] *PL* 23, 355B–C.
[77] See above, p. 43. Cf. *Contra Vig.* 3: *libros . . . quos inter crapulam stertens evomuit.* Also *Adv. Iovin.* i. 1: *quod hesternam crapulam ructans, ita evomuit.*
[78] Cf. Tertullian *De Anima.* 3. 2 (*CC* 2, 785) and Vallarsi's note, *PL* 23, 356.
[79] *PL* 23, 360C. *Textrinas* should probably be corrected to *textrina*.

years before the tract against Vigilantius. Referring to Rufinus, Jerome complains, *inter muliercularum radios et textrina dilanior.*[80] The repetition of such expressions reveals how little Jerome's satiric language changed or developed with time.

We have frequently seen how fond Jerome is of drawing grotesque physical caricatures of his adversaries. Vigilantius too is treated in this manner. Jerome compares him to the pagan god Liber Pater, *pro ebrietate et cantharo ex humeris dependente, et semper rubente facie, et spumantibus labiis, effrenatisque conviciis.*[81] If one read only this work of Jerome, one might think he is here lampooning the actual physical appearance of Vigilantius. In truth Jerome has simply dipped into his well-filled bag of satirically descriptive phrases and come up with details used elsewhere with greater effect. We may compare his portrayal of a drunken clergyman in an earlier work: *ille e diverso . . . trementibus labiis . . . effrenatis conviciis . . . facie inter pallorem ruboremque variata. . . .*[82] In his haste to destroy the venomous serpent Jerome has had to rely upon the vivid phrases coined at a period of greater satiric inventiveness.

Up to the end of this treatise almost all evidence of earlier personal hostility between Jerome and the heretic is suppressed. The only indication of a private quarrel is Jerome's account of Vigilantius' ludicrously indecent behavior at Bethlehem.[83] Jerome's hatred of Vigilantius as his own personal foe appears to have been replaced by his detestation of the enemy of the Church. But at the very end we are sharply reminded that Jerome viewed every attack on orthodoxy as a personal insult and, conversely, held all personal hostility to be a sign of enmity toward God and the Church:

---

[80] Letter 57. 13.   [81] *Contra Vig.* 10, *PL* 23, 364A.

[82] *Comm. in Titum, PL* 26, 601. This work was written about 388, the tract against Vigilantius in 406.

[83] *Contra Vig.* 11 (*PL* 23, 364B).

Quod si Dormitantius in mea rursum maledicta vigilaverit, et eodem ore blasphemo, quo apostolos et martyres lacerat, de me quoque putaverit detrahendum, nequaquam illi brevi lucubratiuncula, sed tota nocte vigilabo, et sociis illius . . . qui nisi tumentes uteros viderint feminarum, maritos earum Christi ministerio arbitrantur indignos.[84]

One could hardly find a better illustration of Jerome's exalted conception of his own position in the Church than his virtual inclusion of himself in the ranks of the apostles and martyrs and his designation of Vigilantius' opposition as blasphemy.

Rufinus

Grim and bitter as Jerome's quarrels with Jovinianus and Vigilantius may appear to us, they were but innocent tiffs in comparison with the lengthy feud between Jerome and Rufinus. A fratricidal conflict between two former friends was naturally more violent than strife between virtual strangers. Jerome himself declares that his battle with Rufinus was more savage than a fight with the gruesome Huns.[85] St. Augustine exclaims, *Quis denique amicus non formidetur, quasi futurus inimicus, si potuit inter Hieronymum et Rufinum hoc quod plangimus exoriri? O misera et miseranda condicio!*[86] The quarrel began in 393 and in spite of superficial reconciliations had not really ended at the time of Rufinus' death in 411. The dispute centered on the heretical views of the great theologian Origen, and Jerome's violence was the direct result of his deep embarrassment.[87] That he, the most vigorous champion of orthodoxy, should be discovered to have unwittingly propagated heresy came as a terrible shock to Jerome. He immediately became entangled in trying to excuse his earlier praise of Origen while slandering the great Alexandrian. Yet try as he might, he was never able to prove

[84] *PL* 23, 368B.   [85] Letter 77. 8.
[86] Letter 110. 6 in the corpus of Jerome's correspondence.
[87] See above, p. 174.

that he had always carefully separated the few good elements from the many bad in Origen's writings.[88] Rufinus, on the other hand, adopted the more honorable position expressed in the phrase, *magistros meos nec accuso nec muto.* In the theologically overheated atmosphere of the late fourth century this spark of disagreement ignited a conflagration as Jerome and Rufinus hurled at each other charges of intellectual dishonesty and moral turpitude.

We deal first with Jerome's satiric assault on Rufinus in his epistles. In the course of the Origenist controversy, St. Jerome had occasion to translate into Latin a letter wherein Epiphanius, Bishop of Salamis in Cyprus, had accused Bishop John of Jerusalem of heretical tendencies. This translation fell into the hands of the partisans of Rufinus, who charged Jerome with having falsified and mistranslated the original document in his own interests. Jerome replied in a long letter addressed to his partisan Pammachius, *De optimo genere interpretandi* (Letter 57), in which he sought to justify his free method of translation.[89] In this epistle Jerome subjects Rufinus to sardonic ridicule.

Quid ais, O columen litterarum et nostrorum temporum Aristarche, qui de universis scriptoribus sententiam feras? ergo frustra tanto tempore studuimus et "saepe manum ferulae subduximus?"[90] egredientes de portu statim inpegimus. Igitur, quia et errasse humanum est et confiteri errorem prudentis, tu quicumque reprehensor es, tu me, obsecro, emenda, praeceptor, et verbum de verbo exprime.[91]

Although Jerome studiously avoids mentioning Rufinus by name, there cannot be any doubt that Rufinus is the object of

[88] See Cavallera, II, n. Q, "Saint Jérôme et Origène."
[89] On the complex circumstances of this letter, see F. X. Murphy, *Rufinus of Aquileia,* 73–75.
[90] Juvenal 1. 15.
[91] Letter 57. 12. Cf. Letter 57. 1: *Ego beatum me in hoc dumtaxat negotio iudico quod apud eruditas aures inperitae linguae responsurus sum.* Also Letter 57. 9: *Haec replico . . . ut reprehensores meos arguam inperitiae.*

this ironic description of literary ignorance. Jerome quotes a correction which Rufinus would have made in his translation and continues:

Haec est Plautina eloquentia, hic lepos Atticus et Musarum, ut dicunt, eloquio, conparandus! Conpletur in me tritum vulgi sermone proverbium: oleum perdit et inpensas qui bovem mittit ad ceroma. Haec non est illius culpa cuius sub persona alius agit tragoediam, sed magistrorum eius, qui illum magna mercede nihil scire docuerunt.[92]

Jerome's pique at the criticism to which his own literary competence had been subjected is clearly visible in these words.

From the following passage it would appear that Rufinus and his followers had charged Jerome with adorning the original letter of Epiphanius with his own rhetorical trumpery. They had alleged that they themselves favored simple and direct language innocent of clever verbal devices. It is probably some such claim which Jerome takes up and perverts into an admission on Rufinus' part of intellectual simplicity and lack of culture:

Nec reprehendo in quolibet Christiano sermonis inperitiam—atque utinam Socraticum illud haberemus: "scio quod nescio" et alterius sapientis: "te ipsum intellige"!—, venerationi mihi semper fuit non verbosa rusticitas sed sancta simplicitas: qui in sermone imitari se dicit apostolos, prius imitetur in vita. Illorum in loquendo simplicitatem excusabat sanctimoniae magnitudo, et syllogismos Aristotelis contortaque Chrysippi acumina resurgens mortuus confutabat.[93]

---

[92] Letter 57. 12. For other examples of the very common proverb, cf. Otto, *Sprich. der Röm.*, 253, s.v. *oleum*. For the last phrase of the passage above, cf. Cicero, *Phil.* ii. 17. 43: *Duo milia iugerum . . . Clodio rhetori assignasti . . . ut populi Romani tanta mercede nihil sapere disceres.* Cf. also *Contra Ruf.* iii. 26: *discipulis tuis, quos magno studio nihil scire docuisti.*

[93] Letter 57. 12. It would appear from Letter 84. 3 that the followers of Rufinus returned the charge of lack of education: *Nec iuxta quorundam praesumptionem ipse me docui*, protests Jerome.

But Jerome cannot confine himself to accusing Rufinus of boorishness and want of education. He insists on believing that his enemies were one and all debauchees, and so he slips almost imperceptibly from deriding Rufinus' rusticity to charging him with sensuality:

Ceterum ridiculum, si quis e nobis inter Croesi opes et Sardanapali delicias de sola rusticitate se iactet, quasi omnes latrones et diversorum criminum rei diserti sint, et cruentos gladios philosophorum voluminibus ac non arborum truncis occulant.[94]

In this sentence Jerome has without warning ceased to employ *rusticitas* in the sense of mental simplicity and instead uses it to mean a simple manner of life. He is saying to Rufinus, "You who live amidst sensuality and wantonness have as much right to boast of your rustic simplicity as murderers have to boast of their learning if they hide their swords behind philosophers' books instead of behind tree trunks." This intricate but trenchant bit of irony is immediately followed by a concluding passage, in which Jerome claims that he can easily wash away any charges brought against him and insists that he will not have anything to do with malicious recriminations.[95]

Throughout the feud with Rufinus, Jerome repeatedly deprecates backbiting and then goes ahead to indulge in malicious personal vilification of his antagonist. It is exactly this kind of hypocrisy against which Rufinus protests in his *Apology*.[96] This conflict between Jerome's earnest pretensions and his actual behavior is clearly reflected in the epistolary handbook on the monastic life (Letter 125), which he wrote for the young Gallic

[94] Letter 57. 12.

[95] Letter 57. 13. Cf. Letter 81. 1, where Jerome repeatedly insists that he will not return Rufinus' evil with evil. In his own *Apology*, Rufinus admits Jerome's claim that he does not return curses for curses. Instead, says Rufinus, Jerome returns insults and curses in exchange for blessings and praise (i. 2).

[96] *PL* 21, 542B. Rufinus' own pretense of avoiding all malice is not fully borne out.

monk Rusticus.[97] One of Jerome's solemn directives is a warning against malicious gossip: "May you malign no man nor think yourself holy by reason of your ill-using others. We often bring accusation against our own behavior and inveigh eloquently against our very own vices, like dumb men judging orators."[98] In his very next words Jerome violates his own precept by thus describing the behavior of one of his carping critics:

Testudineo Grunnius incedebat ad loquendum gradu et per intervalla quaedam vix pauca verba capiebat, ut eum putares singultire, non proloqui. Et tamen, cum mensa posita librorum exposuisset struem, adducto supercilio contractisque naribus ac fronte rugata duobus digitulis concrepabat hoc signo ad audiendum discipulos provocans. Tunc nugas meras fundere et adversum singulos declamare; criticum diceres Longinum censoremque Romanae facundiae notare, quem vellet, et de senatu doctorum excludere. Hic bene nummatus plus placebat in prandiis. Nec mirum, qui multos inescare solitus erat factoque cuneo circumstrepentium garrulorum procedebat in publicum intus Nero, foris Cato, totus ambiguus, ut ex contrariis diversisque naturis unum monstrum novamque bestiam diceres esse conpactam iuxta illud poeticum:

Prima leo, postrema draco, media ipsa chimaera.[99]

This is truly an amazing passage! Jerome preaches against backbiting by painting an acid caricature of a backbiter. There can be no doubt that Jerome is here depicting Rufinus, to whom he repeatedly refers as Grunnius, the grunting pig, an allusion to a character from the popular *Testamentum Porcelli*.[100] The depths of Jerome's hatred of his adversary and his unforgiving nature are well illustrated by this irate libel, for at the time it

[97] On the identity of Rusticus, who appears to have become Bishop of Narbonne and to have corresponded with Pope Leo the Great, see Grützmacher, III, 245.

[98] Letter 125. 18. 1.   [99] Letter 125. 18. 2–3.

[100] Cf. *Comm. in Ezech.*, PL 25, 323A: *Grunniae factionis haeredes, adversum nos latrant*. Note the mixture of animal imagery. Cf. also *Comm. in Jer.*, PL 24, 707A, 825B, 848D, 849A, 889D, 896A.

was written Rufinus had already died.[101] The phrase *intus Nero, foris Cato* and the picture of Rufinus walking abroad amid screeching disciples occur only in this passage, but the rest of the description is a cento of satiric details used by Jerome elsewhere. *Testudineo gradu*, drawn from Plautus' *Aulularia* I. 1. 10, occurs in another satiric portrayal of Rufinus: *Tu qui in Latinis mussitas, et testudineo gradu moveris potius quam incedis.*[102] The same expression is used to lampoon the heavy and arrogant literary style of the heretic Pelagius.[103] The raised eyebrows and the snapping fingers of Rufinus are also found in an earlier mocking reference to him: *Et audet quidam ex eis adducto supercilio et concrepantibus digitis eructare.*[104] In the later passage, however, Jerome reinforces his ridicule by using the diminutive *digitulis*. We may also compare Jerome's depiction of Rufinus in his tract against him as *hominem rugosae frontis adductique supercilii.*[105] Certainly Rufinus was well justified in protesting against Jerome's *venenata lingua* and complaining of the *arma ac tela foecundissimi sui pectoris.*[106]

Another posthumous lampoon of Rufinus, briefer but even more strongly worded, is found in Jerome's *epitaphium* on Marcella (Letter 127). Jerome is describing the commotion Rufinus aroused at Rome by importing the Origenist controversy from the East:

Nec mirum, si in plateis et in foro rerum venalium pictus ariolus stultorum verberet nates et obtorto fuste dentes mordentium quatiat, cum venenata spurcaque doctrina Romae invenerit, quos induceret.[107]

---

[101] Cavallera, II, 54.

[102] *Contra Ruf.* i. 17. The line of verse in the passage quoted above is Lucretius *De rer. nat.* 5. 905.

[103] *Dial. contra Pelag.* iii. 16 (*PL* 23, 614B).   [104] Letter 57. 3.

[105] *Contra Ruf.* i. 13 (*PL* 23, 426A).

[106] Ruf. *Apol.* i. 25 and *PL* 21, 544C.

[107] Letter 127. 9. 2–3. Vallarsi reads *fictus* for *pictus*.

Rufinus is compared to a painted mountebank who goes about the market place trying to attract attention by beating the buttocks of fools and battering the teeth of his critics with a crooked staff. Jerome suggests that the doctrines Rufinus has to sell are worth about as much as the cheap wares of such a quack. Yet here again Jerome is bringing down from his attic a somewhat timeworn satiric painting, for he had already used exactly the same caricature to lampoon Rufinus in an earlier work and had also applied the description to Jovinianus.[108] Jerome realizes the incongruity of maligning a personal enemy in the *epitaphium* for a noble Roman lady, for he fears, *ne . . . videar apud malivolos sub occasione laudis alterius stomachum meum digerere.*[109]

We turn now to Jerome's major attack on Rufinus, his tract *Contra Rufinum.* In the first book Jerome devotes much effort to exposing his adversary's ignorance. In doing so he relies heavily on classical satire:

Praetermitto Graecos, quorum tu iactas scientiam, et dum peregrina sectaris, paene tui sermonis oblitus es: ne veteri proverbio, Sus Minervam docere videar, et in silvam ligna portare. . . . Non eligo quod reprehendam, eligat ipse quod vitio careat. Ne illud quidem Socraticum nosse debuerat: Scio quod nescio:

> Navem agere ignarus navis timet; abrotonum aegro
> non audet, nisi qui didicit, dare. Quod medicorum est,
> promittunt medici: tractant fabrilia fabri.
> Scribimus indocti doctique poemata passim.

Nisi forte se litteras non didicisse iurabit; quos nos illi et absque iuramento perfacile credimus. . . . Vel Graece debes scribere, ut apud homines Graeci sermonis ignaros, aliena scire videaris; vel si Latina tentaveris, ante audire grammaticum, ferulae manum subtrahere. . . . Quamvis Croesos quis spiret et Darios, litterae

---

[108] Cf. *Contra Ruf.* i. 17 (PL 23, 430C) and *Adv. Iovin.* i. 36 (PL 23, 349C).

[109] Letter 127. 10. 4.

marsuppium non sequuntur. Sudoris comites sunt et laboris, sociae ieiuniorum, non saturitatis; continentiae, non luxuriae. . . .

> Cur nescire pudens prave, quam discere malo?

. . . Aliud est, si vulgi lectione contenti doctorum aures despiciunt; et contemnunt illud elogium quo procax imperitia denotatur:

> . . . . . Non tu in triviis, indocte, solebas
> stridenti miserum stipula disperdere carmen?

Quasi non cirratorum turba Milesiarum in Scholis figmenta decantet: et testamentum Suis, Bessorum cachinno, membra concutiat, atque inter scurrarum epulas, nugae istiusmodi frequententur.[110]

In this passage we find three references to Horace (*Sat.* i. 10. 34; *Epist.* ii. 1. 114; and *Ars P.* 88), one to Juvenal (1. 15), one to Persius (1. 29), and one to the *Will of a Pig*, as well as a satiric usage of Vergil, *Eclogue* 3. 26. The reason for Jerome's insertion here of this string of allusions to classical literature is not far to seek: as he lampoons Rufinus' ignorance, he is pointing to his own thorough literary education.[111] Typical of Jerome's malevolence is the suggestion that Rufinus' sensuality and avarice are the chief obstacles to his acquiring an education.

Since Rufinus was the most hated and one of the most feared of his enemies, it was inevitable that Jerome should bring to bear against him some of his most forceful and trenchant satire. Mocking Rufinus' allegedly heretical views on the world to come, Jerome ironically declares: "To be sure, this is our great fear, that we might arrive in heaven without noses or ears, or with our genital parts amputated and cut off, and thus found a city of eunuchs in the celestial Jerusalem."[112] In the third book

---

[110] *Contra Ruf.* i. 17 (PL 23, 420B–430C).

[111] Numerous other references to pagan satire are found throughout the work: *Contra Ruf.* i. 1, *male sarta gratia* (Horace *Epist.* i. 3. 31); i. 13, *audio te Plautino in me sale ludere* (*Ars P.*, 270); iii. 3, *Qui parturis mihi montes criminum* (*Ars P.*, 139); ii. 16, *ad populum phaleras* (Persius 3. 30); ii. 17, *non erit meus, sed tuus* (Martial i. 38. 1–2).

[112] *Contra Ruf.* ii. 5 (PL 23, 447C).

of his tract Jerome insists that his defense against his opponent
will be free of that insane savagery of which, he claims, Rufinus'
own *Apology* is so full.[113] Such brutal malice, he says, befits
only a man who from the one dung heap of his chest (*de uno
pectoris sterquilino*) distills at once the odor of roses and the
stink of rotting corpses.[114] There is no more foul piece of abuse
in all of Jerome's writings than the description of Rufinus which
follows this vilification: so great is Rufinus' purity, *ut ad sudaria
et semicinctia tua demones rugiant.*[115] Jerome makes this comment after he has just denied that he will *insanire contra in-
sanientes et . . . vel falsa, vel vera congerere!* Jerome is fond
of accusing Rufinus of being repellently malodorous. Rufinus
in his own *Apology* had warned Jerome to beware the smell of
his sins. Jerome replies by likening Rufinus to a noisome fuller,
or leather tanner, who has the impudence to warn a perfume
maker to stuff his nostrils when passing his perfumery.[116] Jerome
thinks it best to keep his nostrils tightly closed, "to avoid their
being tortured by the sweet odor of Rufinus' truth and Rufinus'
blessings."[117] "Can you complain," he asks, "if I accuse your
writings of stinking, when you, a church writer, adopt the disgusting behavior seen in comedies and trifle with me like a whore
or a paramour?"[118] Jerome laughs down Rufinus' pretensions
to superior knowledge by quoting the verses of Ennius:

> Tu Maximus ille est
> unus qui nobis scribendo restituis rem.

By replacing *cunctando* of the original with *scribendo* he has
created a piece of cutting irony.[119] Elsewhere Jerome brings to
bear against Rufinus one of his usual satiric techniques, the use

---

[113] Rufinus' *Apology*, although it makes effective sallies, is much less
violent in tone than Jerome's own defense. See Murphy, *Rufinus*, 140–150.
[114] *Contra Ruf.* ii. 42 (*PL* 23, 510B).   [115] *PL* 23, 510C.
[116] *Contra Ruf.* iii. 26 (*PL* 23, 498C).   [117] *Ibid.*
[118] *Ibid.*, iii. 16 (*PL* 23, 490B).   [119] *Ibid.*, iii. 29 (*PL* 23, 501A).

of ridiculing diminutives: his enemy is *religiosulus et sanctulus, supinus et lassulus.* Furthermore he is a *sciolus* who has but an *ingeniolum.*[120]

Jerome's rancor against Rufinus was so bitter that it found expression even in his biblical commentaries, an unusual place for the airing of personal pique. In the commentaries on Nahum and Habakkuk we find Rufinus described as a sybaritic Sardanapalus: *Sibilet igitur excetra et Sardanapalus insultet turpior vitiis quam nomine.*[121] It has been suggested that Jerome's fondness for the insulting appellative Sardanapalus stems from its resemblance in sound to *phallus.*[122] In the light of such remarks we can judge the fairness of Jerome's protest against Rufinus' pun on the name of Jerome's teacher of Hebrew, Bar-Anina, whom Rufinus called Barrabas: *Cavendus homo, et mihi maxime declinandus, ne me repente, dum nescio, de Hieronymo Sardanapalum nomines.*[123] That is, "You, Rufinus, might make an outrageous pun, transforming me from 'the one with the holy name' into a filthy voluptuary."

Jerome's frequent reference to Rufinus as *excetra* has led to the conjecture that he is making a cruelly mocking reference to his former friend when he interprets the *flagellum* of Nahum 3:2 as applying to physical disease:

Quando viderimus hunc morbo regio computruisse, et superesse cadaveri suo, alium intercuti aqua et tumenti natare corpore, crescentibusque membris, formam pristini hominis decrescere, quod nuper in excetra vidimus.[124]

---

[120] *PL* 23, 484B, 445C, 500A.

[121] The expression *Sardanapalus turpior vitiis quam nomine* comes from Cicero *De republica,* iii. frag. 4. Cf. *Comm. in Abacuc, PL* 25, 1307A; *Comm. in Nahum, PL* 25, 1261C.

[122] Süss, "Hieron. u. die Formen," 224.

[123] *Contra Ruf.* i. 13. See Ruf. *Apol.* i. 13 (*PL* 21, 407).

[124] *Comm. in Nahum, PL* 25, 1255B. The application of this passage to Rufinus requires some slight adjustment of Cavallera's chronological scheme. He attributes the *Comm. in Nahum* to 392 (II, 29–30). But the

Such a savage description of Rufinus' physical malady will not
seem shocking when we read Jerome's bitterly triumphant shout
of joy on Rufinus' death in Sicily: *Scorpius . . . inter Encela-
dum et Porphyrionem Trinacriae humo premitur, et Hydra
multorum capitum contra nos aliquando sibilare cessavit.*[125] Even
after his antagonist's death Jerome refuses to call off those dogs,
who, Rufinus had complained, *me per urbes, per vicos, per iter
quoque transeuntem calumniarum latratibus insectantur.*[126]

St. Augustine

St. Jerome's inability to bear competition and criticism calmly
and without rancor is revealed in two quarrels which set him
against the most brilliant and distinguished churchmen of the
day, St. Augustine and St. Ambrose. The circumstances and
progress of the quarrel with Augustine have been thoroughly
dealt with in countless books and articles.[127] We need, therefore,
merely to sketch the background of the dispute and then to pass
on to a consideration of Jerome's verbal attack on Augustine.
The conflict began in 394 when Augustine, the younger man,
wishing to open relations with the renowned scholar of Bethlehem, made the disastrous mistake of sending Jerome a letter

---

quarrel with Rufinus broke out in 393. It would not do too much
violence to this scheme if we put off the Commentary several months to
393.

[125] *Comm. in Ezech., Praefat., PL* 25, 16A. Cf. another savage reference
to the same event, *Comm. in Ezech., PL* 25, 165D: *Putabam, quod medio
serpente confosso, non reviverescerent hydrae novella plantaria, et iuxta
fabulas poetarum, nequaquam in me Scyllaei saevirent canes. . . .*

[126] Ruf. *Apol.* i. 21 (*PL* 21, 559C).

[127] Most recently by G. Folliet, "Nonnulli putaverunt," *Revue des
Etudes Augustin.,* I (1955), 401; G. Simard, "La Querelle de deux Saints,"
Revue de L'Université d'Ottawa, XII (1942), 15–38; P. Auvray, "S.
Jèrôme et S. Augustin," *Recherches de Sc. Religieuse,* XXIX (1939),
594–610; D. de Bruyne, "La Correspondance échangée entre Augustin et
Jérôme," *Zeitschr. für Neutest. Wiss.,* XXXI (1932); E. Malfatti, "Una
controversia tra S. Agostino e S. Girolamo," *Scuola Catt.,* XLIX (1921),
321–328. For earlier bibliography see Bardenhewer, *Geschichte,* III, 647.

questioning certain aspects of Jerome's scholarship. Augustine suggested that Jerome's project of translating the Hebrew Scriptures from the original into Latin was superfluous labor. What was wrong, he asked, with the revered Septuagint text, which in the original or in Latin translation had so long served Christian needs? Furthermore, Augustine took issue with Jerome's interpretation of the passage in Galatians 2:11–21, where Paul rebukes Peter for his continued observance of the Old Law. Jerome had explained this quarrel as a prearranged sham, but Augustine found such an interpretation unacceptable.[128] This questioning of his intellectual authority would alone have enraged Jerome. But his bitterness was immeasurably increased by the manner in which he came to hear of Augustine's criticism. Augustine had given his letter to a certain Profuturus, who was planning a pilgrimage to Palestine, for delivery to Jerome. Profuturus, however, was unexpectedly elected bishop of his native North African town and died soon after. The letter therefore never reached Jerome. Augustine then wrote another letter containing the same criticism and gave it to a certain Paul, who, however, suddenly changed his travel plans and, instead of sailing to the East, journeyed to Rome with the letter. Somehow this missive was circulated in Rome, and Jerome soon heard a rumor that Augustine had written a *libellus* against him. The result was an interchange of twelve letters in each of which Jerome's anger waxed hotter, while Augustine tried to exculpate himself by politeness and restraint.

This quarrel has been more than once described as "aigre-douce," a term that is applicable if we understand "aigre" to refer to Jerome and "douce" to Augustine.[129] Augustine evidently knew that Jerome considered any difference of opinion an insult, for he carefully and courteously wrote:

[128] See *PL* 26, 363–367. Grützmacher (III, 119) points out that this interpretation is taken from Origen.

[129] Cavallera, I, 299; Auvray, "St. Jérôme," 594.

Si forte aliqua in aliquibus scriptis meis reperiuntur, in quibus aliter aliquid quam tu sensisse reperiar, non contra te dictum sed quod mihi videbatur a me scriptum esse, puto te debere cognoscere; aut si cognosci non potest, credere.[130]

In his reply Jerome's deep hostility is barely concealed beneath restrained ridicule:

Ceterum optime novit prudentia tua unumquemque in suo sensu abundare, et puerilis esse iactantiae, quod olim adulescentuli facere consueverant, accusando inlustres vires, suo nomini famam quaerere.[131]

Jerome's oblique allusion to Augustine as an *adulescentulus* in contrast to himself, an *inlustris vir*, is almost incredibly arrogant, even if we consider that at the time of this letter Augustine had not yet won fame as a writer or theologian. Yet Augustine was only about nine years younger than Jerome and was already a bishop, a fact that aroused Jerome's jealousy. Later in this letter he applies to Augustine a passage of Persius: *Sed illa est vera inter amicos reprehensio, si nostram peram non videntes, aliorum, iuxta Persium, manticam consideremus.*[132] Subsequently Jerome compares Augustine to the rash Dares, who at the funeral games held by Aeneas ventured to challenge the elderly Entellus and was struck down by him.[133] Jerome concludes with a threat: in this letter he is merely giving a hint of the invective of which he is capable. Though old, he can still crush an opponent: . . . *memento . . . vulgaris proverbii, quod bos lassus fortius figat pedem.*[134] Jerome's rude remarks in this letter appear to have shocked and wounded Augustine, for he makes frequent reference to Jerome's insults in his letters of reply. Thus he gently

---

[130] Letter 101. 2; Letter 67 in the corpus of Augustine's correspondence, ed. Goldbacher, *CSEL*, XXXVII. For the chronology of the correspondence, see Cavallera, II, 47–56.

[131] Letter 102. 2.   [132] *Ibid.*; Persius 4. 23–24.

[133] *Aeneid* v. 368–484.

[134] Letter 102. 2. See Otto, *Sprich. der Röm.*, 58.

protests against Jerome's allusions to him as an ambitious
adulescentulus:

Si hoc aliquanto securiore libertate dicamus, non incidamus in suspi-
cionem puerilis iactantiae, quasi nostro nomini famam, viros inlustres
accusando quaeramus.[135]

The Dares-Entellus comparison in particular seems to have
offended Augustine, for he mentions it three times:

Iam me arbitror rescriptis tuis, velut Entellinis grandibus atque
acribus caestibus, tamquam audacem Dareta coepisse pulsari atque
versari.[136]

Augustine's protestations of friendship and respect at first
made little impression on Jerome. In reply to Augustine's explanation of the disappearance of the first two letters, Jerome
composed a missive in which he cuttingly portrayed Augustine
as a petty reputation-seeker:

Nonnulli familiares mei et vasa Christi, quorum Hierosolymis et in
sanctis locis permagna copia est, suggerebant, non simplici animo
a te factum, sed laudem atque rumusculos et gloriolam populi re-
quirente, ut de nobis cresceres; ut multi cognoscerent te provocare,
me timere; te scribere ut doctum, me tacere, ut inperitum; et
tandem repperisse qui garrulitati meae modum inponeret.[137]

In this remarkable passage Jerome unwittingly reveals his con-
sciousness that he had been too free with words, for Augustine
had not accused him of *garrulitas;* Jerome had brought the charge
against himself.[138]

Augustine's distress at Jerome's harsh treatment of him is
mirrored in a letter addressed to their mutual friend, Praesidius

[135] Letter 116. 2.

[136] Letter 110 (Augustine's Letter 73), 1. Cf. Letter 110. 4 and 9 for
the other allusions.

[137] Letter 105. 2.

[138] Cf. Letter 50. 5 on his anonymous critic: *Dignetur . . . docendo gar-
rulitatem nostram corrigere.*

(Letter 111). He encloses copies of Jerome's letters to him and of his own to Jerome for comparison and says: "You will easily see by your holy wisdom both my moderation, which I thought ought to be preserved, and his passion, which I justifiably feared."[139]

After about ten years this conflict between the two churchmen died for lack of fuel to feed upon. Jerome wrote an elaborate reply to the objections that had originally begun the quarrel, and Augustine answered in a mild letter appealing for friendship.[140] The dispute highlights the contrast between the two men: Augustine, gentle and reasonable, in search of true knowledge, reluctant to indulge in recrimination; Jerome, irascible, proud, biting, refusing to believe that his own views do not represent absolute truth.[141] Yet Jerome's invective against the Bishop of Hippo is far less harsh than that employed against Vigilantius and Rufinus. There are two reasons for this comparative mildness: Augustine's invariable courtesy and deference tended to cool Jerome's wrath. As Grützmacher says, "Wäre Augustin von gleicher Empfindlichkeit wie Hieronymus gewesen, so wäre jetzt eine literarische Fehde von ähnlicher Heftigkeit ausgebrochen wie die des Hieronymus mit Rufin."[142] Secondly, Jerome saw in Augustine a man of deep piety and outstanding intellect and was reluctant in the midst of the Origenist strife to become further embroiled with this adversary. He knew that the techniques of abuse he had employed against

---

[139] Letter 111. 1.

[140] Letters 112 and 116. For Augustine's eagerness to end the dispute, see esp. Letter 116. 33 and 36. Contrast Jerome's veiled slurs on Augustine, *Comm. in Isa.*, PL 24, 532C and 679C.

[141] However, the following judgment by Grützmacher (III, 126) is too harsh on Jerome: "Der kleinliche Charakter des Hieronymus vermag jenen faustischen Drang nach Wahrheit, der in dem Jüngling wie in dem Bischof Augustin lebte, nicht ergreifen." Jerome too was interested in truth. He simply thought that it lay within himself.

[142] Grützmacher, III, 127.

his other opponents could not be sustained against such a man. Jerome had enough respect for Augustine to combine forces without hesitation some years later in a common battle against the Pelagian heresy.

St. Ambrose

In contrast, St. Jerome's enmity toward the great Bishop of Milan never resulted in an extended quarrel. Indeed, probably Ambrose was entirely unaware that Jerome had made sharply satiric remarks about him, since Jerome never dared to attack openly so powerful a churchman, not at least while Ambrose was alive. It is significant that most of Jerome's open and explicit references to Ambrose are complimentary. In his translation and revision of the *Chronicle of Eusebius* (completed circa 381), Jerome noted under the tenth year of Valentinian I the elevation of Ambrose to the episcopal throne of Milan, adding that upon this event, *omnis ad fidem rectam Italia convertitur.*[143] In his *libellus* to Eustochium on the ascetic life (dated 384) he praises Ambrose's eloquence on virginity as addressed to his sister Marcellina.[144] About nine years later, in defending his opposition to marriage, Jerome supports his views by quoting from Ambrose's work *De viduis.*[145] And yet in composing his book on illustrious Christian writers, among whom Ambrose would naturally figure prominently, Jerome substitutes for the expected biographical and literary information the strange remark: *Ambrosius, Mediolanensis episcopus, usque in praesentem diem scribit, de quo, quia superest, meum iudicium subtraham, ne in alterutram partem aut adulatio in me reprehendatur, aut veritas.*[146] Thus Jerome tries to give the impression of being

---

[143] *Chron.*, ed. Fotheringham, 329.   [144] Letter 22. 22.

[145] Letter 49 (48 Vallarsi), 14.

[146] *De vir. ill.* CXXIV (*PL* 23, 751B). A social factor may have contributed to Jerome's ill feeling toward Ambrose. As a man of the lower-middle class, Jerome may have felt a coldness or arrogance in the high-born Ambrose.

painstakingly fair to Ambrose. Yet the meaning of these words is clear enough: the sharp contrast drawn between flattery and truth must mean that the truth would be highly uncomplimentary to Ambrose. The hostile attitude implicit in this allusion should not come as a surprise to the perceptive reader of St. Jerome's works, for about eight years earlier, in the introduction to his translation of Didymus' work on the Holy Ghost, Jerome had written:

Malui alieni operis interpres existere, quam (ut quidam faciunt) informis cornicula, alienis me coloribus adornare. Legi dudum cuiusdam libellos de Spiritu sancto: et iuxta Comici sententiam ex Graecis bonis, Latina vidi non bona. Nihil ibi dialecticum, nihil virile atque districtum, quod lectorem vel ingratis in assensum trahat: sed totum flaccidum, molle, nitidum, atque formosum, et exquisitis hinc inde odoribus pigmentatum.[147]

Beneath his ridicule can be seen an attack on Ambrose's three books, *De Spiritu Sancto*. The ugly crow of this description first appears in Horace's *Epistle* i. 3. 19–20:

> moveat cornicula risum
> furtivis nudata coloribus. . . .

The phrase *ex Graecis bonis, Latina vidi non bona*, comes from Terence's *Eunuchus*, Prologue, 8:

> Ex Graecis bonis Latinas fecit non bonas.[148]

Rufinus may be subtly referring to this insult when in his *Apology* against Jerome he applies the same quotation from Terence to Jerome's own commentaries,[149] for Rufinus takes Jerome severely to task for the anonymous lampoon above,

[147] *PL* 23, 108A–B. The date is 386–387. There is probably another reference to Ambrose in preface to the *Comm. in Eph.* (*PL* 26, 469C–470A), where Jerome describes an unnamed writer who is accustomed *paene in communibus locis pompaticum iactare sermonem.*

[148] Cf. Hagendahl, *Latin Fathers*, 116.

[149] *Apol.* i. 43 (*PL* 21, 583A).

which he was the first to understand as an attack on Ambrose.[150]

In another of Jerome's works, finished soon after his reworking of Didymus, namely the *Translatio homiliarum Origenis in Lucam* (dated 388–389), we read in the dedication to Paula and Eustochium:

Praetermisi paululum *Hebraicarum Quaestionum libros*, ut ad arbitrium vestrum . . . haec, qualiacumque sunt, non mea sed aliena dictare: praesertim cum a sinistro oscinem corvum audiam crocitantem, et mirum in modum de cunctarum avium ridere coloribus, cum totus ipse tenebrosus sit.[151]

Jerome again calls upon Horace to ridicule his anonymous foe. We may compare *Carmen* iii. 27. 11:

> Oscinem corvum prece suscitabo
> solis ab ortu.[152]

Rufinus picks out these very words as a particularly unpleasant example of Jerome's malevolent tongue and expressly declares that in this passage, too, Jerome is maligning Ambrose.[153] Modern scholars have agreed with Rufinus in seeing the great figure of Ambrose behind Jerome's cackling crow. They point out that Jerome here means to stigmatize Ambrose's recently (388) composed commentaries on Luke.[154]

Veiled slander of Ambrose is probably contained also in Letter 69, where Jerome draws a contrast between a worthy bishop and one who is *heri in amphitheatro, hodie in ecclesia; vespere in circo, mane in altari; dudum fautor histrionum, nunc*

[150] For Rufinus' censure of Jerome's criticism of Ambrose, see *Apol.* ii. 24 (*PL* 21, 603).

[151] *PL* 26, 229–230.   [152] Cf. Hagendahl, 117.

[153] Ruf. *Apol.* ii. 22 (*PL* 21, 601).

[154] See Grützmacher, II, 74–75. Hagendahl, *Latin Fathers*, 116–117. Vallarsi makes a valiant but unsuccessful effort to preserve Jerome's reputation against the charge of malice: *Nemo autem vel jurato Rufino credat, id sentire de Ambrosio potuisse S. Patrem, qui eum plurimi continuo fecit, nec raro in suis libris pro re nata laudavit* (*PL* 26, 229).

virginum consecrator.[155] This passage certainly has the appearance of a scurrilous description of Ambrose's elevation to his bishopric while he was still a catechumen and very much involved in a worldly career.[156] Cavallera (II, 46) dates the letter between 395 and 401. The absence of any open mention of Ambrose, however, implies that he is still living, for after the bishop's death Jerome does not hesitate to disparage him without troubling to conceal his name. Since Ambrose died in 397, this letter should probably be dated between 395 and 397.[157] With this anonymous slur we may contrast a passage in a letter dated 398, the year after Ambrose's death. There Jerome speaks openly of one of his works as merely a compilation from Origen, with additions from Basilius and Hippolytus.[158] In a later epistle (circa 404) Jerome implies that Ambrose's commentary on the Psalms relies too heavily on material taken from Origen.[159] It can hardly be an accident that during Ambrose's lifetime Jerome never makes such freely disparaging remarks.

In his slanderous ridicule of the great Bishop of Milan, Jerome's character appears in dark colors. Plainly, Jerome's personal hostility toward him cannot be explained as the result of intellectual disagreement, for in all the great religious battles of the late fourth century Ambrose and Jerome were on the same side. They were both champions of orthodoxy and proponents of asceticism. They both strove to make known the fruits of Greek theology to the Latin world. But, as Grützmacher remarks, "Gerade die Gemeinsamkeit ihrer Bestrebungen erregte den

---

[155] Letter 69. 9.   [156] See above, p. 83.

[157] Cf. Letter 54. 17, written two years before Ambrose's death, where Jerome ridicules his ignorance of Scripture without naming him.

[158] Letter 84. 7. Cf. *Contra Ruf.* iii. 14 (*PL* 23, 458D). Grützmacher, II, 77, is distorting the text of Jerome for the purpose of his own argument when he translates the word *compilavit* as "sind eine schamlose Kompilation."

[159] Letter 112. 20. Again Grützmacher (II, 77) grossly exaggerates and distorts Jerome's words by translating *secutus est* as "ist ein Plagiat."

Neid des Hieronymus."[160] It could only have been petty jealousy
of Ambrose's powerful position that led Jerome to mock him as
a croaking raven, dressed in colored feathers of other birds.
Jerome could not forgive Ambrose for having reached so high
a station while he himself remained a humble monk. The bitterness Jerome felt toward the challenge to his own intellectual and
moral leadership by the brilliant and successful Ambrose over-
flowed into satire, highly personal, if necessarily anonymous.

Conclusion

Hated for the harshness of his moral strictures and castigated
as a dangerous revolutionary for his new scholarly approach to
the text of the Bible, St. Jerome felt himself constantly threat-
ened by a host of enemies. He frequently found grounds of
consolation for this general dislike. The longest of such pieces
of self-pity is found in the Preface to the second book of the
commentary on Hosea:

He who often goes sailing sometimes experiences a storm; he who
frequently travels the road either suffers or at least fears the attacks
of highwaymen, and in every skilled pursuit praise and detraction
arise according to favorable or adverse winds. . . . For some men,
drawing together their nostrils, condemn and despise whatever we
say as trivial, while others through hatred of our name consider
not facts but personalities. . . .[161] For, while we live and are contained in this fragile vessel, the favor of our friends seems to
profit us and the blame of jealous rivals to harm. But after earth
returns to earth and pale death removes both us who write and
those who pass judgment on us . . . then genius alone is considered
and not the prestige of names.[162]

[160] Grützmacher, II, 76.

[161] Note Jerome's audacity. He complains that *his* enemies are guided
more by personal dislike than simply by intellectual disagreement.

[162] *PL* 26, 859C–861A. Cf. Letter 54. 13: *Fieri quidem non potest ut
absque morsu hominum vitae huius curricula quis pertranseat.* . . . Letter
108. 18: *Semper virtutes sequitur invidia,* "*feriuntque summos fulgura
montes.*" Cf. also *Comm. in Eccles., PL* 23, 1116B and 1124B.

In spite of this protest against his opponents' jealous prejudice, there can be no doubt that Jerome himself delayed the acceptance of his innovations by continually becoming involved in violent personal quarrels with his critics. Jerome's opponents parade through his writings, an incredible band of monsters, ignorant, debauched, foul, ugly, malodorous. He calls upon every one of his many verbal tricks to lampoon them, from cutting irony to the most uncontrolled exaggeration. Strangers as well as personal acquaintances are caricatured with equal vividness.

And yet this ability of Jerome to portray in lively terms adversaries on whom he had never laid eyes raises a suspicion in the mind of the reader; can there be much authentic character drawing or true satiric originality in parodies which are not based on the writer's own observations? When Jerome's attacks on his enemies are read separately they give the impression of brilliant mockery. Yet when considered as a whole, they appear repetitious and monotonous. The same caustic phrases appear over and over again; the same lines of pagan satire are called upon; the same animal terminology is employed. Only on rare occasions, when Jerome is ridiculing an enemy with whom he has had intimate contact, does he succeed in creating brilliantly trenchant satire based on his own perceptions. More usually, even when he is censuring persons whom he knew well, like Rufinus, he is content to make use of his large but somewhat worn supply of mocking expressions. This repetitious quality is often due in part to the speed with which Jerome wrote in his eagerness to cool the unbearable heat of his anger.[163] For *saeva indignatio* and *invidia* are the essence of Jerome's attitude to all who crossed his path, and his cruelly maligned opponents might well agree with the words that Jerome applies to himself, "Happy is he who has arranged his life in so holy and sober a

---

[163] Indeed Jerome himself states that he wrote his tract against Vigilantius in one night. See *PL* 23, 368A–B.

manner that nothing sinister about him can even be imagined, since the greatness of his merit battles against the willfulness of his detractors, and no one dares to concoct what he thinks will be believed by no one."[164]

[164] Letter 148. 23. 2.

CHAPTER VII

Retrospect and Conclusion

WE have been considering from an external and objective point of view those elements of St. Jerome's writings which in their content, if not in their form, represent a Christian continuation and development of classical Roman satire and of traditional oratorical invective. The natural conclusion to such a study is an investigation of Jerome's own attitude toward the bitter, mordant, and mocking features of his works. First, what did Jerome consider to be the nature of satire? Secondly, did Jerome realize the close similarity between his own caustic attack on men and morals and the satire of the pagans? That is, was he a conscious imitator and continuator of the classical writers of satire? Furthermore, as a Christian scholar and monk, what did Jerome believe to be the aim and purpose of his satire? An attempt will here be made to answer these questions on the basis of the evidence to be found in Jerome's own works.

St. Jerome's Own View of His Satire

We begin with those passages in which Jerome specifically refers to himself as a satirist. We saw in Chapter IV that in his twenty-second letter, to Eustochium, Jerome illustrates his denunciations of feminine hypocrisy by describing a ludicrous scene which, he claims, he had recently witnessed. A rich and well-born Roman lady, surrounded by her eunuchs, is distributing alms in the Basilica of St. Peter with her own hands, so that she might seem the more pious. A certain poor and ancient hag, after receiving her coin, returns to the end of the line of alms seekers, hoping not to be recognized and thus to receive another coin. When she again reaches the front of the line, however, she is greeted not with more charity but with a blow in the face, covering her with blood.[1] Jerome interrupts the telling of this tale with the remark, *nomina taceo, ne saturam putes*. This comment is significant, for it provides a clue to Jerome's own views of the essence of satire. Arthur Weston has interpreted Jerome's remark as follows:

The only logical inference to be drawn from '*nomen taceo, ne saturam putes*,' is that the use of the woman's name would, to his mind, have caused him to be satirizing her, which, as it was, he avoided doing. . . . It seems to be the idea of Hieronymus that this use of names is actually an essential characteristic of satire, as such.[2]

This interpretation is unacceptable, for it implies that Jerome was unaware that the pagan satirists, including Horace and Juvenal, had never used the actual names of the living persons they attacked. It is of course impossible that Jerome, who had a thorough knowledge of classical Latin literature, was ignorant of this. The phrase *nomina taceo* cannot, then, mean that Jerome believed the naming of actual persons to be essential to satire. These words should rather be compared with an expression Jerome uses in his commentary on Zephaniah. He is there ridiculing the erroneous and unorthodox opinions of certain *novi prudentes, quorum nomina*, he says, *taceo, ne quemquam*

---

[1] Letter 22. 32.

[2] *Latin Satirical Writing*, 99, and *ibid.*, n. 56. Note that Weston reads *nomen* with Vallarsi instead of *nomina* (Labourt). This is perhaps better, for Jerome was no doubt suppressing the name only of the noble lady, not of the hag too.

laedere videar.[3] In the two passages of ridicule under discussion, Jerome, who was aware that his caustic mockery was winning him innumerable enemies, was extremely anxious to avoid openly wounding individuals. Therefore in both passages, *nomen tacet*. The expression *nomina taceo, ne saturam putes* means then, "I avoid naming the woman involved in this tale, because my intention here is not to ridicule and wound *specific individuals*, but to expose vicious behavior." Jerome expresses himself rather loosely and inaccurately in this passage, but we cannot believe that he thought the omission of personal names would destroy the satiric nature of the tale.

Names or no names, Jerome regards the story as basically satiric in character. It is important to note that Jerome ignores the fact that his story is not in verse, thus accepting without question the concept of satire in prose. His judgment of the story as satiric implies that, regardless of the form it takes, satire is, to his mind, a clear mirror of life wherein human behavior is so accurately reflected that its ludicrous inconsistencies are mercilessly exposed. Hence in telling his tale Jerome strives for detailed accuracy: the lady brings along her eunuchs (*semiviris antecedentibus*) when she distributes alms; she is careful to give only one coin (*singulos nummos*) to each poor person; she uses her own hand (*propria manu*) to pass out the money, *quo religiosior putaretur*; in contrast to her, the old woman is "squalid with years and rags." Moreover, Jerome implies that the spirit of satire is basically vitriolic, by its very nature acid and piercing. For just this reason Jerome has been careful to suppress the names of the actors in the story. Furthermore, satire has a *reforming purpose*. That is why Jerome has included the tale in his exhortation to Eustochium against hypocrisy. It is clear from Jerome's specific designation of this incident as satiric that he views satire as σπουδαιογέλοιον, a mixture of earnest and humor, the aim of which is to convey important moral teachings

---

[3] *PL* 26, 1382C.

in a humorous form.[4] This is in fact the classical Roman concept of satire, formed by Lucilius under the influence of the Cynic and Stoic diatribe, and adopted by Horace, Persius, and even Juvenal, who in his description of the infamous Rubrius Gallus as *improbior satiram scribente cinaedo* implies his belief in the ethical purpose of satiric humor.[5] Jerome strongly implies that he held this classical view of the satirist's role, expressed in Horace's words *ridentem dicere verum*, when, after ridiculing the vices of Vigilantius in bitingly humorous terms, he assures his adversary, *Haec dolentis magis effudi animo quam ridentis.*[6] He thereby suggests that he has noted the mingling of deep seriousness and laughter in his satiric remarks. It is precisely this mixture of earnest and jest that Rufinus justly claims is one of Jerome's favorite literary techniques: *ut ei mos est miscere ridicula seriis.*[7]

We may add that Jerome did not suppress the names of individuals in recounting his tale solely out of a delicate wish to spare a lady's feelings. He is also hoping to avoid reprisals, whether merely verbal recriminations or some more dangerous form of revenge which a rich and powerful matron would have at her disposal.[8] He thus implicitly claims for himself the right to expose the faults of individuals without giving their names, so that even if they recognize themselves as the targets of Jerome's satire they cannot straightway accuse him of malice. A sign of the arrogance with which Jerome viewed his role as a reforming satirist is his refusal to allow the same right to others.

---

[4] Fiske, *Lucilius and Horace*, 143. Cf. Duff, *Roman Satire*, 9.

[5] Juvenal 4. 106. Juvenal's moral purpose has been wrongly doubted by many scholars.

[6] *PL* 23, 355C.   [7] Ruf. *Apol.* i. 7, *PL* 21, 546A.

[8] Jerome here adopts the position of Juvenal, who in his first satire states his fear of openly attacking contemporaries. Jerome is not usually so timorous, especially when his targets have little power to injure him.

In a letter of his later years he writes, *Si me vis corrigi delinquentem, aperte increpa, tantum ne occulte mordeas.*[9]

We turn now to another passage in which Jerome specifically refers to himself as a satirist. In Letter 40. 2, to "Onasus," he writes:

Dico quosdam scelere, periurio, falsitate ad dignitatem nescio quam pervenisse. . . . In quodcumque vitium stili mei mucro contorquetur te clamitas designari, conserta manu in ius vocas, et satiricum scriptorem in prosa stulte arguis.[10]

These words have frequently been misinterpreted. General opinion holds that by using the word *stulte* Jerome is denying the accusation that he is a satiric writer in prose. Vallarsi in his note *ad loc.* expresses the view that the form of satire is the chief question here. Jerome is calling Onasus stupid, claims Vallarsi, because Onasus believes that satire can be written in prose, *ac si quis Italice diceret:* "Scritor di Sonetti in prosa." This is an impossible interpretation, first because, as we have seen above, in Letter 22 Jerome accepts the concept of prose satire and secondly because, if Jerome were saying that his use of prose *in itself* proves him no satirist, surely the phrase *in prosa* would occupy a more prominent place in the sentence. Weston's interpretation of the passage is that, "It is not the fact that he writes in prose that makes it seem foolish to Hieronymus for anyone to call him a *"satiricum scriptorem"* but the fact that he does not call anyone by name."[11] But this exegesis is also wide of the mark, for as we have seen, Jerome was conscious that satire was not necessarily directed at specifically named persons. The plain meaning

---

[9] Letter 125. 19. 5. His reasoning is unexceptionable: *Quid enim mihi prode est, si aliis mala mea referas, si me nesciente peccatis meis, immo detractationibus tuis alium vulneres.* However, Jerome might have observed the same principle when maligning others.

[10] See above, Chapter V.   [11] Weston, 99–100.

of this epistle is that Jerome *is* a satirist and admits to being one, but denies that he has been satirizing Onasus in particular. He begins the letter by saying:

Medici quos vocant chirurgicos crudeles putantur et miseri sunt. An non est miseria alienis dolere vulneribus et mortuas carnes clementi secare ferro? non horrere curantem quod horret ipse qui patitur et inimicum putari? ita se natura habet ut amara sit veritas, blanda vitia aestimentur.[12]

Jerome's implied comparison of his writings to surgery which would wound and pain in order to cure can only mean that he claims for himself the role of a caustically satiric moral reformer. He too will harshly cut and wound, but his aim is to cure moral evils.[13] Jerome restates his claims to a reforming role in even clearer terms later in this letter: *Unde non mirum est si et nos vitiis detrahentes offendimus plurimos. Disposui nasum secare fetentem: timeat qui strumosus est.*[14] Jerome will try to cure the ills of society by lopping off its putrid elements with his cutting remarks. In these words Jerome openly states his pretensions to be considered a satirist and shortly afterward makes good this claim, while also in a subtle manner revealing his descent from the classical satirists, by applying to "Onasus" some acid lines from Persius.[15] Since Jerome is here patently subjecting his foe to satiric treatment, how are we to interpret his words *stulte arguis satiricum scriptorem in prosa?* They mean simply that Onasus is foolish to claim that *he* in particular has heretofore been the object of Jerome's satire. The key word in this letter is *te*, but its significance has escaped the interpreters of this passage:

[12] Letter 40. 1.

[13] Cf. *Comm. in Soph.*, PL 25, 1351C: *Alioquin et scalpellus medici malus erit, quia resecat vulnera, et putridas amputat carnes.* Cf. also Duff's remarks on the role of the satirist: "He would fain purge, blister, cauterize, if so he might work a cure" (*Roman Satire*, 8).

[14] Letter 40. 2.   [15] See above, p. 204.

Dico quosdam scelere . . . ad dignitatem nescio quam pervenisse: quid ad *te*? . . . quadrante dignam eloquentiam nare subsanno: quid ad *te*? . . . volo in nummarios invehi sacerdotes: *tu* qui dives es quid irasceris? . . . quicquid dictum fuerit in *te* dictum putes.

Jerome is striving to make absolutely clear wherein Onasus' stupidity lay; that is, not in claiming that Jerome was a satirist—Jerome himself admits this—but in imagining that he, Onasus, had been the object of Jerome's satire. Jerome is careful in this letter not to attack Onasus by his real name, so as not to validate Onasus' charge. It is certain, however, that Jerome would never have imagined that the use of the pseudonym "Onasus" would destroy his claim to be considered a satirist.

Several important conclusions can be drawn from a study of this letter. In Jerome's view the nature of satire is at once destructive and curative. The object of satire is to arouse fear in the vicious; *timeat qui strumosus est*. But the unfortunate targets of satire are also led to an understanding of their faults: *rancidulam se intelligat cornix*. Thus satire is essentially thera-peutic, a type of literary medicine of which Jerome declares himself to be an expert practitioner. Jerome reveals by quoting Persius that in his role of satiric doctor he is consciously making use of the medicines inherited from his pagan predecessors.

The correctness of the conclusions stated here is confirmed by many other passages in Jerome's writings. In answering an anonymous enemy in his Letter to Domnio (Letter 50, discussed above, in Chapter V), Jerome makes it clear beyond any possi-ble doubt that he considers himself a satirist in the tradition of the pagans. Protesting against his critic's scurrility, he warns:

Det nobis occasionem respondendi disertitudini suae. Possum re-mordere, si velim, possum genuinum laesus infigere; et nos didici-mus litterulas, "et nos saepe manum ferulae subtraximus," de nobis quoque dici potest: "faenum habet in cornu, longe fuge."[16]

---

[16] Letter 50. 5.

Jerome has here strung together a series of passages from the classical satirists. *Genuinum laesus infigere* is taken from Persius 1. 115, a line Jerome frequently borrows.[17] *Manum ferulae subtraximus* is quoted from Juvenal 1. 15, and *faenum habet in cornu* from Horace *Satire* i. 4. 34. This juxtaposition of three passages, one from each of the major pagan satirists, can have only one meaning. Jerome is cautioning his adversary, without specifically saying so, that he is well versed in the techniques of satiric attack and exposure. The quotation from Horace is particularly apposite, for the poet had put these words into the mouth of those timid critics who feared being wounded by satiric barbs. Jerome is surely thinking of these same lines of Horace in a later work when, cautioning Rufinus not to malign him lest he excite his own satiric talents, he warns: *Cornutam bestiam petis*.[18] Of course Horace in the original context of this line specifically denies, in answering his critic's objections, that his intent is to wound, denies that he is a dangerous bull who must be avoided. Jerome, in contrast, proudly accepts the timorous warning, *longe fuge*, as well justified. "You have excellent cause for fear," he implies, "for my satire is sharp and will be aimed openly at *you*." Jerome here makes clear that, although he recognizes himself as the heir of the classical satirists, he will not be copying the genial Horace, who studiously sought to avoid wounding, but will instead employ a more personal and vitriolic method of attack. In this passage Jerome is considering satire not as a moral curative but rather as a powerful weapon of retaliation in personal quarrels. This very same concept of satire is illustrated by a passage in which Jerome gives his readers a rare glimpse into his study. We see him at his desk, making notes for use in future writings:

[17] E.g., Letter 108. 15; *Chronicle of Eusebius*, ed. Fotheringham, 4; *Praefat. in Librum Job, PL* 29, 63B.

[18] *Contra Ruf.* i. 31 (*PL* 23, 433A).

Volo in chartulis meis quaslibet ineptias scribere, commentari de scripturis, *remordere laedentes*, digerere stomachum, in locis me exercere communibus *et quasi limatas ad pugnandum sagittas reponere*.[19]

Thus Jerome admits that part of his literary activity consists in piling up a stock of satiric arrows to be used in the battles with his personal enemies.

Yet Jerome's attitude toward the personal and malicious aspects of satire was highly ambiguous. In the passages above he emphasizes his ability to indulge in personal scurrility, specifically stating, *Possum genuinum infigere*. Yet in other passages he strives mightily to refute the charge, *me hominem maledicum, omnium detractorem, . . . genuinum semper infigere*.[20] Although in the passage from Letter 50 cited above Jerome uses the Horatian words, *Longe fuge, faenum habet in cornu* implicitly to reject Horace's gentle concept of satire, elsewhere he is anxious to call himself a follower of precisely this milder tradition. In Letter 125 he answers the critics of his vitriol: *Ego enim neminem nominabo nec veteris comoediae licentia certas personas eligam atque perstringam*.[21] Jerome is here referring to the opening of the fourth satire of Horace's first book, where the poet shows the relation of Lucilius' personal scurrility to the traditions of Old Comedy. But just as Horace avoided such personal malevolence, so, says Jerome, will he, for his goal is not to

[19] Letter 57. 4. Jerome is here accusing Rufinus of having used dishonest methods to obtain from his study a copy of Epiphanius' letter to John of Jerusalem. See Murphy, *Rufinus*, 74.

[20] *Contra Ruf.* i. 30 (PL 23, 440C). Note that while in Letter 50. 5 Jerome claims for himself the right *genuinum infigere*, he complains in the preface to the *Chronicle of Eusebius* (ed. Fotheringham, 4): *Nec ignoro multos fore qui solita libidine omnibus detrahendi huic volumini genuinum infigant*. Again in the Preface to Job, Jerome bewails the malice of his enemies: because of his efforts to purify the text of the Bible, *mihi genuinus infigitur* (PL 29, 63B).

[21] Letter 125. 5. 2.

insult individuals but to reform them: *Prudentis viri est ac prudentium feminarum . . . indignari sibi magis quam mihi nec in monitorem maledicta congerere.*[22] The inconsistency and even cowardice of Jerome's satiric position here becomes plain: when threatening his enemies he wishes to be known as a brilliant and malevolent satirizer of persons; when, however, he is under attack for his malicious bitterness, he quickly retreats and takes refuge beneath the specious plea voiced centuries before by Martial:

> Hunc servare modum nostri novere libelli
> parcere personis, dicere de vitiis.[23]

We turn now to examine more fully a document that has been in part discussed above (Chapter III)—Letter 117, Jerome's admonition to a mother and daughter in Gaul who had each set up a separate household together with a clergyman. We have seen that his letter is almost surely a rhetorical fiction not based on an actual situation. Such artificiality increases immeasurably the significance of the words which Jerome puts into the mouth of the son and brother of these women as he protests against Jerome's supposed reluctance to compose a caustic exhortation against their immorality: *Nimium, ait, formidolosus. Ubi illa quondam constantia, in qua multo sale orbem defricans Lucilianum quippiam rettulisti?*[24] The speaker is referring here of course to Horace's description of Lucilius:

> At idem, quod sale multo
> urbem defricuit, charta laudatur eadem.
>
> [*Sat.* i. 10. 3]

It would, to be sure, be revealing if the interlocutor had in reality compared Jerome to Lucilius, thus proving that con-

---

[22] *Ibid.*

[23] Martial x. 33. 9–10. Lucilius frequently has to reply to charges of personal malice. See frags. 1014, 1015, 1016, 1022 (Marx).

[24] Letter 117. 1

temporaries viewed Jerome as a brilliant satirist in the classical tradition. More important, however, is Jerome's bestowal of this title upon himself, first because it shows that he was a conscious imitator of the pagans and secondly because it suggests his proud sense of the significance of his satiric role. Highly noteworthy is a slight change which Jerome has made in Horace's words: the pagan poet claimed only that Lucilius *urbem defricuit.* Jerome, on the other hand, speaks of himself as *orbem defricans!* This is truly an arrogant claim, but no more arrogant than the basic idea of this letter, that a monk had come all the way from Gaul to obtain Jerome's epistle of admonition.[25]

Throughout the introduction to this letter Jerome emphasizes the distinction between the reforming or curative aspects of satire and the malicious or abusive. The latter he rejects altogether: his satire is never meant to harm but to cure. Yet he has been sadly misunderstood: *Postquam enim arguendo crimina, factus sum criminosus . . . ipsique parietes in me maledicta resonarunt.*[26] We may compare the complaint voiced elsewhere on the hostile reception given to his reforming satire: *Sermo offendit plurimos, dum unusquisque in se intellegens, quod dicebatur, non quasi monitorem libenter audivit, sed quasi criminatorem sui operis aversatus est.*[27] Hurt and troubled by such misunderstanding Jerome shyly resolves to retire from the satiric battlefield: *Coactus malo tacere didici, rectius esse arbitrans, ponere custodiam ori meo, et ostium munitum labiis meis, quam declinare cor meum in verba malitiae.*[28] As might be expected, Jerome's artificial coyness is eventually overcome and

[25] That Jerome imagined such an incredible journey as the background of the letter is clear from the words at the end of section 1: he tells the monk that if the women do not heed his words, *ego verba perdiderim, tu itineris longitudinem.*

[26] Letter 117. 1.

[27] Letter 130. 19. 4. Jerome is here referring to Letter 22. Cf. Letter 45 6: *Infamiam falsi criminis inportarunt.*

[28] Letter 117. 1.

he persuades himself that a vitriolic exhortation will serve a high moral purpose. As if to emphasize the therapeutic, in contrast to the malicious, purpose of his invective he again employs the comparison of satire to medicine: *Putridae carnes ferro curantur et cauterio: venena serpentino pelluntur antidoto.*[29]

In reading this letter one might easily experience a feeling of revulsion at Jerome's inordinate pride. The laudatory remarks of the interlocutor on the world-reforming power of Jerome's satire were composed by Jerome himself. The timidity with which he undertakes his satiric task is both affected and hypocritical. He had never before hesitated to indulge in the most violent scurrility. His reluctance to give rein to personal malice is of course completely hollow in view of his open admission in passages quoted above that he will make free use of such ridicule whenever he wishes.

The ambiguity of St. Jerome's attitude toward vitriolic ridicule reveals that as a Christian satirist he faced a problem which had not confronted the pagans: he was keenly aware that malevolent backbiting was unchristian and he consequently experienced a feeling of deep guilt over his irrepressible penchant for abuse. The result of this feeling was that throughout his works he inserted warnings against the evil of malevolence, even while himself continuing to indulge in invective. In the same letter in which he subjects Vigilantius to malicious vituperation, he claims, *Christiana verecundia teneor, et cellulae meae latebras nolo mordaci sermone reserare.*[30] In his letter of praise for the Holy Land, Jerome mentions as a particular sign of sanctity that there the *genuinus dens* is not used for tearing at one's fellow man.[31] Warnings against the use of unchristian malice are

[29] Letter 117. 2.
[30] Letter 61. 3. At least at the end of the letter Jerome admits that he had written *mordacius* than he had originally planned.
[31] Letter 46. 10. Cf. 46. 12: *laudare* and *detrahere*, so common in the social life of Rome, are absent from Bethlehem. Cf. also Letter 43. 2: Jerome complains that at Rome *lacerantur absentes.*

particularly frequent in Jerome's educational letters on the ascetic life. He urges Nepotianus: "Be careful to have neither an itching tongue nor itching ears, that is neither slander others nor listen to those who do so."[32] Again, in advising Furia how to live a truly Christian life, he writes, "Self-imposed silence corrects an evil-speaking tongue."[33] It is too simple to say that in making these remarks Jerome is unconscious that the failing he sees in others was very much his own. On the contrary, it is precisely because Jerome was aware of his own uncontrollable penchant for malice that he so urgently admonishes others to avoid it, as if he could absolve himself of his fault by constantly inveighing against it in others. Indeed in a letter written in his old age Jerome expresses his realization that acid critics are in danger of discovering in others their own faults: *Accusamus saepe, quod facimus, et contra nosmet ipsos diserti in nostra vitia invehimur muti de eloquentibus iudicantes.*[34] In writing these words Jerome was probably thinking with misgivings of his own satire. The frequency with which he preaches against malicious detraction suggests that he was almost obsessed by feelings of guilt. "Have the simplicity of a dove, that you may plot treachery against no one," he cautions Paulinus of Nola.[35] "Speak evil of no one and do not consider vilifying others a mark of your holiness," he tells Rusticus.[36] Jerome reproves Helvidius and Rufinus because, as he says in words borrowed from Tertullian, each of them *maledicere omnibus, bonae conscientiae signum arbitratur.*[37] A malicious detractor is a poisonous serpent: "Just as the snake with its bite secretly injects its poison, so does the secret slanderer pour out against his brother the venom of his heart."[38] *Invidia* is one of the most heinous moral crimes, *quia*

---

[32] Letter 52. 14.   [33] Letter 54. 9.
[34] Letter 125. 18. 1.   [35] Letter 58. 6.
[36] Letter 125. 18. 1.
[37] *PL* 23, 193A and 482D. Cf. Tertullian, *Adv. Hermogenem*, 1, *Homo . . . qui . . . maledicere singulis officium bonae conscientiae iudicet.*
[38] *Comm. in Eccles.*, *PL* 23, 1151D–1152A.

anima quae semel possessa fuerit ab invidia difficile est ut virtutes recipiat.[39] The just man when wounded by his enemy must avoid avenging himself by casting malicious slurs *sub velamento prudentiae.* It is better to appear stupid while awaiting God's punishment of evil-tongued foes.[40] In his commentary on the Epistle to the Galatians, Jerome enters into a lengthy analysis of jealousy and contentiousness. While deprecating *muliebre iurgium,* especially over the interpretation of biblical passages, he reveals insight into his own character by remarking, "Yet I know not who among us can be free of this evil."[41] As if in self-defense he mentions a number of biblical figures in whom irascibility and envy were prominent characteristics. His anxiety over his harsh and censorious temperament is again revealed in his comment on the passage from Matthew: *Omnis qui irascitur fratri suo sine causa, reus erit iudicio* (Matthew 5:22). Jerome asks, as if excusing his own tendencies, *Quis nostrum potest huic vitio non subiacere . . . ?*[42] Again, in the commentary on Ecclesiastes, Jerome sounds as if he is thinking with unusual gentleness of his many personal enemies and regretting his fondness for satirizing them maliciously when he says that the Preacher *docet penitus non curandum iusto homini, quid homines loquantur, dicens: Quomodo novit conscientia tua, quod tu de multis locutus es, et saepe aliis detraxisti: sic et aliis debes ignoscere detrahentibus.*[43] Elsewhere, he feels called upon to defend the virulence with which he had been attacking men and morals. He announces in the preface to the *Dialogus contra Pelagianos* that he will give his interlocutors fictitious names "in order to prove before all that I do not hate men but rather

---

[39] *Anecdot. Mared.,* III. 2. 336.
[40] *Comm. in Eccles., PL* 23, 1145B–C.   [41] *PL* 26, 444C–445C.
[42] *Dial. contra Pelag.,* ii. 11 (*PL* 23, 570C).
[43] *PL* 23, 1124B, on Eccles. 7: 22: *Etenim frequenter scit cor tuum, quia et tu maledixisti aliis.*

their errors, and that I do not seek to defame some men but rather grieve for the fate of those led astray."[44]

These passages show that Jerome was fully aware that malice and acid bitterness have no place in the Christian heart. He would hardly have mentioned the odiousness of *invidia* so frequently had he not felt deeply uneasy about his own penchant for malevolence. He senses that a propensity for waspish malice was an ineradicable part of his temperament and thus is compelled to defend and justify his position as a violent critic of his contemporaries. It is precisely for this reason that he so often emphasizes the reforming purpose of his satire. If he can show that his satire serves to improve morals, then he has escaped the charge of malevolent lack of charity. In Letter 24. 1, we find Jerome urging, "Let no one find fault with me because in my letters I praise some men and ill-use others, since when I bring accusations against evil men, others too are reproved, and when I praise those of excellence, the enthusiasm of good men for virtue is aroused." Jerome here claims that his scurrilous carping at individuals is above malice because such mordacity serves the cause of moral improvement. The same claims are put forward in even prouder and loftier terms in Letter 109. 3. Jerome has just written a scathing personal attack on Vigilantius in this letter addressed to his friend Riparius. Realizing that his correspondent might view such backbiting as malicious, he writes:

Tacita me forsitan cogitatione reprehendas, cur in absentem invehar. Fateor tibi dolorem meum; sacrilegium tantum patienter audire non possum. Legi enim siromasten Finees, austeritatem Heliae, zelum Simonis Chananaei, Petri severitatem Ananiam et Sapphiram trucidantis, Paulique constantiam, qui Elymam magum viis Domini resistentem, aeterna caecitate damnavit. Non est crudelitas pro Deo pietas.[45]

In this passage Jerome openly admits the cruelty of his invective

---

[44] *PL* 23, 520A. [45] Cf. above, p. 222.

but seeks to vindicate it by reference to cruel acts described in the Bible. Just as Paul was justified in striking with eternal blindness the sorcerer who opposed Christ, so he, Jerome, is justified in making the most caustic and venomous remarks about his own enemy Vigilantius, who of course is also the enemy of God. Nowhere is Jerome's certainty that his own opinion represents absolute truth more clearly expressed than in the commentary on the Epistle to the Galatians, where, expounding Paul's injunctions against *rixae* and *dissensiones*, Jerome writes: *Quantum enim in nobis est, nullius esse debemus inimici, sed cum omnibus habere pacem.*[46] But he realizes that he can hardly lay claim to such pacific and charitable behavior and, pricked by his conscience, he undertakes a defense of his invective and of the quarrels to which it had given rise: *Quod si loquentes veritatem, aliquos meremur inimicos: non tam nos inimici eorum sumus, quam illi inimici sunt veritatis.*[47] Jerome identifies the targets of his satiric malice not as his own enemies, but as the enemies of irrefutable truth. Against the foes of truth it is permitted to say anything. The same concept of Jerome's satiric role is also applied in a passage of the treatise against Jovinianus. On the point of launching into an abusive description of the clergy, Jerome states his belief that he will necessarily offend some people: *Dicam aliquid quod forsitan cum multorum offensa dicturus sum; sed boni mihi non irascentur, quia eos peccati conscientia non remordebit.*[48] Jerome is here claiming that his vitriolic portrayals are really unobjectionable because only evildoers will be offended. Good men can but agree with him and rejoice in his censoriousness. For just this reason Jerome did not hesitate, as Juvenal did hesitate, to attack his own contem-

---

[46] PL 26, 444A.   [47] *Ibid.*

[48] *Adv. Iovin.* i. 34 (PL 23, 269C). Cf. *ibid.*, ii. 11 (PL 23, 425A–B): *Quando sine nomine contra vitia scribitur; qui irascitur, accusator sui est. Prudentis hominis fuerat, etiam si dolebat, dissumulare conscientiam; et cordis nubilum frontis serenitate discutere.*

poraries. The forces of God and of right-thinking men are on his side as he denounces and excoriates evil. This belief is clearly implied in a statement Jerome makes in the preface to his revision of the *Chronicle of Eusebius.* He has been prevented from continuing the work down to his own day, asserts Jerome, not by the fear of maligning living men, but simply because of the uncertainty of the age: *non quo de viventibus timuerim libere et vere scribere, timor enim Dei hominum timorem expellit.*[49] Jerome thus unmistakably identifies his own cause with God's. He is certain beyond any possibility of doubt that the objects of his revealing remarks, who might take offense at his frankness, are God's enemies, and therefore Jerome is not only permitted to speak the unvarnished, even though venomous, truth, but he is actually obligated to do so. It is this close identification of Jerome's view of evil with God's which justifies, or even demands, his free use of the most vitriolic and mocking invective.

St. Jerome's lofty conception of his own mission as a moral reformer who is not bound by the usual rules of charity but has been granted license to indulge in malice and scurrility in the pursuance of his goals may strike the modern reader as intolerably arrogant. And yet if this conception is viewed from Jerome's own point of view it becomes more understandable. It is, first of all, necessary and inevitable for a satirist, any satirist, to assume a higher moral position than his fellow men, for his task is not to censure his own failings but those of others. When a satirist is working in the cause of religion, this higher moral stand is even better justified, for then the satirist's concept of the vicious behavior he chooses to ridicule is determined not by his own private views but by the principles of religion. St. Jerome was a highly religious man, not only in the sense of having a deep feeling of devotion toward God but in being zealous for the growth of the Church and for its progress and success in

[49] *Chronicle of Eusebius,* ed. Fotheringham, 5.

its task of moral reformation. His unusual ability keenly and penetratingly to perceive the faults of men and his irascible and waspish character naturally determined the manner in which he chose to further the goals of the Church. Since he always believed himself to be employing his satiric talents in the service of the Church, he assumed that the forces of good and right supported his use of ridicule and exposure. Moreover, though Jerome was a man of intense personal ambition, he always saw this ambition as closely related to the welfare of the Church. Therefore, when attacked personally he believed that the Church too was on the defensive. His satiric invective against his enemies was justified, he held, because he was at the same time defending both God's cause and his own. It is possible, then, to describe St. Jerome's satiric efforts in the words of his contemporary Rutilius Namatianus, words which Jerome would doubtless have been glad to see applied to himself:

> Restituit veterem censoria lima pudorem
> dumque malos carpit, praecipit esse bonos.[50]

Conclusion

St. Jerome is the author of the final chapter in the brilliant volume of ancient satire, one of the chief glories of Latin literature, whose first pages had been written by Lucilius more than five hundred years previously. The satiric book must now be sealed, since for centuries to come no one will possess that special combination of native wit, literary education, and reforming zeal necessary for reshaping satire to the requirements of a new and ruder age. We have completed our detailed examination of Jerome's satire and must now sketch his contribution to the genre as a whole, asking ourselves what makes his satire far more significant than that of other Church Fathers. St. Jerome is the most important of the Christian satirists, not because he

[50] *De reditu suo* i. 605–606.

always achieves the keen subtlety of which Tertullian is fre-quently capable nor because he regularly attains the height of brilliant inventiveness occasionally reached by Arnobius, but rather because he has studied and absorbed more thoroughly than any other of the Fathers the spirit and language of the great classical satirists and because satiric attitudes more con-sistently shape and determine the character of his own writing.

This appraisal is not meant to deny that much in Jerome's satire may appear unoriginal, repetitious, or excessively studied. Indeed, does not the material of his satire show a disconcerting resemblance to that *crambe repetita* of the ancient intellect, the *loci communes* ceaselessly rehearsed in the diatribes of popular Cynic-Stoic philosophy, in the *suasoriae* and *controversiae* of the schools of rhetoric, and in the show speeches of the halls of declamation? We are here asking of Jerome the very question which has incited students of Juvenal to frenzied controversy during the last century: do the obviously artificial and declama-tory style of Juvenal and his equally obvious lack of philosophic originality detract from the sincerity of his moral indignation and hence undermine the value of his satire? This controversy has made very slow progress because the detractors of Juvenal have been content simply to point out similarities between cer-tain passages of the satires and the rhetorical writings of the elder Seneca and others and then to pronounce that Juvenal is a mere declaimer, reheating tired commonplaces. Juvenal's de-fenders, on the other hand, curiously cite many of the same satiric passages as examples of their author's deep and original ethical thinking.[51] Neither side in this quarrel stopped to ask itself whether this controversy made any sense in terms of

[51] E. Marmorale, *Giovenale* (2d ed.; Bari, 1950) and A. Serafini, *Studio sulla satira di Giovenale* (Florence, 1957) are the latest contribu-tions to this debate. Marmorale's first chapter is a strong attack on Ju-venal's moral sincerity, while Serafini's second chapter is an even stronger defense of the satirist.

ancient literary theory. The same questions which have arisen
over Juvenal's satire may likewise be asked of Jerome's, but in
asking them we must avoid the mistakes of the Juvenal scholars.
Whoever studies the problem of originality and imitation in
ancient literature should take to heart the words of Quintilian,
*Neque enim dubitari potest quin artis pars magna contineatur
imitatione.*[52] The essence of ancient satire had always been the
combination of original social portraiture with popular moralistic
reflections of a timeless character.[53] These are the two aspects
of satire which Fritz Gauger has designated as "Zeitschilderung"
and "Topik," implying, however, that there is a conflict between
the two and that a satirist is great to the extent that he emphasizes personal commentary on society and avoids traditional
moralizing and borrowing from predecessors.[54] But the ancients
would have judged literature by no such canons. Gauger's standards belong wholly to nineteenth-century romanticism, which
viewed individuality rather than adherence to tradition as the
hallmark of literary greatness. St. Jerome, however, when he
writes satire is deeply conscious that though his language is
prose he is in fact writing in the genre of Horace and Juvenal,
and ancient literary concepts would never have suggested, much
less demanded, that Jerome divorce himself from the traditions
of this genre. Furthermore, we may well wonder whether obedi-
ence to generic laws is fatal to literary freedom. The ancient
rhetorical commonplaces constituted merely a corpus of literary
formulae, and each rhetorical writer had complete liberty in
choosing whichever formulae best suited his own thinking and
his own intentions. The Homeric epics, though formulaic in
character, reflect nonetheless the poet's own mind and art. In

---

[52] Quintilian x. 2. 1. Cf. x. 5. 12 and Cicero *Orator* 118.
[53] Fiske, *Lucilius and Horace*, 52.
[54] Fritz Gauger, *Zeitschilderung and Topik bei Juvenal* (Greifswald,
1936).

similar fashion rhetorical prose literature, though constructed in part of inherited formulaic materials, are the products of the writer's own craftsmanship and thought.

In such a genre as satire with its constant preoccupation with the spirit of the individual and society, with its insistence upon the principles which mould character, with its frank, popular, and humorous expression of these social and moral laws, there was accumulated, so to speak, a vast mass of human and social material. In so far as human and social experience repeats itself in every age, this material had some measure of fixity.[55]

If then it has been shown that St. Jerome, while drawing upon the wealth of inherited commonplaces, restores this traditional wisdom to meaningful life by using it to censure and correct the faults of a new society, the Christian society coming into being in his own day, his place as the last of the great line of Roman satirists will be secure. Jerome does, for the most part, succeed in this undertaking. Just as Christianity was remaking the pagan world as a whole, so did Jerome recast the popular philosophy of paganism into a vehicle of Christian propaganda. The many similarities between the Cynic-Stoic *philosophia vulgaris* and Christian principles greatly facilitated Jerome's task of adaptation, but we usually sense that he sincerely and strongly appreciated the truth and moral value of the time-honored *loci communes*. Of course Jerome does occasionally make such unthinking use of standard rhetorical material that the reader wonders whether frigid artifice rather than fervid indignation is guiding his pen. When Jerome advises a friend who he knew had become immured in the monastic life to cease building rich porticoes and to find happiness in simplicity or when he draws up for a pious and wealthy lady an elaborate contrast between the misery of city life and the delights of the country, urging

[55] Fiske, *Lucilius and Horace*, 55.

her to indulge with him in rustic pleasures, so unreal is his argumentation that we are forced to admit that at these points Jerome's moralism is hollow and his satire unsuccessful.

Jerome is without question at his best as a satirist when he abandons such preaching altogether and expresses his moral wrath by drawing those ludicrous pictures of contemporary society which prove how well endowed he was with the keenness of observation and power for detailed description on which all satire is ultimately based. As we observe Jerome passing from trenchant irony through parody, burlesque, and mimicry to bitter vituperation, revealing a penetrating insight, almost unparalleled in antiquity, into the vagaries and incongruities of human behavior, can we deny that here is a great satiric talent?

Yet we may be inclined to judge Jerome harshly when we find him driving to death certain of his favorite lines from pagan writers and plundering his own writings so habitually that the same acid phrases are found over and over again, even in works separated chronologically by nearly a lifetime. But the monotony the reader may feel in considering Jerome's satiric passages *in toto* is not justly to be blamed on the writer himself. Jerome did not, after all, intend that satiric sections be sliced from the body of his writings and then placed under a microscope for purposes of examination and comparison. Jerome's tendency to repeat identical phrases, to repaint the same satiric pictures, proves that his language, even when vehemently passionate, is always under the careful control of his intellect. The same is proved by the large store of declamatory techniques upon which Jerome is constantly drawing. Hyperbole, asyndeton, polysyndeton, alliteration, apostrophe, rhetorical questions, carefully placed *sententiae*—these are the stock in trade of the school-trained writer of antiquity, and we should not be surprised to find Jerome availing himself of them in order to increase the effectiveness of his satire. It is difficult for moderns to realize the hold that rhetoric exercised over the ancient intellect, but the reader who feels that an inevitable conflict exists between calculated writing and the expression of sincere emotion is judging by modern standards.[56] Jerome's satiric language proves that the characteristic ancient emphasis on style and form in literature is maintained until the end of antiquity.

Jerome's studied elaboration of his satire and his frequent borrowings could justly be condemned only if they tended to obscure his own individuality as a writer. But no one would venture to make such a charge. Beneath almost every satiric phrase, the borrowed as well as the original, there glows a powerful personality—bitter, witty, ambitious, discontent, abusive, and fiercely moral. Eduard Norden's general dictum that in Christian writing the individual personality of the author is far less prominent than in pagan literature is clearly inapplicable to St. Jerome, for Jerome in his satire depicts his own character, his loves and hates, his ideals and disappointments, with greater vividness and vigor than any of the pagan satirists, including Juvenal, reveal themselves in theirs.[57] Jerome's unique greatness as a satirist lies precisely in his ability to fuse passionate personal feelings with a moral system imposed from without. Jerome's fervent attachment to Christianity and his championship of adamantine orthodoxy in no way embarrass or restrain the vigor of his satire but on the contrary promote it. Indeed, in the very possession of a firm and certain moral system Jerome is distinguished from all the leading pagan satirists except Persius, for Horace admits that he wanders from school to school, while

[56] Cf. E. Norden, *Die antike Kunstprosa*, II, 457: "Behandelte einmal ein Schriftsteller realistische Stoffe des täglichen Lebens, so stilisierte er sie doch mehr als uns modern empfindenden Menschen lieb ist."

[57] Norden, *Antik. Kunst.*, II, 455. The endless debate over Juvenal's true beliefs and hopes would obviously never have begun if he had expressed these clearly in his satires. Of course, Juvenal indicates plainly enough whom he hates, but not whom he loves.

Juvenal has no clearer idea of what society should be than any intelligent but completely unphilosophic man.[58] To Jerome the world is no more pleasant a place than it is to the earlier satirists, but Jerome, unlike the pagans, knows how he wants it to be reformed. His attack on society thus acquires a direction and reforming purpose quite foreign to most classical satire, which usually tends toward purely negative social criticism.

This earnest reforming aim of Jerome's does much to explain certain puzzling elements of his satire. The excessive vividness of many of his scenes of immorality may shock the reader who fails to remember that obscenity is native to the satiric genre and that the purpose of Jerome's indecency is to disgust and thus reform the evildoer. Jerome's free use of venomous and malicious ridicule toward his personal enemies may leave him open to the charge of prostituting his satiric gifts, elsewhere used in the service of the Church, for private ends. But since Jerome did not readily distinguish his own foes from those of the Church, even his malevolence toward individuals, though it frequently arose from petty jealousy, seemed to him to serve the cause of moral improvement. Blind though Jerome was to the many faults of his own character and harshly unsympathetic to the natural human weaknesses of others, he nonetheless always believed that his harshness served the cause of Christianity in general and the ascetic movement in particular. Thus the history of Roman satire ends on a positive note. The world is a dismal place, but it can be made better, and Jerome has both a reform program—Christian asceticism—and an instrument for putting this program into effect—satire. If we consider St. Jerome's profound dismay at the decadent world in which he lived and his earnest belief that only through Christianity could life become worth living, if, furthermore, we understand the innate irasci-

---

[58] See Horace *Epist.* i. 1. 13–19 and Juvenal 13. 120–124 for the satirists' philosophic confusion.

bility of his temperament and appreciate the thoroughness of his acquaintance with pagan and Christian letters, we must agree that Jerome could justly apply to himself the words of Juvenal: *Difficile est saturam non scribere.*

Bibliography

Editions of St. Jerome

S. Eusebii Hieronymi opera omnia. (*Patrologiae Latinae cursus completus*, XXII–XXX.) Ed. by J. P. Migne. Paris 1854–1890. Based on the second edition of D. Vallarsi, Venice, 1766–1772.

S. Hieronymi Presbyteri commentarioli in Psalmos. (*Anecdota Maredsolana*, III, pt. i.) Ed. by G. Morin. Maredsou, 1895.

S. Hieronymi Presbyteri tractatus sive homiliae. (*Anecdota Maredsolana*, III, pts. ii and iii.) Ed. by G. Morin. Maredsou, 1897 and 1903.

S. Eusebii Hieronymi epistulae. (*Corpus scriptorum ecclesiasticorum Latinorum*, LIV–LVI.) Ed. by I. Hilberg. 3 vols. Vienna and Leipzig, 1910–1912.

S. Eusebii Hieronymi in Hieremiam Prophetam libri sex. (*Corpus scriptorum ecclesiasticorum Latinorum*, LIX.) Ed. by S. Reiter. Vienna and Leipzig, 1912.

Eusebius Hieronymus. *Eusebii Pamphili chronici canones.* Ed. by J. K. Fotheringham. London, 1923.

Selected Letters of St. Jerome. Ed. and tr. by F. A. Wright. ("Loeb Classical Library.") London and New York, 1933.

Saint Jérôme. *Lettres.* (Collection Guillaume Budé.) Ed. with a French translation by Jérôme Labourt. 7 vols. Paris, 1949–1961.

Saint Jérôme. *Sur Jonas.* Ed. with a French translation by P. Antin. Paris, 1956.

St. Jerome. *The Satirical Letters.* Tr. into English by Paul Carroll. Chicago, 1956.

S. Hieronymi Presbyteri opera: pt. i, *Opera exegetica;* pt. ii, *Opera homiletica.* (*Corpus Christianorum*, LXXII and LXXVIII.) Turnhout, 1958 and 1959.

Editions of Other Authors

S. *Ambrosii opera*, pt. ii. (*Corpus scriptorum ecclesiasticorum Latinorum*, XXXII.) Ed. by C. Schenkl. Vienna and Leipzig, 1897.

Ammiani Marcellini rerum gestarum libri qui supersunt. Ed. by V. Gardthausen. 2 vols. Leipzig, 1874–1875.

Anthologia lyrica Graeca. Ed. by E. Diehl. 3d ed. Leipzig, 1952.

Aphthonius. *Progymnasmata.* Tr. by Raymond E. Nadeau. *Speech Monographs*, XIX (1952), 264–285.

The Apocryphal New Testament. Tr. by Montague Rhodes James. Oxford, 1924; reprinted 1945.

Arnobii adversus nationes. (*Corpus scriptorum ecclesiasticorum Latinorum*, IV.) Ed. by A. Reifferscheid. Vienna, 1875.

Arnobius. *The Case against the Pagans.* (*Ancient Christian Writers*, VII and VIII.) Tr. and with a commentary by George McCracken. Westminster, Md., and London, 1949.

S. *Aurelii Augustini epistulae.* (*Corpus scriptorum ecclesiasticorum Latinorum*, XXXIV, XXXXIV, and LVIII.) Ed. by A. Goldbacher. Vienna, 1885–1923.

Cicero. *In Pisonem.* Ed. by R. G. M. Nisbet. Oxford, 1961.

Claudianus. *Invectives contre Eutrope.* Ed. by P. Fargues. Paris, 1933.

Comicorum Atticorum fragmenta, I. Ed. by T. Kock. Leipzig, 1880.

Epigrammata Bobiensia, II. Ed. by F. Munari. Rome, 1955.

Epistulae imperatorum pontificum aliorum. (*Corpus scriptorum ecclesiasticorum Latinorum*, XXXV.) Ed. by O. Guenther. Vienna, Leipzig, and Prague, 1895.

Festi opera. Ed. by W. M. Lindsay. Leipzig, 1913.

Gennadius. *De viris illustribus.* Ed. by E. C. Richardson. In Oscar von Gebhardt and Adolf Harnack, *Texte und Untersuchungen*, XIV, no. 1 (Leipzig, 1896), 57–97.

Grammatici Latini, I. Ed. by H. Keil. Leipzig, 1857.

Gregorii Nazianzeni opera. (*Patrologiae Graecae cursus completus*, XXXVI.) Paris, 1886. Based on the edition of A. Caillau (Paris, 1778 and 1840).

Gregorii Nysseni contra Eunomium libri. Ed. by W. Jaeger. Leiden, 1960.

Q. Horatii Flacci opera. Ed. by F. Klingner. Leipzig, 1959.

Iovinianus: Die Fragmente seiner Schriften, die Quellen zu seiner Geschichte, sein Leben und seine Lehre. Ed. by W. Haller. In Oscar von Gebhardt and Adolf Harnack, *Texte und Untersuchungen,* XVII, no. 2 (Leipzig, 1897).

Joannis Chrysostomi opera. (*Patrologiae Graecae cursus completus,* XLVII–LXI.) Paris, 1862–1863.

D. Junii Juvenalis saturarum libri V. Ed. by L. Friedlaender. 2 vols. Leipzig, 1895.

Lactantii opera, pt. i. (*Corpus scriptorum ecclesiasticorum Latinorum,* XIX.) Ed. by Samuel Brandt. Vienna, Leipzig, and Prague, 1890.

C. Lucilii carminum reliquiae. Ed. by F. Marx. Leipzig, 1914.

Minucius Felix. *Octavius.* (*Corpus scriptorum Latinorum Paravianum.*) Ed. by M. Pellegrino. Turin, 1950.

Palladius. *The Lausiac History.* Ed. by J. A. Robinson, in *Texts and Studies, Contributions to Biblical and Patristic Literature,* VI (Cambridge, 1904).

Sancti Paulini Nolani epistulae. (*Corpus scriptorum ecclesiasticorum Latinorum,* XXVIII.) Ed. by G. de Hartel. Vienna, 1893.

A. Persi Flacci et D. Iuni Iuvenalis saturae. Ed. W. Clausen. Oxford, 1959.

A. Persius Flaccus. *Satires.* Ed. by John Conington. Oxford, 1893.

Petronii saturae. Ed. by F. Buecheler. 6th ed. Berlin, 1922.

Prudentius. *Works.* Tr. by H. J. Thompson. ("Loeb Classical Library.") London and Cambridge, Mass., 1953.

Quintilian. *Institutio oratoria,* xii. Ed. by R. G. Austin. 2d ed. Oxford, 1954.

Rhetorica ad Herennium. Ed. and tr. by H. Caplan. ("Loeb Classical Library.") London and Cambridge, Mass., 1954.

Rufini opera omnia. (*Patrologiae Latinae cursus completus,* XXI.) Paris, 1878. Based on the edition of D. Vallarsi (Verona, 1745).

Rutilius Namatianus. *De reditu suo.* Ed. by Charles H. Keene. London, 1907.

Seneca. *Epistulae morales.* Tr. by R. M. Gummere. ("Loeb Classical Library.") London and New York, 1921.

Suetonii opera. Ed. by A. Reifferscheid. Leipzig, 1860.

Suetonius. *De poetis.* Ed. by A. Rostagni. Turin, 1956.

Sulpici Severi libri qui supersunt. (*Corpus scriptorum ecclesiasticorum Latinorum,* I.) Ed. by C. Halm. Vienna, 1886.

Tertulliani apologeticum. (*Corpus scriptorum ecclesiasticorum Latinorum,* LXIX.) Ed. by Heinrich Hoppe. Vienna and Leipzig, 1939.

Tertulliani opera. (*Corpus scriptorum ecclesiasticorum Latinorum,* LXX.) Ed. by Aemilius Kroymann. Vienna and Leipzig, 1942.

Tertulliani opera. ("Opera Montanistica," pt. ii, of *Corpus Christianorum, Series Latina,* II.) Turnhout, 1954.

The Theodosian Code. Tr. by Clyde Pharr. Princeton, 1952.

General Works

Altaner, B. *Patrologie.* 5th ed. Freiburg-im-Breisgau, 1958.

Bardenhewer, O. *Geschichte der altkirchlichen Literatur,* III. Freiburg-im-Breisgau, 1912.

Baron, Salo W. *A Social and Religious History of the Jews,* II. 2d ed. New York, 1952.

Caspar, E. *Geschichte des Papstums,* I. Tübingen, 1930.

Courcelle, P. *Les Lettres Grecques en Occident, de Macrobe à Cassiodore.* (*Bibliothèque des Ecoles Françaises d'Athènes et de Rome,* Fascicle CLIX.) Paris, 1943.

Daniel-Rops, H. *The Church in the Dark Ages.* Tr. by A. Butler. London, 1959.

A Dictionary of Christian Biography. Ed. by W. Smith and H. Wace. 4 vols. London, 1887.

Dictionnaire de Théologie Catholique. 15 vols. Paris, 1930–1950.

Dill, Samuel. *Roman Society in the Last Century of the Western Empire.* 2d ed. London, 1899.

Duff, J. Wight. *Roman Satire.* Berkeley, Calif., 1936.

Festugière, A.-J. *Les Moines d'Orient.* Paris, 1961.

Gaudemet, H. *L'Eglise dans l'Empire Romain, IVe–Ve Siècles.* Paris, 1958.

Geffcken, Johannes. *Der Ausgang des Griechisch-Römischen Hei-dentums.* Heidelberg, 1929.

Gibbon, Edward. *The History of the Decline and Fall of the Roman Empire.* Ed. by J. B. Bury. 7 vols. 2d ed. London, 1929.

Glover, T. R. *Life and Letters in the Fourth Century.* Cambridge, 1901.

Graetz, Heinrich. *History of the Jews,* II. Tr. by J. K. Gutheim. Philadelphia, 1893; reprinted 1941.

Harnack, Adolf. *Das Mönchtum, seine Ideale und seine Geschichte.* Giessen, 1881.

Hatch, Edwin. *The Influence of Greek Ideas on Christianity.* (Hibbert Lectures, 1888.) Ed. by A. M. Fairbairn. London and Edinburgh, 1891; reprinted New York, 1957.

Juster, Jean. *Les Juifs dans l'Empire Romain.* 2 vols. Paris, 1914.

Knoche, U. *Die Römische Satire.* 2d. ed. Göttingen, 1957.

Labriolle, P. de. *Histoire de la Littérature Latine Chrétienne.* 3d ed. 2 vols. Paris, 1947.

———. *La Réaction Païenne.* Paris, 1934.

Laistner, M. L. W. *Christianity and Pagan Culture in the Later Roman Empire.* Ithaca, 1951.

Leon, Harry. *The Jews of Ancient Rome.* Philadelphia, 1960.

Lukyn-Williams, A. *Adversus Iudaeos.* Cambridge, 1953.

Norden, Eduard. *Die antike Kunstprosa.* 5th ed. Stuttgart, 1958.

Otto, A. *Die Sprichwörter und sprichwörtlichen Redensarten der Römer.* Leipzig, 1890.

Palanque, J.-R., G. Bardy, and P. de Labriolle. *Histoire de l'Eglise de la Paix Constantinienne à la Mort de Theodose.* (Vol. III in Fliche and Martin, *Histoire de l'Eglise.*) Paris, 1950.

Pauly-Wissowa-Kroll. *Realencyclopaedie der Klassischen Alter-tumswissenschaft.* Stuttgart, 1893 ff.

Rand, E. K. *Founders of the Middle Ages.* Cambridge, Mass., 1928; reprinted New York, 1957.

The New Schaff-Herzog Encyclopedia of Religious Knowledge. 12 vols. New York, 1908.

Schanz-Hosius-Krüger. *Geschichte der Römischen Literatur.* (Iwan von Müller's *Handbuch.*) 4 vols. Munich, 1914–1935.

Schneider, Carl. *Geistesgeschichte des antiken Christentums*. 2 vols. Munich, 1954.

Simon, Marcel. *Verus Israel*. Paris, 1948.

Smalley, Beryl. *The Study of the Bible in the Middle Ages*. 2d ed. Oxford, 1952.

Stein, Ernst. *Histoire du Bas-Empire*. French translation by J.-R. Palanque. 2 vols. Paris and Bruges, 1959.

Terzaghi, N. *Per la storia della satire*. Turin, 1933.

Vogt, Joseph. *Von der Gleichwertigkeit der Geschlechter in der bürgerlichen Gesellschaft der Griechen*. Wiesbaden, 1960.

Wendland, Paul. *Die Hellenistisch-Römische Kultur*. Tübingen, 1907.

Zeller, E. *Outlines of the History of Greek Philosophy*. Tr. by L. R. Palmer. 13th ed. London, 1955.

Special Studies on St. Jerome

Antin, P. *Essai sur Saint Jérôme*. Paris, 1951.

Auvray, P. "S. Jérôme et S. Augustin: La Controverse au Sujet de l'Incident d'Antioche," *Recherches de Science Religieuse*, XXIX (1939), 594–610.

Bardy, Gustave. "Saint Jérôme et ses Maîtres Hébreux," *Revue Bénédictine*, XLVI (1934), 145–164.

Basabe, E. "San Jeronimo y los Clasicos," *Helmantica*, II (1951), 161–192.

Baur, C. "S. Jérôme et S. Jean Chrysostome," *Revue Bénédictine*, XXIII (1906), 430–436.

Bickel, E. "Das asketische Ideal bei Ambrosius Hieronymus, und Augustinus," *Neue Jahrbücher für das klassische Altertum*, XXXVII (1916), 437–474.

Brochet, J. *Saint Jérôme et ses Ennemis*. Paris, 1905.

Bruyne, D. de. "La Correspondance Echangée entre Augustin et Jérôme," *Zeitschrift für die neutestamentliche Wissenschaft*, XXXI (1932), 233–248.

——. "La Lettre de Jérôme à Sunnia et Fretela sur le Psautier," *ibid.*, XXVIII (1929), 1–13.

Cavallera, Ferdinand. *Saint Jérôme, sa Vie et son Oeuvre. (Spicilegium Sacrum Lovaniense.)* 2 vols. Louvain and Paris, 1922.

Collombet, F. Z. *Histoire de Saint Jérôme, Père de l'Eglise au IVe Siècle, ses Ecrits et ses Doctrines.* Paris, 1844.

Courcelle, P. "Paulin de Nole et Saint Jérôme," *Revue des Etudes Latines,* XXV (1947), 250–280.

Delhaye, P. "Le Dossier Anti-Matrimonial de l'*Adversus Jovinianum* et son Influence sur Quelques Ecrits Latins du XIIe Siècle," *Medieval Studies,* XIII (1951), 65–86.

Demougeot, E. "Saint Jérôme les Oracles Sibyllins et Stilicon," *Revue des Etudes Anciennes,* LIV (1952), 83–92.

Diederich, M. D. "The Epitaphium S. Paulae: An Index to St. Jerome's Classicism (epist. 108)," *Classical Journal,* XLIX (1953–1954), 369–372.

Duckworth, G. E. "Classical Echoes in St. Jerome's Life of Malchus," *Classical Bulletin,* XXIV (1947–1948), 29–30.

Eiswirth, Rudolf. *Hieronymus' Stellung zur Literatur und Kunst. (Klassisch-Philologische Studien,* ed. by Herter and Schmidt, XVI.) Wiesbaden, 1955.

Favez, Charles. "La Satire dans les Lettres de Saint Jérôme," *Revue des Etudes Latines,* XXIV (1946), 209–226.

Goelzer, Henri. *Etude Lexicographique et Grammaticale de la Latinité de Saint Jérôme.* Paris, 1884.

Gonsette, M. "Les Directeurs Spirituels de Démétriade," *Nouvelle Revue Théologique,* LX (1933), 783–801.

Grützmacher, G. *Hieronymus: Eine biographische Studie zur alten Kirchengeshichte.* 3 vols. Berlin, 1901, 1906, 1908.

Harenzda, G. *De oratorio genere dicendi, quo Hieronymus in epistulis usus sit.* Bratislava, 1905.

Hritzu, J. N. *The Style of the Letters of St. Jerome. (Catholic University of America Patristic Studies,* LX.) Washington, D.C., 1939.

Hughes, L. *The Christian Church in the Epistles of St. Jerome.* London, 1923.

Kelly, Sister M. Jamesetta. *Life and Times as Revealed in the Writings of St. Jerome Exclusive of His Letters. (Catholic University of America Patristic Studies,* LXX.) Washington, D.C., 1944.

Kunst, C. *De S. Hieronymi studiis Ciceronianis.* (*Dissertationes philologae Vindobonenses.*) Vienna, 1918.

Levy, Harry. "Claudian's *In Rufinum* and an Epistle of St. Jerome," *American Journal of Philology*, LXIX (1948), 62–68.

Luebeck, Aemilius. *Hieronymus quos noverit scriptores et ex quibus hauserit.* Leipzig, 1872.

Malfatti, E. "Una controversia fra S. Agostino e S. Girolamo: Il conflitto di Antiocha," *La Scuola Cattolica*, XLIX (1921), 321–338, 402–426.

Miscellanea Geronimiana: Scritti varii publicati nel XV centenario della morte di San Girolamo. Rome, 1920.

Mohrmann, C. "St. Jérôme et St. Augustin sur Tertullien," *Vigiliae Christianae*, V (1951), 111–112.

Morin, Dom G. "Un Passage Enigmatique de S. Jérôme," *Revue Bénédictine*, XXX (1913), 174–186.

Murphy, F. X., ed. *A Monument to St. Jerome.* New York, 1952.

Pease, A. S. "The Attitude of Jerome towards Pagan Literature," *Transactions and Proceedings of the American Philological Association*, L (1919), 150–167.

——. "Medical Allusions in the Works of St. Jerome," *Harvard Studies in Classical Philology*, XXV (1914), 73–86.

——. "Notes on St. Jerome's Tractatus on the Psalms," *Journal of Biblical Literature*, XXVI (1907), 107–131.

Pence, M. A. "Satire in St. Jerome," *Classical Journal*, XXXVI (1941), 322–336.

Penna, Angelo. *Principi e caratere dell' esegesi di S. Girolamo.* Rome, 1950.

——. *S. Girolamo.* Rome and Turin, 1949.

Préaux, Jean-G. "Procédés d'Invention d'un Sobriquet par Saint Jérôme," *Latomus*, XVII (1958), 659–664.

Pronberger, N. *Beiträge zur Chronologie der Briefe des hl. Hieronymus.* Amberg, 1913.

Puech, A. *Saint Jean Chrysostome et les Moeurs de son Temps.* Paris, 1891.

Rahmer, M. *Die hebräischen Traditionen in den Werken des Hieronymus.* Breslau, 1861.

Schultzen, F. "Die Benutzung der Schriften Tertullians de monogamia und de ieiunio bei Hieronymus adversus Iovinianum," *Neue Jahrbücher für deutsche Theologie*, III (1894), 485–502.

Seliga, S. "De Hieronymi scriptorum colore satirico," in *Charisteria Gustavo Przychocki* (Warsaw, 1924).

——. "Quibus contumeliis Hieronymus adversarios carpserit," *Eos*, XXXIV (1932–1933), 395–412.

Simard, Georges. "La Querelle de Deux Saints, Saint Jérôme et Saint Augustin," *Revue de l'Université d'Ottawa*, XII (1942), 15–38.

Stade, W. *Hieronymus in prooemiis quid tractaverit et quos auctores quasque leges rhetoricas secutus sit.* Rostock, 1925.

Steinmann, J. *Saint Jérôme.* Paris, 1958.

Süss, Wilhelm. "Der heilige Hieronymus und die Formen seiner Polemik," *Giessener Beiträge zur deutschen Philologie*, LX (1938), 212–238.

Zöckler, D. *Hieronymus, sein Leben und Wirken aus seinen Schriften dargestellt.* Gotha, 1865.

Studies on Related Topics

Anderson, W. S. "Juvenal and Quintilian," *Yale Studies in Classical Philology*, XVII (1961), 3–93.

Baur, C. *John Chrysostom and His Times.* Tr. by Sister M. Gonzaga. 2 vols. Westminster, Md., 1959.

Bickel, E. *Diatribe in Senecae Philosophi fragmenta.* (*Fragmenta de matrimonio*, I.) Leipzig, 1915.

Bitterman, H. "The Beginning of the Struggle between the Regular and Secular Clergy," in *Medieval and Historical Essays in Honor of J. W. Westfall* (Chicago, 1938), pp. 19–26.

Bloch, Herbert. "A New Document of the Last Pagan Revival in the West, 393–394 A.D.," *Harvard Theological Review*, XXXVIII (1945), 199–244.

Buck, Sister M. Joseph Aloysius. *S. Ambrosii De Helia et Ieiunio: A Commentary with Introduction and Translation.* (*Catholic University of America Patristic Studies*, XIX.) Washington, D.C., 1929.

Capelle, W., and H. I. Marrou. "Diatribe," in T. Klausner, ed.,

Reallexikon für die Antike und Christentum, III (Stuttgart, 1957), cols. 990–1009.

Caplan, Harry. "The Four Senses of Scriptural Interpretation and the Mediaeval Theory of Preaching," *Speculum*, IV (1929), 282–290.

Courcelle, P. "Commodien et les Invasions du Vᵉ Siècle," *Revue des Etudes Latines*, XXIV (1946), 227–246.

Decker, J. de. *Juvenalis declamans*. Ghent, 1913.

De Lacy, Phillip. "Cicero's Invective against Piso," *Transactions and Proceedings of the American Philological Association*, LXXII (1941), 49–58.

Delehaye, H. *Les Légendes Hagiographiques*. 3d ed. Brussels, 1927.

Dirking, A. S. *Basilii Magni de divitiis et paupertate sententiae quam habeant rationem cum veterum philosophorum doctrina*. Münster, 1911.

Dudden, F. Homes. *The Life and Times of St. Ambrose*. 2 vols. Oxford, 1935.

Ellspermann, G. L. *The Attitude of the Early Christian Latin Writers toward Pagan Literature and Learning*. (*Catholic University of America Patristic Studies*, LXXXII.) Washington, D.C., 1949.

Fiske, G. C. *Lucilius and Horace*. Madison, 1920.

Froebel, E. *Quid veteres de Horatii poematis iudicaverint*. Jena, 1911.

Gauger, F. *Zeitschilderung und Topik bei Juvenal*. Greifswald, 1936.

Geffcken, J. *Kynika und Verwandtes*. Heidelberg, 1909.

Grant, M. A. *The Ancient Rhetorical Theories of the Laughable*. (*University of Wisconsin Studies in Language and Literature*, XXI.) Madison, 1924.

Hagendahl, Harald. *Latin Fathers and the Classics*. (*Studia Graeca et Latina Gothoburgensia*, VI.) Göteborg, 1958.

Harnack, Adolf. *Die Altercatio Simonis Iudaei et Theophili Christiani nebst Untersuchungen über die antijüdische Polemik in der alten Kirche*. In Oscar von Gebhardt and Adolf Harnack, *Texte und Untersuchungen*, I, pt. iii (Leipzig, 1883).

Haury, A. *L'Ironie et l'Humeur chez Ciceron.* Leiden and Paris, 1955.

Hendrickson, G. L. "Satura—the Genesis of a Literary Form," *Classical Philology,* VI (1911), 129–143.

——. "Satura tota nostra est," *Classical Philology,* XXII (1927), 46–60.

Hertz, M. *Analecta ad carminum Horatianorum historiam.* Breslau, 1876–1882.

Highet, Gilbert. *Juvenal the Satirist.* Oxford, 1954.

——. "The Philosophy of Juvenal," *Transactions and Proceedings of the American Philological Association,* LXXX (1949), 254–270.

Knoche, U. *Handschriftliche Grundlagen des Juvenaltextes, Philologus,* Suppl. Vol. XXXIII (1940), fascicle 1.

Kraus, S. "The Jew in the Works of the Church Fathers. VI: Jerome," *Jewish Quarterly Review,* VI (1894), 225–261.

Leclerq, H. "Cénobitisme," *Dictionnaire d'Archéologie Chrétienne et de Liturgie,* II (1925), cols. 3047 ff.

——. "Monachisme," *ibid.,* XI (1934), cols. 1774 ff.

Marrou, H. I. *S. Augustin et la Fin de la Culture Antique.* Paris, 1939.

McGuire, Martin R. P. *S. Ambrosii De Nabuthae: A Commentary with an Introduction and Translation.* (Catholic University of America Patristic Studies, XV.) Washington, D.C., 1927.

Meyer, L. *Chrysostome Maître de Perfection Chrétienne.* Paris, 1934.

Murphy, F. X. *Rufinus of Aquileia* [345–411]: *His Life and Works.* (Catholic University of America Studies in Medieval History, n.s. VI.) Washington, D.C., 1945.

Myers, J. N. L. "Pelagius and the End of Roman Rule in Britain," *Journal of Roman Studies,* L (1960), 21–36.

Petit, P. *Libanius et la Vie Municipale à Antioche au IV Siècle après J.-C.* Paris, 1955.

Pétré, Hélène. *Journal de Voyage.* Paris, 1948.

Praechter, Karl. *Hierokles der Stoiker.* Leipzig, 1901.

Reich, H. *Der Mimus: Ein litterarentwicklungsgeschichtlicher Versuch,* I. Berlin, 1903.

Reville, A. *Vigilance de Calagurris.* Paris, 1902.

Säflund, Gosta. *De Pallio und die stilistische Entwicklung Tertullians.* Lund, 1955.

Schneider, Carl. *Juvenal und Seneca.* Würzburg, 1930.

Schütz, R. *Juvenalis ethicus.* Greifswald, 1905.

Scott, Inez G. *The Grand Style in the Satires of Juvenal.* ("Smith College Classical Studies.") Northampton, Mass., 1927.

Strong, H. A. "Ausonius' Debt to Juvenal," *Classical Review*, XXV (1911), 15–16.

Thompson, E. A. *The Historical Work of Ammianus Marcellinus.* Cambridge, 1947.

Viller, M., and K. Rahner. *Askese und Mystik in der Väterzeit.* Freiburg-im-Breisgau, 1939.

Wageningen, Jacobus van. "Seneca et Juvenalis," *Mnemosyne*, n.s. XLV (1917), 417–429.

Weston, A. *Latin Satirical Writing Subsequent to Juvenal.* Lancaster, Pa., 1915.

Wilde, R. *The Treatment of the Jews in the Greek Christian Writers of the First Three Centuries.* (*Catholic University of America Patristic Studies*, LXXXI.) Washington, D.C., 1949.

Zappala, M. "L'inspirazione cristiana del "De Pallio" di Tertulliano," *Ricerche Religiose*, I (1925), 132–149.

Index

Albina, Roman matron, 28
Ambrose, St., Bishop of Milan, 49n., 83, 100–101n., 117, 121n., 210n., 212, 213n., 235, 240–244
Ammianus Marcellinus, 2n., 3, 21, 25, 27, 30n., 66, 70n., 109, 111, 124n., 134, 136n., 166
Anderson, W. S., 172
Aphthonius, rhetorician, 115, 220
Apocalypse of Paul, 66, 67, 117
Apollinarius of Laodicea, 167
Arianism, 109, 167, 173
Aristophanes, 57, 113–114, 220
Aristotle, 153, 172n.
Arnobius, 169, 265
    satiric attack on paganism, 15–16
Ascetic movement, 42, 46–47, 63, 66–68, 74, 86–90, 104, 111
Asella, Roman matron, 28
Atarbius, 174
Augustine, St., Bishop of Hippo, 19n., 23n., 115n., 145, 177, 213n., 225
    quarrel with Jerome, 235–240
Ausonius, 4

Bar Anina, 189, 234
Basil, St., 169
Biblical exegesis, 54, 95–96, 189–190
Bickel, E., 28n., 153–157, 159n.
Blesilla, daughter of St. Paula, 31, 125n., 128–129

Caplan, Harry, 95n., 172n.
Carmen ad senatorem, 18
Carmen contra paganos, 18

Cavallera, Ferdinand, 10n., 12, 40, 48, 73n., 82n., 85n., 140–141, 201n., 209n., 213n., 218, 234n., 243
Chrysostom, St. John, 34, 44, 48, 134, 139, 163n., 165, 169, 189, 191n., 192
Cicero, 4, 10–11, 58, 68–69n., 72, 88, 168, 171n., 172, 176, 182n., 183n., 186, 187, 198, 203–204, 209, 212, 217, 220, 227n., 234n., 266n.
Claudian, 4
Commodianus, 15
Courcelle, P., 8, 9, 15n., 37n., 40n.
Cynic diatribe, 114, 170–171
Cyprian, Bishop of Carthage, 106n., 189

Damasus, Pope, 30, 66, 69, 71, 106, 117, 173
Demetrias, 35, 145, 175
Diomedes, grammarian, 1
Domnio, 206, 207, 208, 253
Donatus, Aelius, 7
Duff, J. Wight, 2n., 250n., 252n.

Eiswirth, R., 8, 10n., 36n.
Ellspermann, G. L., 8
Ennius, Quintus, 233
Ephraem Syrus, 189
Epiphanius, Bishop of Salamis, 226, 227, 255n.
Euripides, 113
Eusebius, Bishop of Caesarea, 189
Eusebius of Cremona, 105
Eustochium, daughter of St. Paula, 32, 70, 76, 118, 119, 123–128, 137, 140, 240, 247, 249

Fabia Aconia Paulina, 195–196
Fabiola, Roman matron, 138
Favez, C., 194n.
Fiske, George C., 72n., 170n., 171n., 250n., 266, 267
Furia, Roman matron, 131–134, 136, 157, 259

Gauger, Fritz, 266
Gibbon, Edward, 48, 51
Gluttony, satiric attack on, 24–25, 27, 43–44, 77–79, 134–135, 182–183, 192, 211, 212
Gnosticism, 111, 116, 127n., 163, 167, 177
Gregory Nazianzen, 66, 106n., 117, 169
Gregory of Nyssa, 167–168
Grützmacher, G., 11, 26n., 35–36, 39–40, 47, 71, 81, 83n., 128, 131, 194n., 213n., 236n., 239, 242n., 243

Hagendahl, Harald, 8, 10n., 11n., 17n., 194n., 212, 241n., 242n.
Hatch, Edwin, 168, 169n.
Heliodorus, Bishop of Altinum, 33, 75, 81
Helvidius, 148–152, 259
see also Jerome, works, *Adversus Helvidium*
Hendrickson, G. L., 1n., 2n.
Heretics, 57, 167–188, 197–198, 200
see also Arianism, Gnosticism, Helvidius, Jovinianus, Origen, Pelagianism, Rufinus, *and* Vigilantius
Hesiod, 113
Hilary of Poitiers, 167
Hilberg, I., 8, 85n.
Hippolytus, St., 185n.
Horace, 1, 2, 4, 9, 24, 34n., 61, 109, 187, 248, 250, 254, 255, 266, 269
popularity of in late antiquity, 5
works:
Ars Poetica, 217, 232
Epistles:
i. 1: 55, 215
i. 2: 52, 59, 192

i. 3: 204, 232n., 241
i. 4: 52, 214
i. 5: 204n.
i. 11: 173–174
ii. 1: 37, 232
ii. 2: 170
Odes:
ii. 14: 49
ii. 15: 33
iii. 27: 242
Satires:
i. 1: 54–56, 60
i. 2: 44–45
i. 3: 140
i. 4: 171, 208n., 254
i. 6: 74, 140
i. 8: 17
i. 10: 55, 85n., 98n., 171, 232, 256
ii. 2: 79n.
ii. 6: 29, 46

Innocent, Pope, 145

Jerome, St.:
classical learning of, 7–10, 62, 268–271; see also Cicero, Horace, Juvenal, Persius, Petronius, Plautus, *and* Terence
education of, 7–9, 170, 189–190, 232
Hebrew learning of, 189–190
hostility toward, 31, 36–37, 82, 127–130, 200–203, 206, 209–212, 244, 257–258, 262
motives for his satire, 46–47, 92, 111–112, 151–152, 167–173, 197–198, 257–264, 270–271
personality of, 11, 31, 38, 47, 62, 200–201, 239, 263–264, 269–271
relationships with women, 38, 76, 118, 164
settlement at Bethlehem, 32
translation of the Bible, 200–202, 211, 236, 244
WORKS:
Adversus Helvidium, 14n., 42, 148–152
Adversus Iovinianum, 14, 42, 52, 91, 116, 151n., 155–160, 213, 217

Jerome, St., works (*cont.*)
  Chronicle of Eusebius, 240, 254n.,
    255n., 263
  commentaries:
    on Amos (*In Amos*), 58, 181, 183,
      184n., 193–194
    on Daniel (*In Danielem*), 22
    on Ecclesiastes (*In Ecclesiasten*),
      50n., 54, 56, 96–97, 259, 260
    on Ephesians (*In Epist. ad Ephe-
      sios*), 5, 56, 57, 98, 99, 173, 211,
      241n.
    on Ezekiel (*In Ezechielem*), 60, 63,
      67, 98, 108–109, 182, 183, 184,
      185, 186, 187, 192, 196n., 197,
      229, 235
    on Galatians (*In Epist. ad Gala-
      tas*), 97, 170, 196, 260, 262
    on Habakkuk (*In Abacuc*), 234
    on Hosea (*In Osee*), 181, 183, 184,
      185, 186, 187, 210n., 212, 244
    on Isaiah (*In Isaiam*), 6, 59, 107–
      108, 118, 121, 122, 161, 162,
      163, 182, 183, 184, 186, 191, 192,
      193, 211, 239n.
    on Jeremiah (*In Jeremiam*), 110,
      182, 183, 184, 219n.
    on Jonah (*In Jonam*), 182, 185
    on Malachi (*In Malachiam*), 107
    on Matthew (*In Evang. Matthaei*),
      105, 196
    on Micah (*In Michaeam*), 57–58,
      102–103, 181, 183, 184, 194, 210,
      212, 216n.
    on Nahum (*In Naum*), 185, 192,
      234–235
    on Obadiah (*In Abdiam*), 195,
      196
    on Titus (*In Epist. ad Titum*), 160,
      192–193, 224
    on Zechariah (*In Zachariam*),
      35n., 58, 106, 181, 192, 194
    on Zephaniah (*In Sophoniam*),
      104–105, 118, 185, 192, 248
  Contra Joannem, 66, 167n.
  Contra Rufinum, 5, 6, 211, 212, 227n.,
    231–234, 243n., 254; *see also*
    Rufinus of Aquileia

  Contra Vigilantium, 84, 92, 159n.,
    219, 222–225; *see also* Vigilantius
    of Calagurris
  De Nominibus Heb., 193
  De Viris Illustribus, 94n., 117n., 118,
    240–241
  Dial. contra Luciferianos, 65n.
  Dial. contra Pelagianos, 53, 112, 161–
    162, 166, 177–179, 197, 230, 260;
    see also Pelagianism
  Homilies, 60n., 93–95, 179–180, 194
  Letters:
    6: 201
    7: 68–69
    14: 33, 46
    16: 173–174
    21: 69
    22: 2n., 8, 10n., 14, 28, 47, 70–73,
      89n., 119–127, 147, 203n., 205n.,
      240, 247, 251, 257n.
    23: 125n., 195–196
    24: 26, 37n., 261
    27: 37n., 74, 128, 201–202, 204
    33: 24, 26, 41, 175, 209n.
    37: 130
    38: 30, 74, 129, 130, 161
    39: 31, 74, 190
    40: 2n., 203n., 204–205, 251–253
    43: 27–29, 46, 258
    45: 31–32, 38, 41, 47, 74, 91n., 130,
      190n., 200–201, 257n.
    46: 32–33, 35–36, 41, 258
    47: 131n.
    49: 130–131, 190, 240
    50: 2n., 131n., 206–209, 238n., 253,
      255
    52: 34–35, 75–81, 259
    53: 37–40
    54: 131–137, 155, 156, 243n., 244n.,
      259
    57: 226, 228, 230, 255
    58: 17n., 35, 38–40, 80–82, 169n.,
      219n., 259
    60: 22–23, 75, 81, 173, 190
    61: 219–221, 258
    65: 174
    66: 41–43, 137, 155
    68: 199

Jerome, St., *Letters:* (cont.)
  69: 82–83, 174, 176–177, 242
  70: 8, 14, 196
  72: 193
  75: 163, 177
  77: 138–139, 225
  79: 139–140, 156
  84: 7, 164, 189, 190, 194, 227n., 243
  97: 174
  98: 175
  100: 44n.
  101: 237
  102: 237
  105: 238
  106: 22
  107: 21, 44, 141, 196
  108: 2n., 32n., 138n., 141–142, 244n., 254n.
  109: 220–223, 261
  110: 225, 238
  111: 238–239
  112: 239, 243
  116: 238, 239
  117: 2n., 84–86, 143–144, 215, 256–258
  119: 209n.
  120: 89n.
  121: 176, 190
  123: 23, 45, 121, 131n., 144–145
  125: 29n., 45, 86–89, 220n., 228–229, 251, 255, 259
  127: 89, 90n., 230–231
  128: 45–46, 145, 147n.
  129: 191n.
  130: 35, 68, 89, 145–147, 155, 175, 257
  133: 177, 220n.
  139: 195
  147: 92, 216
  148: 36n., 245–246
Liber Heb. Quaest. in Genesim, 209, 211n.
Life of Malchus (Vita Malchi), 50–51, 65
Life of Paul (Vita Pauli), 48–49
translations:

  of Didymus' *De Spiritu Sancto,* 26n., 210n., 241
  of Ezekiel, 10
  of Job, Preface, 254, 255n.
  of Origen's *Homilies on Luke,* 242
Jewish learning, 54, 189–190, 193
Jews, 81, 188–194, 198
John, Bishop of Jerusalem, 40, 226, 255n.
John Chrysostom, St., *see* Chrysostom, St. John
Jovinianus, 51–52, 152, 206, 208n., 213–218, 220, 225, 231
  see also Jerome, works, *Adversus Iovinianum*
Julian, Roman Emperor, 196
Justin Martyr, St., 167
Juvenal, 2, 3, 24, 28n., 33, 54, 61, 109, 114, 129, 172, 248, 250, 260–263, 265–266, 269, 270, 271
  popularity in late antiquity, 3–4
  references to in Jerome, 9–10, 53n., 137n., 151n., 153, 155, 157, 202, 207–208, 226
Satires:
  1: 20, 78, 171n., 208n., 226, 232, 254
  2: 58, 79–80
  3: 29, 46
  4: 25
  5: 133
  6: 53n., 101, 120n., 126n., 129n., 138, 148, 153, 155, 157, 163
  8: 205
  9: 202
  11: 21n., 29, 43–44, 46
  13: 10, 16n., 20, 75
  14: 21n., 25n., 56n., 189n.

Knoche, Ulrich, 2n., 4n.

Labourt, Jérôme, 205, 248n.
Lactantius, 3, 4, 88, 169
  as a satirist, 16–18
Laeta, daughter-in-law of St. Paula, 140–141
Legacy-hunting, satiric attack on, 26, 51, 76

Lucan, 23
Lucian, 17, 80n., 168
Lucilius, 1, 2, 3, 4, 17, 18, 24, 68, 87, 109, 114, 171, 187, 204n., 250, 255, 256, 257, 264
Lucretius, 229n.
Luebeck, Emil, 4n., 8, 9, 28n.

Marcella, Roman matron, 26, 28, 32, 36, 37n., 38, 76, 90, 118, 230
Martial, 25, 109, 147, 176n., 232n., 256
Methodius, Bishop in Lycia, 116
Monasticism, *see* Ascetic movement
Morin, Dom G., 93

Nepotianus, 33, 35, 75–76, 78–79, 81, 173n., 259
Nicaeus, editor of Juvenal, 4
Norden, Eduard, 186n., 269

Oceanus, 82
"Onasus Segestanus," 203–205, 212, 251–253
Origen of Alexandria, 24, 54, 174–175, 189, 210, 219, 225, 236n., 239, 242, 243
Ovid, 203n.

Paganism, 194-199
   see also Ammianus Marcellinus, Vettius Agorius Praetextatus, *and* Virius Nicomachus Flavianus
Palladius, 11
Pammachius, Roman senator, 41–43, 47, 137, 186, 226
Paula, St., companion of St. Jerome, 2n., 28, 32, 42, 118, 137–138, 141–142
Paula, granddaughter of St. Paula, 141
Paulina, daughter of St. Paula, 42
Paulinus of Nola, 35, 37–40, 80, 81, 129n., 218, 259
Pease, A. S., 8, 10n., 75
Pelagianism, 53, 107, 146, 177–179
   see also Jerome, works, *Dial. contra Pelagianos*
Peregrinatio ad loca sancta, 135

Persius, 1, 2, 3, 9, 24, 61, 109, 250, 252, 253, 269
popularity of in late antiquity, 5
Satires:
   1: 10n., 20, 30, 45, 53n., 86, 110, 126, 133, 143n., 171n., 208n., 215, 216, 232, 254
   2: 17, 131, 191, 205
   3: 38n., 80, 88, 98, 191, 204n., 208n., 214, 217, 232n.
   4: 237
   5: 88, 204
   6: 17, 25, 202
Petronius, 24, 78, 147
Plautus, 9, 179, 183n., 201, 202, 206, 212, 217, 230
Plutarch, 114, 153
Polycarp, St., 167
Porphyry, 28n., 52n., 115, 153, 154, 196
Praesidius, 238
Préaux, J.-G., 203–205
Probus, commentator on Juvenal, 4
Profuturus, 236
Prudentius:
   Apotheosis, 189
   Contra Symmachum, 19
   Peristephanon, 21n.
   Psychomachia, 26–27

Quintilian, 29, 88, 169, 172, 266

Reich, H., 72n., 122, 158n.
Rhetorica ad Herennium, 210–211
Rufinus of Aquileia, 5, 6, 7, 9, 70n., 73, 99, 163, 179n., 189n., 201n., 209n., 224, 225–235, 239, 241, 242, 245, 250, 254, 255n., 259
   see also Jerome, works, *Contra Rufinum*
Rusticus, Gallic monk, 86, 88, 228–229, 259
Rutilius Namatianus, 189, 264

Sabinianus, 216
Sallust, 88
Salvina, 139–140

Satire:
　in the Christian apologists, 11–19,
　　167–169; *see also* Arnobius, Lac-
　　tantius, *and* Tertullian
　nature of in antiquity, 1, 171–172,
　　247–250, 253, 257, 261, 263, 265–
　　267, 270
　popularity of in late antiquity, 3–6
Semonides of Amorgos, 113
Seneca the Elder, 265
Seneca the Younger, 2, 20–21, 33, 50,
　61, 62, 63n., 86, 101, 114, 153, 154,
　159n., 215n.
Servius, 4
Silvia, St., 212
　see also Peregrinatio ad loca sancta
Siricius, Pope, 97, 152
Stoicism, 61–62, 116, 196, 198, 265–267
Süss, Wilhelm, 10n., 72, 207n., 210,
　234n.
Suetonius, *De Poetis*, 1n.
Sulpicius Severus, 11, 36n., 55n., 66,
　82n.
Sunnia and Fretela, 21–22

Tatian, 116

Terence, 9, 124n., 127, 179, 194, 209–
　210, 241
Tertullian, satiric tone of his writings,
　12–14, 24, 45n., 46n., 49, 68n., 101,
　116, 119n., 134, 149, 167, 169, 175–
　176, 188, 190n., 220, 223n., 259, 265
Theophilus, Bishop of Alexandria, 44n.,
　175
Theophrastus, 114, 152, 153, 155, 156,
　158, 164

Vallarsi, Domenico, 49n., 202, 215,
　230n., 242n., 248n., 251
Varro, M. Terentius, 1n., 23, 24, 114
Vergil, 41n., 49, 55n., 70, 204n., 209, 232,
　237
Vettius Agorius Praetextatus, 66, 195–
　196
Vigilantius of Calagurris, 84, 201n.,
　218–225, 245n., 250, 258, 261, 262
Virius Nicomachus Flavianus, 18

Wageningen, J. van, 154–155, 157
Weston, Arthur, 2n., 3n., 16n., 101n.,
　117n., 194n., 248, 251
Will of a Pig, 6, 232